Birds, Beasts & Bureaucrats

A Naturalist on a Caribbean Island

Herbert A. Raffaele

*Author of "Guide to the Birds of the West Indies" and
"Guide to the Birds of Puerto Rico and the Virgin Islands"*

Cold Tree Press
Nashville, Tennessee

Published by Cold Tree Press
Nashville, Tennessee
www.coldtreepress.com

Printed in the United States of America
ISBN 978-1-58385-111-1

6/6/07

Dear Lanie,

I very much appreciate the focus & hard-work you bring to bear & conservation.

All the best,
Herb Raffaele

To everyone, young and old, who enjoys nature and desires a sense of how better to make a difference towards its conservation.

Acknowledgements

I thank my old friends and co-workers in Puerto Rico who were part of the process of learning by the seats of our pants how best to achieve conservation. Particularly in this regard I want to acknowledge Ruben Freyre, Mitch Fram, Alvaro Yamhure, Jim Wiley, Noel Snyder, Gilberto Cintron and Pete Weaver among many others. Also, I thank and apologize to my kids, Nina and Herb who had to put up with me being away from home so regularly while conducting field work. I hope at least that they came through the experience with a greater appreciation for nature than they might have otherwise. To my wife Jan I sincerely thank her for her patience, tolerance and support while I dabbled on this manuscript. Special appreciation goes to my parents, Tom and Florence Raffaele who always supported me in my life choices and who waited so long for what was a phantom manuscript to become a reality.

I am pleased to recognize Ms. Chistine Hicks for the cover design on which she worked so conscientiously. To Ms. Barbara Dean I owe a debt of gratitude for her comprehensive and insightful comments on an earlier version of the manuscript. Appreciation is also extended to Karen Eckert of WIDECAST for the use of the photo upon which the sea turtle sketch is based.

Table of Contents

Prologue

Though it penetrated into my skull only bit by bit, one incident as much as any other convinced me that I was in the wrong profession.

Entering an eighth grade biology class on the first day of a new semester, only one student had yet arrived. Or maybe I was just oblivious to the presence of any others. Regardless, all my attention was focused on a husky, if not somewhat obese, boy in the middle of the room bounding about like a buffoon in an attempt to imitate a gorilla—and doing a mighty fine job of it.

This spectacle, of course, was staged specifically for me, a new teacher in this school and one who at that very moment was wondering what in the world I had done to deserve such treatment; whether I hadn't made a serious mistake in entering the teaching profession; how a kid like this could possibly have reached the eighth grade and be permitted in a class where learning was to take place; and most importantly at the moment, what in the world I was going to do about this ridiculous situation.

I do not recall the details of how I got my ape-mimic to settle down. It was but one of many confrontations I had with him. As often as not I shipped him off to the principal's office since he frequently wreaked havoc in my classroom. It made for a long year.

By June I was ready not only for a summer vacation, but also for a change, a change in careers. Though I very much enjoyed teaching, it was now perfectly clear that I was not cut out for it in the traditional classroom setting. The time had come to explore alternative methods of earning a living.

My timing was unfortunate. My Master's degree in teaching completed one year earlier would now be of limited value. Worse, at home was my wife with our two-year old daughter and six-month old son. Supporting our young family did not allow for recklessness.

Yet some factors fell on the positive side of the ledger. During the previous year we had lived with my parents, thus enabling us to save a few dollars from my teacher's salary. This provided at least a little latitude for shifting into a new profession.

But into what profession was I to move? I considered various areas in which I had some expertise or interest. In none was there much promise of employment. Finally, I opted for the long shot, an area where the chances for employment or financial reward were less than slim, but the potential for satisfaction was great; I decided to write a bird book.

A bird book you say? Is that being responsible to your family? Aren't there already ten million bird books on the market? And, even if you succeed in getting the book published, it might be years before royalties are received.

Yes, yes, I understand, but let me explain. There is a bit of rationality here.

For one, I had long been addicted to observing birds. Though, as a Cub Scout I had scorned the idea of learning five birds to obtain a silver arrow on my bear badge. At the time I believed all birds were either black, brown, or black and brown. That's what happens when you spend your entire childhood growing up in the confines of New York's city streets. Nevertheless, at the age of 15 when I saw a "real" bird, one with some colors on it, out in the forests of Long Island, I was hooked on these feathered marvels. Nothing would suit me more than to work with them professionally.

My idea was to prepare the first field guide to the birds of Puerto Rico. While visiting the island six years earlier, I had become enthralled by its rain forests, deserts, palm trees, exotic birds. For a young man interested in nature, Puerto Rico was heaven. On top of that I had also become enchanted with one of the island's young senoritas which ultimately led to my having in-laws in San Juan. Yet, I was equally appalled by the absence of an adequate field guide for identifying the island's avifauna. With over a million tourists visiting Puerto Rico every year, there might be a market for such a book. The first publisher I consulted showed strong interest.

Meanwhile, I would not completely depart from reality. During this self-created sabbatical, I would continue to seek employment as a teacher, but in a much less formal setting such as at an outdoor education facility.

With our plans set, I first spent several months in New York libraries reviewing the published literature on Puerto Rico's birds. It was then off to the island for a few months of intensive field work.

One morning with the sun just beginning to peep over the horizon, I waded into a field of lush grass that was nearly over my head and drenched with dew. Struggling forward in chest high rubber waders to keep from getting soaked, I halted suddenly as a flock of a half dozen small finches, scarcely 30 feet in front of me, fluttered to a fallen limb. Slowly I raised my binoculars to identify them.

The only small flocking finches expected in San Juan sharply contrasted a dark throat and upper chest with a white belly and abdomen. Focusing on the flock before me I could make out the dark throat and upper chest, but...the remaining underparts were not white. Despite being unable to see sharply in the diffuse light of dawn, it was clear that the lower chest on downward was covered with delicate dark ringlets over a white background. No bird known from Puerto Rico had a plumage anything like that of the birds before me.

A perusal of bird guides covering the West Indies and Central and South America showed that my unusually marked mystery bird was from none of these neighboring landmasses. Over the course of the next few days, therefore, I absorbed myself in visiting pet shops and scrutinizing books on cage birds in an attempt to identify my phantom species. It took a while, but in one pet shop in downtown Santurce I found my mystery bird—a spice finch, also called a nutmeg mannikin, native from India through southeastern Asia to Taiwan, Indonesia, and the Philippines.

It was exciting discoveries such as this that indicated Puerto Rico's avifauna was not as well studied as it had first appeared. Ranges of some species had expanded, others had contracted, and none of this was reflected in the literature. If I were going to prepare an accurate guide, more than a few months of research would be necessary. It was at this juncture that I began to contemplate the possibility of finding a job locally; thus I took a day off from field work and paid a visit to the Division of Fish and Game of the Puerto Rico Department of Agriculture.

As it so happened, it looked like opportunity, at least in some obscure sense of the word, was knocking. The head of Fish and Game casually informed me that their field biologist responsible for Puerto Rico's southwest corner and the island of Mona, a unique remnant of uplifted ocean floor lying halfway between Puerto Rico and the Dominican Republic, had apparently died in a plane crash on his way to Mona, disappearing without a trace. Thus, that biologist position was now vacant, and the Division head was enthusiastic about me filling it. Of course, his enthusiasm may have derived at least in part from there being no other applicants for the job.

Regardless, I was satisfied. Despite the obvious difficulties, I knew we could make it. The salary was only $320 per month, one fourth of what I had earned as a teacher; but taxes would be zilch, and we'd live in the least expensive part of the island. I would have to spend two weeks a month on Mona and leave my family behind, but we could put up with this for a while until I could transfer to purely main island duties. The important thing was that it was a job—a job as a wildlife biologist in a New York City boy's paradise! While I might be flying in rickety planes over the treacherous Mona Channel, I felt it was a good sign that at least the Division head had not inquired about how well I could swim, or whether I had a comprehensive life insurance policy.

Content with my good fortune at being in line for one of the only existing wildlife biologist positions in Puerto Rico, I contemplated how much field work I could accomplish on this job before starvation struck my family, or my plane struck the

Mona Channel. Little did I suspect that opportunity had not finished with me and was about to pay another house call.

Sometimes I wonder why the newspaper was ever invented. Information can often be transmitted by word of mouth at a rate that makes the modern printing press pale in comparison. Such is what happened with the news that I was in search of a wildlife position. Over my in-law's back fence and across to Santurce, the word spread until I was invited for another interview, this with the newly-formed Area of Natural Resources within the Department of Public Works. There I met with Ruben Freyre, a middle-aged man of average build and easy-going temperament. Freyre was chief of the Division of Flora and Fauna, a prestigious enough sounding position except that his entire staff consisted of one sole secretary.

Apparently Ruben was reasonably enough satisfied with my credentials, particularly my knowledge of birds, that he took me to see the head of the entire Area of Natural Resources, an extremely intimidating personage who was as cold as Ruben was mellow.

"This agency has too many chiefs and not enough indians," he boomed at me in his not-to-be questioned manner.

"Yes sir," I replied eloquently.

"I understand you have a B.A. in geology," he asked somewhat challengingly.

"Yes sir," I responded once more.

"Well," continued the cacique (big chief). "There is a position open as a geologist, and you can start in it tomorrow. A biologist position is presently up in the air pending approval of our request for additional funds. We won't know about that position for another two months."

"I'd rather wait for the biologist position on the chance that it is funded," I blurted out, using little bureaucratic moxie in my decision. Had I known anything about the budgetary process, I would have realized that the chances of the biologist position ever being created were slim at best. On top of that, it would not have been unacceptable had I taken the geologist post and later transferred to the biology spot once it became available. Those types of manipulations, however, were not my style. Despite the odds, I would go for broke. Geology was interesting, but a distant second to wildlife. That had become perfectly evident to me when, during a field course in the Rocky Mountains as an undergraduate, the geology professor, standing at the base of a large sedimentary outcrop, was describing the formation while I scanned the cliff crevices for rock wrens.

The Area of Natural Resources job had more appeal than that with the Department of Agriculture. I would be responsible for avifauna inventories virtually throughout Puerto Rico, not just in the southwest, and I would not have to leave my family two weeks of each month to stay on Mona. Furthermore, when I had told Ruben during my interview that I would settle for any salary equal to or more than the $320 offered by the Department of Agriculture, his response was, "Either we pay well, or not at all," which certainly made me feel good and gave me a lot of respect for this man.

As things turned out, my luck held. Though I heard nothing official from the Department of Agriculture which continually assured me that final papers were being prepared, scarcely two months had passed since my Area of Natural Resources interview when I received a call from Ruben asking me to come and see him.

"The biologist position is available, and we will hire you for the job," he told me as I sat brimming with excitement, "and, your salary will be $700 per month."

I was flabbergasted. Seven hundred dollars a month, travel expenses, and official status to continue on a long-term basis what I had been doing on my vacation! Things were looking good, and I was rarin' to go.

I had not been in the Area of Natural Resources job one week when I received a letter from the Department of Agriculture:

> *Dear Mr. Raffaele:*
> *Please come to...on...to receive a preliminary interview for the position of Biologist...*

Thus began seven years of adventures and misadventures on the island of Puerto Rico.

Birds, Beasts & Bureaucrats

A Naturalist on a Caribbean Island

A Night on Rat Island

I had never been alone in the sea with a shark before. Or more accurately put – in the great expanse of the world's oceans, this was the first time that a shark and I would simultaneously share such a minuscule portion of this vastness that we would become intimately aware of one another's existence. But everything was under control – so it seemed. Actually, the shark and I weren't alone. Peter had entered the water with me, and I should have heeded the knot in the pit of my stomach when, almost as an afterthought, he had reached back into the boat and pulled out his glistening spear gun.

"Put that back!" I demanded, being all too familiar with stories of thoughtless divers who had wounded sharks or even so-called "harmless" fish only to learn a lesson at the expense of a limb or portion thereof.

"Oh, don't get excited," groaned Peter, dismayed at what he perceived as clearly unjustified hysteria. "The gun's not loaded."

Peter was a handsome young fellow, huskily built and deeply tanned. A general technician in the Area of Natural Resources, he was assigned to our program on a temporary basis when we needed additional field assistance. During this particular venture, he was primarily along to handle the boat.

The boat was a small, fiberglass 12 footer with a 20 horsepower motor, more than adequate for surveying the numerous small islets that dot Puerto Rico's southern coastal waters. These cays, sometimes just coral rubble, but more often covered with dense mangrove forests, were the object of our expedition because many of them had never yet been surveyed for breeding colonies of nesting waterbirds such as pelicans, frigatebirds, terns, and the many species of herons.

You will notice I said "breeding" colonies. Breeding is the operative word. Many waterbirds occur commonly around Puerto Rico's entire coastline. When it comes to breeding, however, most of these waterbirds congregate in but a few dense colonies. Take the brown pelican for example, a bird recognized by everyone. Any tourist brochure to a tropical island in the Caribbean that is worth its salt will likely show one of these distinctive birds soaring low over a calm bay or sitting on a pier waiting for a handout of fish. This perception belies the true status of the bird through much of its range, including in Puerto Rico.

As common as the brown pelican appears to be, the only regularly active breeding colony known to exist in Puerto Rican waters was Cayo Conejo near Vieques island, a site rather far from Puerto Rico proper. Around the main island of Puerto Rico only three pelican breeding islands had ever been recorded and all of these were used only intermittently and did not appear presently to be active.

What is so special about Cayo Conejo that it should serve as the only permanent breeding site for brown pelicans? Probably its most unique feature is its location adjacent to a military bombing range.

Say what?

Yes, well, believe it or not, there are some small upsides to bombs being dropped. One is that bombing areas have zones around them which reflect degrees of threat from bombing exercises. Cayo Conejo, to approach the islet without special permission. This circumstance, as peculiar as it might be, offers inordinate protection to the pelicans from human disturbance.

And it is human disturbance which is probably the single greatest bane to pelican breeding. All pelicans among the seven or eight species which presently exist, are extremely sensitive to human disturbance and will abandon their nests and eggs when minimally bothered. Desertion of the former nesting colonies at

La Parguera, Montalva Bay and Anasco Bay in western Puerto Rico might well have been due to significant increases in boat traffic around these areas in recent years.

Needless to say, this circumstance did not present a pretty picture regarding survival of the brown pelican in Puerto Rico. The breeding population on Cayo Conejo was a small one, yet Puerto Rico appeared to sustain many hundreds, if not thousands of birds around its coastline. While some of these were migrants from North America during winter, the island supported substantial numbers of birds during all months of the years. All indications were that despite the apparent abundance of brown pelicans in Puerto Rico, many of the birds were either not breeding, or were leaving the island to breed elsewhere in the Caribbean.

Brown pelicans mature at three to four years of age, consequently, a healthy population should support a fair number of immature birds. And this is what I found to be the case. This finding eased my concern that the birds might not be breeding, but it raised the issue of whether Puerto Rico's brown pelicans were breeding in some other nation's territory and subsequently wandering to Puerto Rico to take advantage of local fishing grounds. While such a scenario might suffice temporarily, what would happen if the breeding islands of this neighboring territory became overstressed?

This was an issue which would require expanded communication to neighboring islands in the Caribbean, but first it was important to pin down the situation with regard to circumstances in Puerto Rico. This is what I was attempting to achieve with this present survey. I had chosen to survey Puerto Rico's southeastern offshore islands because they were among the least studied and perhaps least disturbed of any surrounding the main islands.

We had spent most of the day surveying before deciding to take a refreshing afternoon dip in the tepid Caribbean. About 100 yards to the lee of the islet Cayo Ratones, we anchored where the placid water was particularly inviting.

Against my better judgment, but deferring to Peter's logic, I ceded that he take the unloaded speargun. This issue decided, together we snorkeled out confidently over the shallow reef leaving the final member of our party behind in the boat in a state of total befuddlement.

Mitch, my field assistant, had a very youthful face and general demeanor which in no way hinted at his age of 29. He was very bright, so doubtless it was taxing his cranial synapses to give meaning to the events of the moment as Peter and I swam off.

You see, Mitch had told us there was a shark nearby. He was the first of us in the water and had come racing back to the boat, boarding it with an unusual alacrity on his part. "There's a shark around here!" he sputtered as he fought to gain his composure.

"What kind is it?" asked Peter.

"No idea," replied Mitch.

"Was it resting on the bottom?" I queried.

"Yes."

"Was it light rusty brown?"

"Yes."

I had heard enough. Though hardly an expert on sharks, it was clear that Mitch had encountered a common nurse shark, a species known for its tameness – as sharks go. To Mitch, a shark was a shark, certainly a wise philosophy for a beginning skin diver, but one by which my actions could in no way be understood. Leaving him in his confusion and awe at the lunacy of his companions, I determined that this was a golden opportunity to see safely my first shark in its own milieu.

The world's several hundred species of sharks share many similarities yet possess dramatic differences. One over-riding similarity is that their skeletons contain no bones. Sharks evolved over 300 million years ago and, along with their relatives the skates and rays, were among the earliest vertebrates to inhabit the planet. Sharks virtually identical to some that exist today have been found in fossil deposits dating back approximately 200 million years. That's quite a lengthy piece of time when we consider the case for our species, Homo sapiens, which scarcely goes back half a million. Bone as we know it was not a "common commodity" then. Sharks and skates made due with cartilage.

Cartilage is the relatively soft tissue in our outer ears and the tips of our noses which give them form and flexibility, but limited strength. Needless to say, however, the sharks and their relatives have gotten by quite well thank you. One reason for this success is that while their skeletal makeup has not changed, other aspects of their body plan have evolved significantly. One of these is the shark's ability to locate prey. The shark uses several highly evolved mechanisms for this purpose. This begins with the lateralis system which is located on the fishes head and sides and serves to detect vibrations in the water, such as those generated by a struggling fish. The ampullae of Lorenzini, sensory organs on the head, detect electrical impulses, even those generated by a fish or invertebrate hiding beneath the sand. Then there are the shark's eyes which have various special adaptations for vision in murky, dark water.

Sharks have been so successful in their evolution that they range in size from the miniature green dogfish, only a foot long, to the whale shark measuring to over 60 feet, the largest fish in the world. Interestingly, the whale shark, like many other of the globe's largest marine animals, notably whales, feeds on some of the sea's smallest creatures – plankton. Unlike whales, however, the whale shark does not have modified teeth to strain these small creatures from the sea. Rather, it has adaptations on its gills that serve as strainers. The shark's mouth pretty much serves as a gigantic vacuum pump to suck in water and prey indiscriminately.

Why I wanted to be in the water with a shark had Mitch flabbergasted and, to be fair, was not entirely clear to me. Certainly I had no intention of disturbing the animal. I have always had a more than healthy respect for wild creatures, and my sympathies have been on their side in practically every confrontation between man and beast. I had no intention of confrontation! It was rather a combination of several factors, one being an inner drive to see new animals in their natural environments. Another was to partake of an experience infamous throughout the annals of humankind. Clearly all this was tempered, and I mean tempered, by my knowing the type of shark with which we were dealing and of its reputation for being docile. That I was seeking out a nurse shark is what gave me confidence in the safety of the mission. A doubly reinforced shark cage might not have been enough to satisfy me had practically any other species of shark been involved. Peter also was eager to see the critter and doubtless would have been equally enthusiastic had Mitch seen a 12 foot hammerhead or, for that matter, an 18 foot great white.

The boat lay at anchor in about four feet of water but, as we swam in search of the huge brain coral under which Mitch had said the shark was resting, the water depth was gradually increasing. Simultaneous with the increase in water depth and distance from the boat, my courage began to dissipate. Though we were swimming in a magnificent world of blue and yellow grunts, colorful parrotfish and wrasses, and damselfish darting among the coral heads, I was finding it impossible to enjoy these striking creatures.

Suddenly Peter and I passed over the precipitous lip of the reef into a basin about 15 feet deep. Gone were the numerous corals – staghorn, finger, brain, elkhorn – all competing for the limited substrate of the reef. Now there was just sand. Gone were

Squirrelfish

the tiny squirrelfish and tang, the snappers and the fanworms. Now there was empty, wet space. Gone was my confidence – totally.

We were clearly in the shark's domain. What in the world was I doing here? This could be an aberrant nurse shark, and it might have wakened from its nap with severe hunger pangs or a taste for a new dish. Why, at this moment, it might be.... But, at that moment, an immense brain coral loomed in front of us, and simultaneously Peter and I spotted our quarry. Beneath the huge coral, its peculiar tail fin sticking out in plain view, lay the shark.

That was enough for me. What a relief! Simply knowing the location of the shark and that it was not on the prowl gave me a big boost. That it was resting with a full 25 feet between us gave me further relief.

I signaled to Peter that we should leave. After all, seeing part

Nurse Shark behind coral

of a shark was as good as a whole shark under these circumstances and, I had used up my ration of courage for the week, if not for the year and was fast developing a tremendous craving for dry land.

In response to my signal, Peter did the unthinkable. He dove on the shark with his arm outstretched – the arm with the spear gun! I was paralyzed. There was nothing I could do. Doubtless my hair stood on end despite being in the water.

As I have already mentioned, nurse sharks are relatively tame. That is to say unprovoked attacks on humans are virtually unknown. Those attacks which have been recorded generally resulted from nurse sharks being speared. While the mouth of a nurse shark is not particularly large – as sharks go – sharks have an adaptation regarding their teeth which is particularly annoying from a human's perspective. Each tooth has beneath it a band of developing teeth. This allows for tooth replacement on a regular basis, as frequently as every eighth day, so that these predators have a constantly renewed set of choppers for dealing with slippery prey. Nurse sharks in particular have been known to bite like a bulldog, holding on to their adversary until the shark is killed or the prey is drowned – neither a pretty picture.

Peter rapidly approached the shark and jabbed it in the back with his gun, while through my mind passed countless scenarios of all the painful consequences that could result from such fool-hardiness. As the shark scooted out from under the coral head in a cloud of sand, a massive bellow welled up inside me and blasted out through my snorkel.

"No-o-o-o-o-o!"

Fortuitously, the shark disappeared. Whether this was a result of the sonic blast emanating from my snorkel, or simply the nature of the species, I'll never know, but the question is moot. Suffice it to say that we made it back to the boat without further incident whereupon I had very few words for Peter.

7

"Did you see the shark?" Mitch inquired.

"Yeah," was my curt reply.

Noting that relations appeared strained between Peter and me, Mitch decided to let the matter drop and moved to the bow to hoist anchor. He was leaning over the side, pulling up the line, when he suddenly stopped and partially turned his head to speak over his shoulder. Curiosity had finally gotten the best of him.

"Oh, by the way, what was that booming noise I heard when you guys were out on the reef?"

The sun was already melting into the calm Caribbean as we maneuvered up to the pier of Cayo Ratones. Rat Island, as the name translates to English, was typical of Puerto Rico's southern offshore cays. No more than a mass of coral rubble several acres in size, the island had accumulated enough coralline debris and calcareous sand, through deposition by innumerable storms, to rise a few feet above the sea and sustain a dense forest of salt tolerant trees, primarily mangroves and sea grapes. Though the island had a narrow concrete pier, perhaps three feet wide and 100 feet long, to which we had moored, a quick reconnaissance indicated that the island was uninhabited. For what purpose such a solid pier had been constructed was no longer evident. The heyday of Cayo Ratones apparently had passed. Forest covered the island to within a few feet of the beach, the latter consisting not of sand, but rather of coral and shell fragments.

In the rapidly descending twilight, we chose our sleeping quarters. Mitch decided to cross to the windward side of the island and set up a hammock near the shore in hopes that the breeze would keep down any bugs – a commendable selection. Peter, not ceasing to amaze me, chose to sleep in the boat, which contained nary enough flat surface for a dwarf – a decision as incomprehensible as another he had made earlier that day. Disliking the debris strewn shoreline, because the litter often harbors sand flies, and being intimidated by what the name of the island suggested (Ratones means mice in Spanish, but it was just as likely that their larger cousins might be around), I chose to sleep at the absolute tip of the pier with my head seaward. The logic behind this was indisputable. The pier got me away from potential bugs and rats while exposing me to maximum breeze. Should, perchance, a rat happen to wander out on the pier, it would have little reason to pass the foot of my sleeping bag, not to mention a certain amount of difficulty in doing so.

Satisfied that my years of Boy Scout camping had been put to good use, I settled down in my sleeping bag upon a comfortable air mattress and lay gazing at the star-flecked sky.

It was unbelievable. Not just the sky, in which danced twice as many stars as ever I remember seeing as a youth in New York City, but just being here, on this island in the tropics, studying birds. So I lay on the pier recalling my good fortune and gently drifted off to sleep.

My slumber was comfortable and deep, but not of long duration. I suddenly became fitful; something was not right. I opened my eyes.

I simply was not prepared for what it was I saw. Particularly considering the intricate calculations that had gone into the selection of my sleeping quarters. No more than a foot from my face a large, brown rat was sniffing near my shoulder, doubtless searching for its evening meal. Well, he (I'll call the rat a "he" for the sake of argument, as I had no time nor inclination to check out its gender) was not there very long. No sooner had our eyes met, in far from a romantic sort of way, than we both reacted compulsively, the rat quicker than I. Up went the rat vertically, a good foot above my shoulder, with his feet frantically churning the air but simply not getting anywhere. When he finally came back down, however, he was ready to go. The rat literally flew down that pier. In the split second it took him to dash to the island, I was firmly convinced the rat had barely touched solid ground. The entire frenzied sprint seemed to occur a good six inches above the dock, and the fact that the rat's feet whirled so fast as to look like propellers may have contributed to his airborne appearance.

My own reaction might certainly have been more severe were it not for the rat's panic which gave me solace, and the creature's flight which was so ludicrously funny. Further, and doubtless most importantly, I was substantially constrained by my zippered sleeping bag.

After a few shudders I felt the top of my head to determine whether my hair was yet laying flat. Several minutes later I had regained my composure enough to reevaluate my strategy concerning the selection of optimal sleeping quarters on Cayo Ratones. Clearly I had erred in assuming that a rat would not explore the end of the pier. Rats are intelligent creatures with an acute sense of smell and while the unusual odors emanating from the dock might have caused a rat some caution, the scent might also have piqued the beast's curiosity. By the same token, I was convinced that being the smart critter that it is, this rat had had enough. He had certainly been scared out of his wits, and I felt confident the rat had been happy to escape with his life and would not explore the pier again that night.

Satisfied that I had reanalyzed the situation thoroughly, and this time taken the curiosity, intelligence, and just the general psychology of rats into careful consideration, I lay back down, though a bit less secure than earlier, to resume my slumber.

You should know that rats did not always exist on Cayo Ratones. In fact, prior to European colonization rats did not exist anywhere in Puerto Rico. How they came to Puerto Rico is easy to explain. They were common stow-aways on ships and readily came to land when these vessels moored at wharves on the island. Not surprisingly such invasions by rats, while entirely unintentional, took place around the world. In most of the New World, including the Caribbean, it took place in three phases. From Columbus' voyage until about 1700 only the European black rat seems to have been transported to the region. For the next 150 years, however, basically from the early seventeen hundreds until about 1850 the Norway rat was the unintentional invader. And from 1850 on both species have been regular colonizers. This pattern reflects a shift in rat abundance which had taken place in Europe, the cause of which is not well understood. Be that as it may, the impacts of two aggressive and resourceful predatory mammals on an island which previously had none has had numerous impacts on the island's ecology, much of which can never be reversed, not to mention the impacts on agriculture, human health and so on.

While this general history may sound reasonable, it would be fair to ask just how rats reached Cayo Ratones – an abandoned island. The pier suggests the answer. Cayo Ratones could never have supported agriculture, but it might well have served as a fine intermediary point for harvesting conch, lobsters, fish, sea turtles, or other marine organisms. The pier, though small, was finely constructed of concrete and brick rather than wood, suggesting a major commitment of resources to this site and, consequently heavy usage. Frequent trips by boats mooring ashore, especially medium-sized boats, would make a rat infestation inevitable.

Initially the rats would have gorged on a smorgasbord of marine organism refuse, but upon human abandonment of the islands, the rats were left to their own devices. Doubtless their population would have crashed, but their omnivorous habits and resourcefulness would have enabled them to survive on land and marine crabs, lizards, bird eggs and nestlings, and vegetation of various types. The rat which had visited me, likely a Norway rat, had just been searching for some new entrée.

Little by little the peaceful night, the gentle ocean breeze, and the water lapping at the pier calmed my nerves. I began to ease off to sleep.

But once more I had erred. No sooner was I on the brink of tranquil repose than I felt something nibbling at my hair. I sprang up, not to be denied by the constraints of a sleeping bag, as another rat (I presume the first one was still recuperating) sprinted down the pier. But this time I did not find things so amusing. I drew the line between rodents exploring my shoulder versus messing around in my hair. Besides, I wanted to get some sleep, and it had suddenly become abundantly clear that sleeping on the pier was now out of the question.

Recomposing myself for a second time, I snatched up my gear and implemented Plan 2.

Plan 2 was based on simple logic, the value of which I had managed to underestimate in Plan 1. If you want to avoid rats, sleep in a hammock. It so happened I was completely prepared for this contingency having brought along a light, compact hammock my wife and I had woven at home out of high-test fishing line. Quickly locating two stout, well-spaced trees on shore, I slung up the hammock and was soon settling down once more for a cozy rest.

Nestled in the hammock, my mind wandered back over my family's long history of conflict with the indomitable rat and its kin. My grandfather, a sailor in his youth around the turn of the century, had the most serious encounters. One incident followed what was probably the worst gale of his seagoing career. All three masts of the ship on which he sailed had snapped, and the crew was left drifting helplessly at sea in what remained of the vessel. Nearly out of food and water, men and rats vied for the few remaining foodstuffs that might keep them alive. The ship's rats did not stand by idly. Upon waking one morning one of the crew members who typically worked without shoes set his feet on the floor to arise from his bunk. Instead of standing up he actually catapulted into the air with pain. Apparently during the night the starving rats had nibbled the thick calluses completely off the sailor's feet, down to the raw flesh. It was days before his feet healed enough for him to walk.

Unlike my grandpa, my father was a landlubber at heart and never strayed any further from land than he could get in a rowboat. Nonetheless, being raised in Brooklyn there was no scarcity of rats and mice with which to carry on the feud. As a youth, he read late into the night as was his habit by lamp light. Engrossed in his typically cerebral version of entertainment, in this case Plato's "Credo," he glimpsed from the corner of his eye an unusual movement. Turning his attention from the tome, he noticed in the shadows a tiny gray mouse searching hither and yon as mice incessantly seem to do. Apparently thinking my father a statue, or at least ignoring his presence, the brazen little rodent strayed further and further into the open until it was prowling around the room with reckless abandon. Irked at this disturbance and at the mouse's ignominious nerve, my father slowly reached for a toy air rifle which happened to be at hand. Loading it with improvised ammunition, he fired a wooden match at the interloper with extraordinary results. Bull's-eye! The match struck the mouse squarely on the butt, doubtless a jolt to the critter in and of itself. More amazingly, the match burst into flame upon contact with the rodent heightening the trauma of the event to the extent that it is a wonder the creature didn't simply expire from shock on the spot.

Gradually my mind drifted from the thoughts of rats and mice. However, no sooner had I started to doze off than the light breeze ceased, and a total calm prevailed. Immediately following the calm, I felt a few raindrops upon my face.

I sprang from the hammock and rummaged through my pack for a protective covering as the sky opened up. Within seconds I was back in the hammock, not much the worse for wear, cloaked in an old shower curtain I had brought along for just such a contingency. The cloudburst let up shortly, dwindling to a light drizzle. I lay in the hammock restfully though hardly in total comfort, as raindrops beat on the plastic an inch from my ear. At least I was satisfied that I had coped adequately with all that mother nature had thrown at me. Considering how I dislike going into the field loaded with equipment, I was content that I had brought along the key necessities: an air mattress, a tiny hammock, an old shower curtain – items which had done their jobs admirably well. Carrying the hammock on my field trips was my one concession to "extravagant" camping and, in fact, in most tropical areas of the world, due to the danger of poisonous snakes, it is the only safe method of sleeping. Lying on the ground is usually a no-no.

Puerto Rico is unusual in this regard because it is an island – an island that never had a continental connection. This means that the first representatives of virtually every group of organisms which inhabit this chunk of land, whether they be bird or beast, tree or toadstool, had to arrive by crossing a large expanse of ocean. As oceans are inhospitable environments for most terrestrial creatures, only a small fraction of the species that inhabit continents are ever able to invade oceanic islands. Furthermore, the greater the water gap between continent and island, the fewer the number of species able to establish themselves. For example,

13

Hawaii, well out in the Pacific Ocean, has but one native mammal, a single bat. Except for a questionable lizard, it also has no native snakes or other terrestrial reptiles. The islands that make up New Zealand are another example. Though New Zealand presently has stoats, various species of deer, boar, and many other wild mammals, all were introduced by early settlers. The only native mammals are two species of bats, their ability to fly obviously aiding in their dispersal. How islands have come to possess the faunas and floras that they do, known as the study of island biogeography, is a fascinating field that in recent years has received significant attention.

Though Puerto Rico is not nearly as remote from a continental landmass as is Hawaii, it is nonetheless reasonably isolated. As a consequence, its vertebrate fauna, particularly mammals, is quite depauperate. Presently the only surviving native mammals on the island are nearly 20 species of bats. About a half dozen small ground dwelling mammals formerly inhabited Puerto Rico, but these became extinct in the not-too-distant past for reasons that are obscure in most cases. One of the important natural benefits of Puerto Rico's isolation as compared to neighboring Central America with its continental connections is that difficulties of dispersal have thus far inhibited poisonous snakes from colonizing the island. The poorly controlled importation of exotic pets, including venomous snakes, and the accidental escape of such species, could reverse instantaneously a situation which nature has managed to maintain unaltered for tens of thousands of years. But that is a separate issue. Basically, the absence of poisonous snakes and large predatory mammals in Puerto Rico makes its rain forests among the safest in the world. One must only be wary of creatures the likes of centipedes, tarantulas, and scorpions. In general these critters are sheltered under bark, in burrows, or in one protected place or another, thus limiting their potential threat to human beings. Though Puerto Rico is an exception, the use of a hammock while camping in the tropics is generally necessary.

Within a half hour the rain had stopped. Gleefully I cast off the shower curtain so that I could again bask in the fresh night air – but my rejoicing was premature. Though the rain had let up, it was not followed by a cool breeze. Rather, it was succeeded by a deathly calm. Unfortunately, the calm and the rain had combined to bring forth another pestilence which to that point had remained dormant. They arouse the sand flies of Cayo Ratones' coastal strip.

Sand flies, or majes (pronounced "ma-hess") as they are called locally, are also known as biting midges and no-see-ums, as well as by a host of unmentionable descriptors. Majes are minute, scarcely visible blood sucking flies with a bite, totally disproportionate to the creature's size. Indeed, though examining one under a microscope might demonstrate that no-see-ums are, in fact, flies, in the field one is hard pressed to believe that they are anything but a set of flying jaws. Certainly it was no-see-ums that served as the prototype for the popular video game Pac-man.

The most common type of biting midge in Puerto Rico goes by the scientific name of *Culicoides furens*, though many other species inhabit the island. In actuality, there are well over 5,000 species of biting midges worldwide, so *Culicoides furens* has a lot of competition. But there is no doubt in my mind that this little critter is ready to take on all comers.

Only female no-see-ums bite. A hearty meal of blood is important for her capacity to synthesize eggs of which she lays about 50 to 100 per meal. Females feed and lay eggs several times during their approximate month or less of life. Recently it has been determined that females locate their hosts by sensing their emission of carbon dioxide. Had I know that while on Cayo Ratones I might have tried holding my breath.

Male sand flies on the other hand take the high road. They do not suck blood. They feed on nectar and apparently play an important role in pollination of some important crop plants such as cacao (chocolate) and rubber trees. They use their antennae to detect a female reputedly by sensing the tone of her wing beat.

Another disconcerting feature of no-see-ums is that the bite of each individual seems to have a synergistic effect on the bites of others. That is to say that while bites by one or a few flies

15

may not be particularly irritating, the more majes that are biting, the more distressing each individual bite seems to be. A last perturbing attribute is that while no-see-ums can be deterred to some extent by insect repellent, they have the ungodly habit of homing in on those few areas of skin to which repellent cannot be applied – the eyes, nose, lips, ears. Repellent, then, is not a complete antidote.

To say that Cayo Ratones' sand flies were aroused is to severely understate the matter. These tiny pests went into a feeding frenzy that would have made piranhas proud. Not only did these beasts have ravenous appetites, but the sheer number of no-see-ums was far beyond anything I had ever encountered. To this day I wonder how such an immense population of these pesky flies could be sustained on that small island. Visitations by unwary travelers, like myself, though clearly providing a banquet to be remembered, could not be expected to feed this vast horde. The detritus on the beach, too, though plentiful, seemed an insignificant food source when compared to the number of majes. I hesitate to say it, but I often feel that my error may lie in thinking that these flies were only those of Cayo Ratones. All indications at the time were clearly that I had stumbled upon one of those events in the world of nature rarely if ever witnessed by Homo sapiens – something on the order of "The Bimillennial Convention of the Sand Flies of the Caribbean and Adjacent Regions." Of this I was pretty much convinced, and what remained as a puzzle was only whether I was merely paying for my intrusion or was, inadvertently, the main course.

As I had no way at all of resolving this question, and being that every second I remained in the hammock appeared to double the number of flies flitting to the feast, I burst from my filamentous cocoon and dashed to the pier. Out in the open air, away from the trees and the beach, the no-see-ums were quickly left behind to continue their festivities in private and not at my expense.

I felt an instant sense of relief at escaping the no-see-ums. But the wet pier reminded me of the furry visitors I had encountered while trying to sleep here. I began to lament my misfortune at the prospect of now having nowhere to bed down.

My self-pity immediately evaporated, however, as I approached our moored boat. There in its bowels sat Peter, drenched to the skin, the image of resigned suffering. His arms hugged his chest in a vice-like grip to retain the precious body heat rapidly being leached from his torso. His soaked sleeping bag was tossed to one side and with the gentle rocking of the boat little rivulets of rainwater which had collected in the craft washed across his bare toes. Despite my earlier displeasure with him over the shark incident, I could not help but feel sympathy for this forlorn fellow.

Quickly I found a towel and some dry clothes to help restore him to feeling human again. Then, since neither the pier nor the shore provided acceptable sleeping conditions, we sat by the boat chatting and munching on peanuts.

After about an hour I felt it was safe to reoccupy my hammock, so I bid Peter good night and returned to shore. Sure enough, the sand flies had called it quits, and I quickly settled comfortably in the hammock to take full advantage of the few remaining hours of darkness. No sooner had I begun to doze off, however, than a few light drops of rain roused me immediately. The few drops, in turn, transformed into a light drizzle as I reached for my shower curtain. Moments later I was huddled in my hammock, muttering and sputtering as a deluge pelted the plastic about my ears. Hadn't I had enough for one night? Was somebody upstairs playing games with me? I lay beneath my multi-purpose synthetic shroud, ruing my treatment by the fates, when in short order the rain ceased.

Though gratified that the rain had stopped, I was hardly euphoric. I lay expectantly not knowing whether the sand flies had reached their quota of activity for the night and were now lying contentedly with full stomachs in their cozy domiciles, or whether they still had some spunk left in them despite the un-godliness of the hour.

I was not left to wonder for long. Within seconds after the rain had halted these tiny pests again sallied forth and immediately sent me scurrying to the pier. There once again I encountered Peter looking more miserable, if possible, than he had before. Soaked and shivering, there was not much that could be done to dry him out, so we sat on the pier and let the breeze do the job.

The peanuts were long gone and our conversation had passed to silence for some time before I cautiously made my way down the pier to assess the temperament of the sand fly population on the beach. To my amazement, good fortune was with me. Not only had the majes settled down, but as I reinstalled myself into the hammock, I noticed that the sky had cleared, reducing the potential for rain in the immediate future. At last, content that my trials and tribulations were over, I was determined not to be denied of sleep for what remained of this tumultuous night.

And such was the case. I was not denied sleep for the remainder of the night. But, there was one small hitch. As I lay in the hammock drifting off to sleep, I thought I felt the bites of sand flies. Yet, this couldn't be. There had been no more rain; I must be imagining things. Suspiciously, I became more alert and confirmed to my bewilderment and dismay that indeed the sand flies were active once again and in fact were increasing the intensity of their attacks. I sat up with alarm, concerned about the biting flies and equally so about their puzzling behavior. Then I saw it. It was only a trace far off on the otherwise black horizon. A sinuous vein of pink had inserted itself into the vast darkness. Dawn was coming – the night was almost over. Outraged that I had been deprived of even a few short winks of comfortable repose, I slipped from the hammock and returned to the pier, pacing in deep thought. Why, I couldn't recall that I had actually fallen asleep for even a moment during the entire night. I had come prepared for every contingency and yet that hadn't been good enough. The hammock for sleeping among the trees, the sleeping bag and air mattress for the ground, and the shower curtain for the rain, had not sufficed. Rats, rain, and flies had cooperated in total unison to deprive me of sleep, to damage my pride, and to abuse my person – a series of indignities that was difficult to take. I was not aware how long I pondered when, before I knew it, the rapidly brightening sky snapped me back to the present. There was only one thing to do: pack my belongings, write off the night as just one of those things that happens when man and mother nature meet face to face – and consider never going camping again.

But it was not quite that simple. When I returned to the beach I encountered invisible bedlam. Dawn and dusk, not to mention after rain showers, are the principle periods during which the aggravating sand flies are typically most active, and this day was no exception. As I gathered my belongings the ravenous little majes attacked relentlessly showing no indication that the meal I had provided them during the night had in any way satisfied their insatiable appetites. Moreover, whatever the gala occasion might have been that accounted for such vast hordes of no-see-ums at Cayo Ratones during the night, that event paled in comparison to the numbers present at dawn. I lurched about the beach rapidly gathering the few items that lay loose, while ineffectively trying to beat away my tormentors. But it was hopeless. Custer had a better chance at the Little Big Horn. The few minutes that it took to gather my belongings seemed endless. Yet, ultimately I was able to scramble to the safety of the pier with all of my articles except one – the hammock.

As often happens during the course of a night, my precious homemade sleeping apparatus, because of my weight, had actually gouged grooves into the two trees from which it hung, due to tightening of the supportive nooses at either end. As a result, the hammock was now effectively fastened at both ends by vise-like bonds that even under the best of circumstances are not easily unraveled. But, what normally would have been the inconsequential struggle of untying the knots had now ballooned into a monumental undertaking.

Standing on the pier, a safe distance from shore I assessed the situation. I seriously considered whether I should cede to the sand flies and abandon the hammock which had taken several days to weave. Was it worth it?

I decided to give it a shot and reclaim the hammock, as much to sustain my already wounded pride as for the hammock itself. Determined, I gritted my teeth and charged to shore. Rushing to the first knot, I worked on it feverishly, but it would not budge. I ran to the second – the same result. Meanwhile, the no-see-ums had not been idle. They swarmed over me in unbearable waves making it impossible to concentrate on untangling the knots for more than a few seconds at a time. Furthermore, the inching of the sun over the horizon seemed to continually augment the numbers of these beasts rushing to the fray. Under their fierce and relentless attacks, my conviction to retrieve the hammock waned substantially, and I doubted that I had made the right decision. Yet, something drove me on and with desperate determination I gradually loosened the knots and tore the hammock free.

In a single motion I scooped up the hammock and bolted down the pier by which time I was certain not a single square inch of skin on my body had been left unscathed by those pernicious little demons. Phenomenally, both Mitch and I arrived at the boat simultaneously and by the briskness of his pace and his less-than-contented countenance, it did not take much to surmise that his night had been somewhat less than pleasant. However, this was no time for words. Quickly we flung our gear on board and then ourselves as Peter, half stupefied from lack of sleep, unmoored the boat and revved up the engine. In a matter of seconds our launch was racing out into the balmy Caribbean towards a new unexplored island, our enthusiasm still intact, though our pride as outdoorsmen sorely wounded.

Cayo Ratones was dwindling astern, but not rapidly enough for us. Collectively we hoped beyond hope that the island would emulate Atlantis and disappear into the sea. Knowing that this was unlikely, we were at least certain of one thing – that Cayo Ratones' furry and winged denizens would surely have to wait for *Homo sapiens* other than ourselves for any further contact with the human race.

Reflections

Why was I out surveying off-shore island birds anyway? Because that is the thing natural resource managers did. We checked on the status of the local fauna and flora. Then we presumably would use this information to make informed decisions regarding the wise use and management of these resources.

The only problem was, rarely did we ever get around to the latter. And when we did, who was there to listen?

Natural resources cannot be managed effectively without minimal financial resources. I mean, funds to hire personnel, to train them in some fundamental skills, to provide the simplest of supplies and materials, perhaps have vehicles for transportation. How about some gasoline? Most of the time I worked for the Department of Natural Resources, gas stations would not accept our government credit card because of our poor credit rating!

And financial resources for a governmental agency such as the DNR come from a strapped Commonwealth budget with a litany of higher priorities than resource conservation. Items such as health, housing, poverty, human services, transportation, you name it, come to mind. I would be hard pressed to think of a lower budgetary priority than natural resources conservation on the island.

Does it have to be that way? Not really. It is that way because we are too busy counting things. It is that way because we have adopted a North American approach to conservation that does not fit the needs of Puerto Rico nor the Caribbean as a whole. It is because someone once said "science is the backbone of conservation," and we took this as some sort of dogma that made us forget that the backbone is only one part of our body, and a small part at that. We need to remember the other body parts – like the heart and soul.

Natural resources management on a small island such as Puerto Rico is very sellable. Tourism, an ever-growing industry, depends on sparkling beaches and pristine reefs. Ample clean drinking water is a must. Rainforests are a fine tourist attraction. So are the numerous endemic birds and other forms of wildlife.

But the connectivity of wise natural resources management to these other important objectives does not happen by osmosis. It takes education and lots of it. It means constant communication with other more powerful agencies. It means reaching out to the public to develop pride in the island's unique resources. It

21

means engaging school children at the earliest ages, through all the school systems of the island, so that they appreciate all the things that are so special about Puerto Rico's fauna and flora.

At one point, after much data collection on birds, mangroves, reefs and whatnot, several of us went to our assistant secretary and suggested a meeting with the Ministry of Education to explore integration of the scientific information we had gathered into the school curriculum. We were told with great firmness that if we wanted to become teachers we could transfer to the Ministry of Education. If we wanted to be biologists, we should get back to work!

Pride among the people is the soul of conservation. Once the local populace recognizes the importance and value of their natural resources there is the potential to generate the political will necessary to undertake effective conservation efforts. Unless natural resource agencies such as the DNR place outreach much, much higher on their agendas, they shall continue to be ineffective.

While I and my fellow field-workers conducted surveys in Puerto Rico, the Forestry Division on a much less endowed island further south in the Caribbean, St. Lucia, was following this more practical tack. The outcome was spectacular. Having reached out to nearly every school child on the island, a ground-swell of support was created to conserve that island's endangered parrot. In just a few years the bird's numbers quintupled from 100 to over 500 parrots in the wild. Puerto Rico has a lot more to learn about conservation from some of its neighboring islands than it does from the United States. I certainly found that to be the case based upon my experience.

Puerto Rico taught me to get away from counting and monitoring things – as much as I like to do this. Such endeavors have to be done very selectively and tied to very specific management needs. Further, there has to be buy-in by the managers before surveys are even begun or their usefulness may well come to naught.

The abundant no-see-ums on Cayo Ratones were probably the most aggravating pest I have ever encountered, chiggers in St. Kitts being a close second. Despite this annoyance, however, that is all they were – an annoyance. Imagine then what Puerto Rico must have been like when its wetlands were full of mosquitoes – mosquitoes carrying malaria and yellow fever. It is no wonder that natural resource managers have an uphill battle conserving such areas. I visited virtually every fresh water marsh in Puerto Rico and I do not recall one which was not channelized to reduce standing water. Yet, our agency seemed inordinately insensitive as to just how to promote wetlands conservation. Again, we tended towards finding scientific reasons to justify the conservation of wetlands but we developed no strategies for communicating this information far and wide across the island. While we at the DNR were charged with protecting mangroves, other agencies were eager to destroy them. We had a communications problem which we never faced.

I learned one extraordinary lesson regarding how isolated we were as an agency following the assignment of a natural resources staff person to the Planning Board. This assignment was aimed at getting this particular individual out of our agency's hair. But, it turned out that each time this fellow reported back to our agency concerning happenings at the Planning Board, he would invariably disclose some huge revelation. This gentleman was acquiring more useful information that any ten of us combined. By being our sole pipeline to an agency much more powerful than our own and one whose actions had tremendous impacts on us, he had become invaluable. What an unexpected outcome!

Ancient Bones
and Underground Rivers

Not long after the offshore island survey, I was invited to participate in a totally different type of ornithological investigation being organized in Puerto Rico. Unlike censusing islands for colonial waterbirds, this survey focused on birds that were already extinct. It involved limestone caves and digging for fossils.

The preservation of fossils can only occur under unusual environmental conditions – conditions that prevent the destruction of a dead animal's bones either by scavengers or physical weathering. Rapid burial of the organism, either in the muck of a swamp, the sand of a desert, or the silt of a sea floor greatly facilitates fossilization. It so happens that by the nature of its geology, Puerto Rico has some ideal localities for the development and preservation of fossils. The best of these areas are the myriad caves that dot the haystack hills of Puerto Rico's north coast.

The haystack hills derive their common name from their strong resemblance to a seemingly endless series of round hay mounds albeit they are green in color. This same terrain is referred to as cockpit country on the island of Jamaica and among geologists goes by the term "karst topography," a name derived from the Kars region of Yugoslavia where this geological formation was first described. Mogotes (pronounced "mo-gó-tes") is the local Spanish expression applied to this peculiar terrain. Composed of limestone, the haystack hills were formed from what was once sea floor that was uplifted above the sea surface millions of years ago. Once exposed to weathering, particularly by rainwater, the massive slab began eroding in a unique way. This is because limestone dissolves readily in water. In any pocket of the rock where water might accumulate or flow, limestone is taken into solution and ultimately carried away leaving an ever deeper cavity or crevice. Over time, in this case millions of years, this relentless process of dissolution and removal of the limestone has resulted in the development of numerous caves honeycombing the region and a number of rivers that, for stretches, flow underground. Over 1,000 caves of various sizes have been systematically identified amongst the mogotes of Puerto Rico and certainly many others remain to be discovered.

Many of the fabulous geological features that decorate such caves, such as stalactites and stalagmites, are, likewise, the result of the same process of water interacting with limestone. These features, however, result when water saturated with dissolved limestone comes in contact with relatively dry air. The water is then evaporated leaving behind a limestone precipitate or residue that gradually accumulates into magnificent structures.

Miniature stalactites resulting from this same process can readily be observed in many areas of the world where bridges of stone and concrete were built as recently as a few dozen years ago. Rainwater drains through the cement between the impermeable stones and gradually forms stalactites hanging from the tunnel below. Some bridges in New York City around 50 years old already have developed stalactites nearly a foot in length.

As for Puerto Rico's caves, the drier ones are ideal for the conservation of fossil material. Any small creature that might accidentally fall into a crevice, or meet its end by other means, likely would not be dismantled and destroyed by a large scavenger; Puerto Rico had no such native animals that might enter a cave. Rather, the deceased animal would gradually be decomposed by insects and bacteria leaving its bones intact to gradually dry out and be preserved.

Another peculiar yet fascinating way in which extensive bone deposits accumulated in some of the island's caves was the result of owls. Owls are notorious for swallowing their prey whole and having the capacity to digest all components with the exception of the bones, fur, and feathers. These remains are then regurgitated by the owl as an impressively clean, odorless, and compact pellet from which one can easily extract and identify the bones of the hapless victim. It so happens that Puerto Rico once supported an endemic species of barn owl, now believed extinct. This, and to a lesser extent the still common and much smaller Puerto Rican screech owl, at times roosted on ledges at cave entrances and consequently regurgitated many of the tell-tale pellets into the protective environment of the cave. Droppings, accumulated over hundreds if not thousands of years, form bone deposits that at times could weigh tons.

Despite the excellent conditions for the formation of fossil material provided by Puerto Rico's caves, only one major fossil survey had ever been undertaken. This was a survey of Puerto Rico's living and extinct mammals conducted in 1916 by zoologist H.E. Anthony. All told, Anthony's inventory, combined with limited more recent contributions, set the island's mammalian fauna at 14 species of bats, three of which were extinct, and six species of terrestrial mammals only known from fossil remains. These included one insectivore and four small rodents, plus a ground sloth, quite massive, but minuscule in size when compared to the largest of its extinct continental cousins which was larger than an elephant. Rather, the local species was more the size, though not the structure, of the living tree sloths of Central and South America.

The reason for the extremely limited representation of mammalian species, with two thirds of them being bats, can be explained by Puerto Rico's history of never having had a land connection with the continental mainland. Bats can readily disperse across water barriers, and the ancestors of the few small-to medium-sized terrestrial mammals apparently survived a precarious journey on flotsam of some sort such as a fallen tree. Such journeys were indeed hazardous and their outcomes almost invariably fatal. This is attested to by the scant handful of mammals that have proved successful colonists in the thousands, if not tens of thousands, of years represented by cave deposits, not to mention the millions of years prior to the laying down of the deposits during which colonization and continued survival was possible.

What led to the demise of all the ground dwelling mammalian species is somewhat more puzzling. It appears that at least five of the six forms expired only a few thousand years ago, some possibly surviving nearly to the present. That all these species would become extinct simultaneously prior to human impacts on their populations is rather curious and cannot be explained without additional information. The last species, however, *Isolobodon portoricensis*, a rodent, clearly lived into recent times as evidenced by its bones commonly being present among the archeological deposits of the Arawak and Carib Indians. There is even good reason to believe that it was carried to several neighboring islands by these indigenous peoples specifically to serve as a food source.

Despite the interesting questions surrounding Puerto Rico's extinct mammals, the focus of the present expedition was primarily the island's fossil avifauna. Among the bones collected by Anthony were a good number representing fossilized birds. These were subsequently passed to the eminent ornithologist Alexander Wetmore who, from this collection, described five extinct forms including a snipe, crow, caracara, quail dove, and the previously discussed barn owl. In 1918 he also described the flightless DeBooy's rail named for the first collector of this bird's remains, bones which came from Indian deposits. Since Wetmore's limited work on the bones collected by Anthony, however, virtually no research had been done in this field in the transpiring half century.

Recognizing the potential to realize new discoveries in Puerto Rico and deeply interested in island species, Storrs Olson, a paleo-ornithologist from the U.S. National Museum of Natural History, came to the island.

Storrs was a young, good-natured fellow. Of average height and with a husky frame, the highlight of his features was a coppice of straight saffron locks and a boyish face that gave little indication of the profoundness of his knowledge of fossil birds nor the relentless intensity with which he pursued this interest. Accompanying Storrs was an impressively non-vocal assistant by the name of Tim.

Among the local biologists to join Storrs and Tim were myself and Peter, along with Noel Snyder, the U.S. Fish and Wildlife Service's ornithologist who was burdened with the formidable task of bringing the Puerto Rican parrot back from the brink of extinction. Few people could possibly have met this challenge as effectively as Noel, who was an indefatigable biologist and a super guy. Of course, one would never glean this from Noel's appearance. He had a distinctive presence, not derived from his medium stature and slight paunch, but rather from his grizzled black beard already generously threaded with gray and his weathered facial features and often bloodshot eyes, characters belying his continual exposure to the natural elements and the inordinate number of hours per day that he bled into his research at the expense of sleep. Nor did Noel's dress help diminish his imposing appearance. Always in beat-up old field clothes, he looked like he had just come out of the jungle – and in most cases he had! But one could bet that every nickel Noel ever saved on new boots or a modern field pack went directly to a more needy cause – research into the conservation of some endangered organism.

The expedition set off in two vehicles in the predawn of what was to be a bright sunny morning, as practically all mornings are in Puerto Rico, heading west from San Juan along the coastal highway. Quickly the large buildings dotting San Juan gave way to the urban sprawl of Bayamon. Here the vendors of chicharon (fried pork rind), who made this portion of the road famous, had not yet assumed their traditional positions lining the highway. By the time the heavy flow of traffic to San Juan had begun, we were already speeding past the extensive sugar cane fields of Dorado followed by the pineapple plantations of Vega Baja. Shortly beyond Vega Baja we turned off the main highway and headed inland. Abruptly we left behind the flat, cultivated coastal plain and plunged amongst the precipitous haystack hills. The road twisted and turned incessantly around the protruding mogotes making one travel three times as far by car as a bat might fly to reach the same destination. The flat tops of these hills were cloaked in vegetation with wild strangler figs and other vines draping the sides. In the scant red soil of the valleys, amidst white limestone boulders that had broken loose from the cliffs, local farmers cultivated their subsistence crops of bananas, plantains, and yautia, or pastured their few cattle which grazed virtually every blade of grass to the rock face. Not surprisingly, this region, due to its remoteness, is one of the least modified portions of the island, its inhabitants living not that differently than they had scores of years before. It may even have been, at the time, the only area of Puerto Rico experiencing a population decline. Attracted by industrial jobs and better wages in towns, local residents were abandoning marginal agricultural areas with the consequence that these lands were reverting to forests. More importantly, the substitution of bottled gas for charcoal as a fuel source several decades earlier allowed the forests of the hilltops and other unarable lands to go uncut, fostering a regeneration of native vegetation to levels unknown in this region perhaps for 100 years.

A long half-hour later, after countless S curves and switch-backs, we parked our vehicles along the road edge. Donning our packs we scurried down an embankment to a fairly open plain dissected by a shallow creek which we easily crossed on exposed rocks without wetting our feet. We then trekked through a steep valley among the mogotes. Noel and Storrs had carefully studied Anthony's manuscripts and had selected several of the caves to revisit from among the 54 Anthony had explored. Using the limited guidance supplied by Anthony's writings and directions from local residents, we were able to encounter our first cave with surprising facility. Perched high on a hillside, its dark, gaping entranceway dominated the valley. Our small party of fossil hunters scurried up the hillside excitedly, eager to rekindle this unusual quest left without standard bearers for more than a half century.

The wide cave entrance allowed in enough light to permit

the rapid exploration of this large chamber. The cave was dry in its interior, a good sign for fossil preservation, but our spirits flagged when we saw how extensively the fine cave soil had already been excavated. Though partially due to Anthony, the bulk of the extraction in this relatively accessible cave had doubtless been carried out by local farmers. That is because this cave's soil was guano, a substance extremely rich in nitrates and phosphates making it an extraordinary natural fertilizer. The guano in this cave and most others on Puerto Rico proper is the product of bat droppings. In other areas, however, such as the famous guano islands off Peru, seabirds are responsible for the deposits. Bat and seabird guano are so similar that after aging for a period it is impossible to distinguish from which of the two sources the guano originated. In addition to being a fertilizer of a value ten-fold that of cow manure, it was discovered in the nineteenth century that guano could serve as an important component for making explosives. As a consequence, the value of guano surged even higher and men killed over these bird and bat feces. An impressive 20 million tons of guano were removed from Peru's famous guano islands in a span of only 27 years, from 1848 to 1875.

A good example of the voracity with which guano was exploited can be found on nearby Monito Island. Monito is a tiny uninhabited islet a few acres in size lying halfway between Puerto Rico and the Dominican Republic. Though Monito's only neighbor, the substantially larger island of Mona, was heavily mined for guano, this is easily understood. Mona has numerous caves and half decent landings; consequently, it is not surprising that during its heyday in the late 1800's the island supported over 150 miners. Monito, however, is another story. This islet has only a single diminutive cave, over 100 feet up on its flank. But that is the least of the problem. More serious is that Monito is virtually surrounded by sheer cliffs except at a single point. All that point provides is the opportunity for a brave soul to make a precarious leap, on a day of calm seas, from a rocking dingy to a knife-sharp ledge. From this ledge, the cliff can be scaled, but not without significant exertion.

Given these impediments, it is striking that every inch of what could not have been more than several cubic yards of guano has been mined from Monito's cave and removed from the island by those earlier dauntless intrepids, in what manner who knows. To this day it remains difficult to fathom how valuable this material must have been to make worthwhile the execution of such a hazardous and arduous undertaking.

The deposition of guano, whether in caves occupied by hordes of bats or on islands carpeted with millions of birds, is a slow process likely measured in small fractions of an inch per year. It was, therefore, very impressive to peer about our fossil cave and notice from the stains upon the walls that, prior to being extracted, the guano had accumulated in places to as much as several yards in depth. This suggested occupation of this cave by bats for probably thousands of years.

Unfortunately, between the guano mining and Anthony's digging, little was left for us to excavate. Following a cursory perusal to confirm that this was indeed one of the important caves Anthony had visited, we packed up our gear and moved on. Within a short time we located several other caves in the vicinity which had apparently gone unexplored for fossils. Two of these produced large numbers of preserved bones.

It was late in the afternoon by the time we had sampled the new caves adequately and decided to call it a day. In short order our gear and collections were packed away, and we were filing out of the cave and down the narrow trail to the open valley among the mogotes. From here it was a brief ten minutes to our vehicles and a relaxed evening in a rustic hotel, formerly the hacienda of a large coffee plantation in the mountains.

At least, we all presumed it was ten minutes to our cars. That was the amount of time it had taken to get from our vehicles to the cave. It was, consequently, a total shock to all of us when we found our calculations to be off by well over an hour.

Rounding the last bend amidst the haystack hills we came out on the open plain where we could see our cars on the road no more than 200 yards distant. This grassy corridor was as we had left it a few hours earlier except for one thing – the creek was gone! In place of the shallow trickle which had not wet the soles of our boots on the outward journey, there was now a raging torrent! Apparently a storm upstream had filled the river to brimming without as much as a raindrop falling in our vicinity.

Standing before the swiftly flowing river, now no less than 20 feet in width, we pondered our next move. To the south, the direction from which it came, the torrent appeared to continue on indefinitely; to the north, it flowed for about one quarter of a mile and then abruptly plunged into the bowels of the earth. There it would flow underground, etching out new chambers in the limestone before reemerging, disappearing again and re-emerging several times before flowing on to the sea. Unusual under most circumstances, this disappearing act of a river is common in karst terrain.

Where the river vanished below ground, the mogote under which it flowed appeared formidably precipitous. Not excited about the prospect of a long and difficult climb over the haystack hill, and not particularly exuberant about being thwarted within a few yards of the road by an overgrown creek, we opted to ford the river where we stood. Most of us that is.

"I can't cross this river," mumbled Peter as the rest of us contemplated strategy. All faces turned towards the dissenter.

"Tonight I have a Bible meeting I must lead. I can't be wet for that, so I'll have to cross over the hill."

"Well, then Peter," Storrs queried. "Would you mind taking my camera and lenses with you so they don't get wet?"

"Sure, no problem," responded Peter.

"I have some camera equipment too, "chimed in Noel. "Would you mind taking that?"

"OK," agreed Peter, good naturedly.

"How about mine?" asked Tim.

"I have some also," I inserted.

"OK, OK," Peter responded in turn.

And so we loaded Peter down with our delicate equipment: four cameras, umpteen lenses, and sundry other photographic paraphernalia. Shortly thereafter, off he staggered with straps and bags slung around his body every which way, making him look something like a bipedal porcupine. Laden now with over 40 pounds of equipment, Peter appeared prepared for a stint no less than two years in the deepest jungle as chief photographer of some high caliber documentary.

Turning our attention back to the river, we noticed that a fallen palm tree was fortuitously lying right near the bank where we stood. If a rope were tied to its smaller end, and we could just get someone with the line to the opposite shore, it looked as though the tree was long enough to span the river. Thereafter the remainder of the group could shimmy across the trunk and stay reasonably dry. The plan sounded good, in fact very good considering the absence of any other reasonable alternatives. The only problem was how to get someone across the river and who was that someone going to be.

With no hesitation Storrs tied a rope to the narrow end of the tree, coiled up the remaining line, and stepped down the bank to the river's edge. His decisiveness was impressive considering the swiftness of the torrent and its disappearance underground not far downstream. I wondered whether perhaps I was not overreacting, that the river might prove only two or three feet deep and would be forded effortlessly.

Storrs stripped off his shirt, grabbed the coiled rope, stepped into the river – and disappeared. When he bobbed to the surface, he had already been swept a good distance downstream.

Flailing against the churning flow, he was well below us before he gained the far shore.

Despite the ominous look of the river, it had still managed to surprise me with its power. Storrs was a burly fellow, and it threw him around like a leaf. Now, aware of just what we were facing, it became even more apparent that the "tree strategy" was a good idea; swimming was simply too dangerous. Storrs had lost the rope in his frenetic plunge, so we recoiled it and cast one end to him. Then, with Storrs pulling from the opposite shore and the rest of us lending what assistance we could, the palm was gradually, after considerable exertion, maneuvered so that it nearly bridged the rapid current.

Noel was next. But before mounting the tree for the crossing, he decided that his recently purchased second-hand boots were too valuable to get soaked. So, sitting on the bank he removed one, stood, and flung it across the river. Storrs, high on the opposite bank, reached out for the boot, but the toss was a bit short and the boot eluded his grasp. Striking the crest of the embankment, Noel's precious footwear, ever so slowly, flip-flopped down the slope, at one moment appearing to have lost momentum and the next making one more turn towards the river below. Completing its descent the boot lay on the shore, its toe dangling over the edge and lapped at by the angry river. We all stood helpless as the boot and the river played out their drama. The only person with a chance to end the epic was Storrs, but one audacious act for the day was doubtless enough for him. Had he flung himself down the bank after the boot he might well have ended up once again in the drink and besides, the boot seemed to have expended its energy and was lying inertly on the shore. But, again we had underestimated the power of the river. Tickling the toe of the boot, the river gradually enticed it, little by little, until Noel's recently purchased pride plopped over the edge into a swirling eddy. For a moment the boot spun slowly in place, its rate of rotation gradually accelerating. By this time Storrs had worked his way down the slope and it appeared that all might be saved, but at that instant the boot burst from the eddy, like a race horse out of its starting gate and surged into the main current.

I glanced at Noel as this drama climaxed and had to restrain a chuckle when I saw the incredulous look on his face – eyes bulging, his mouth agape – but what could he do? Clearly Noel and I were not thinking along the same track, for as the boot accelerated downstream, Noel burst into action. Dashing along the top of the embankment parallel to the river, Noel pursued the bobbing boot. Of course, he had the odds stacked against him. For one, the boot started with a 20 foot lead and was making good time in the swift current. Furthermore, the path along the embankment was hardly that. Overgrown with tall grass it substantially hindered the forward progress of any hiker and, moreover, hikers plying their trade with only a single boot in place. But despite the odds there was one factor that overwhelmed all others: Noel was not the typical hiker – far from it. He blazed along that embankment, limping heavily on his unshod foot like a wounded elephant charging through the undergrowth. Nothing could stand in his way. Consequently, about 150 feet past where we stood, Noel finally caught up with the boot whereupon he catapulted himself into the river, snatched up the prize, and struggled to the opposite shore some distance further downstream, soaked, but unvanquished.

Two were across. Neither got many points for execution, but they were across. It was Tim's turn.

Learning from the experience of Noel, Tim decided to keep his footwear in place. Straddling the log, he cautiously edged out into the current. As he proceeded his feet gradually disappeared beneath the water as the tree sagged due to his weight and the absence of mooring on the far bank. Soon his knees and lower thighs were below water, but the rest of him was dry, and he was nearly halfway across the torrent. Suddenly there was a shriek of pain and Tim reversed himself. That is to say that for the moment the parts of him that had been below the surface, namely his feet and knees, rotated to the top of the log and the remainder of his torso that had an instant before been high and dry, had now vanished into the watery depths. In appearance Tim gave the impression of an oversized aquatic tree sloth hanging from the bottom of the limb, as arboreal sloths typically do. However, despite the vividness of the image he provoked, Tim was not adapted for such an aquatic existence, and he quickly sputtered to the surface.

"I got caught on the barbed wire!" he yelled as he rebalanced himself on the trunk, now as soaked as his predecessors. Clearly this had been Tim's loudest outburst during the trip, and we were all significantly impressed. Typical of Tim, he only commented when it mattered – and this mattered. We had forgotten about the loose piece of barbed wire, about a yard in length, no doubt once part of a boundary fence, that we had unthinkingly left dangling from the trunk. The remaining river crosser would have to take this into careful consideration so as to avoid Tim's fate.

Tim made what was left of the crossing without further event. His leg wound looked nasty, but was superficial. It now remained for the final warrior – myself – to cross the miserable 20 foot barrier which had divided us from a good meal, rest, and relaxation. I was determined to make a successful go of it.

The past hour of turmoil had provided me with two important lessons – keep my footwear on and look out for the wire near midstream. I eased onto the trunk and sidled out into the current. The chilly water rushed about my feet, my calves, and then my knees as I approached midstream. At that point I began looking and touching cautiously for the barbed wire which I knew was lurking beneath the surface. Fortunately I found it and negotiated by the spiny barrier with moderate difficulty since by this point my balance was precarious due to the rocking tree and the velocity of the current. From that point on all went impressively well, especially considering the overall misfortune of my companions. I managed to join them on the far shore, wet nearly to my waist, and having been spared the dangers of a desperate swim.

Reunited, we climbed the low slope to the road expecting to find Peter sitting there chortling at our blundering efforts, but he was nowhere to be found. Somewhat surprised and at the same time concerned, we deliberated as to what might have delayed his arrival for such an inordinate amount of time. An obvious explanation was the precipitousness of the mogotes in the area, a consideration instrumental in our decision to ford the stream. So, we did what we could by driving up the road to the mogote under which the torrent flowed and then sat and waited.

Ten minutes later Peter appeared. And was he a sight to behold. Not only did the description of his disheveled appearance as an erect walking porcupine become even more apropos, but he was wet. Soaked was more like it. As one might suspect, this resulted not from a battle with the torrent, but rather from the sheer exertion of toting all of our gear over the forbidding haystack hill. Peter's selection of the arduous mogote route in an effort to remain dry had proven a poor choice indeed, though it was of invaluable worth from our perspective of preserving our photographic gear. Had Peter chosen to ford the torrent with us he would certainly have become no wetter for his meeting that night than he was as a result of his hike.

And so our first day of fossil hunting came to a close. As the bedraggled group hiked to the cars, I cast one last glance at Peter. The poor fellow was waterlogged from perspiration and looked as wet and deflated as he had during the rainy night on the pier of Cayo Ratones. At that juncture I could only hope his bible meeting that evening dealt with the great flood. Regarding floods, Peter could now at least speak from first-hand experience, and in his drenched state who there would possibly doubt his word!

A pleasant evening was spent at Hacienda Rosa, a restored central residence of a formerly prosperous coffee plantation, now a delightful hotel. One of the benefits of coffee growing, at least as far as wildlife is concerned, is that coffee trees of many varieties need shade. As a consequence, taller, dense canopied vegetation, oftentimes orange trees, are grown to provide cover for the coffee, thus coincidentally providing food and shelter for a diversity of forest organisms. This was apparent the next morning when we hustled outside at the crack of dawn to enjoy the abundance of birdlife that thrived about the hacienda.

Puerto Rican screech owls were uttering their last tremulous trills as we emerged from our quarters, the sun just peeking over the horizon. For some reason these diminutive owls are blamed virtually islandwide for feeding on coffee beans and damaging the crop. This despite extensive proof to the contrary, based on examination of numerous stomachs, that the vast bulk of their diet consists of insects, and many noxious ones at that. No vegetable matter of any kind forms a component of this owl's food. This owl is also, according to local lore, a cure for asthma. That is, if it is prepared properly. An owlet must be fried without oil in a skillet and eaten without seasoning. Given the uses and abuses attributed to the poor Puerto Rican screech owl, a species known only from Puerto Rico and the Virgin Islands, it is a wonder that the creature still survives. Yet, all indications are that it is coping reasonably well with its tormentors.

Local owls have a worse rap on some other Caribbean islands. In Jamaica folklore goes that if a duppy owl (duppy means ghost) flies over screeching, you must say, "Salt and pepper, your mama and your papa, you brute you." And you had better say it fast because if the owl stops calling before you are done, you will have bad luck. The neighboring Dominican Republic has lore which urges you to put salt in the corners of your home to keep away owls which would, otherwise, suck the blood of your children. Owls, there, are believed to be witches – quite a challenge for conservationists!

As the screech owls trailed off, we began to hear a cacophony of other birds including the ventriloquial coo of the ruddy quail-dove, a secretive bird of the undergrowth, the hardy "cheer-y, cheer-y" of the dapper red-legged thrush, and the distinctive chatter of the Puerto Rican woodpecker, another species endemic to Puerto Rico.

Shortly after dawn we had the good fortune of discovering the tiny nest of a green mango humming-bird, another of the island's unique species. One of five species of hum-mingbirds on the island, the green mango is confined primarily to the central and western mountains. Coffee plantations are one of the principal habitats where this bird abounds. Distinguished by its rela-tively large size – a full five inches – and its totally emerald-green un-derparts, this attractive bird feeds

Puerto Rican Emerald

heavily on insects and spiders as well as nectar, a feeding regi-men typical of all the island's hummers. Undigested animal parts are compacted into pellets and regurgitated. To extract nectar from flowers, hummingbirds are equipped with long tongues for reaching deep into the corollas. Hovering before a flower their wings beat nearly 50 times per second as they suck up a meal. Though Puerto Rico supports two species of hummers substantially smaller than the green mango, even these are large compared to the smallest tyke of them all which inhabits the nearby island of Cuba. The bee hummingbird, endemic to Cuba, is the smallest bird in the world. It takes 14 of these mites to equal a single ounce.

The green mango nest we found was fascinating. Two diminutive white eggs, the universal clutch size of hummingbirds, were nestled in its finely woven cup-shaped interior. Snugly placed in the fork of a branch about head height, the nest was coated with lichens, an extremely effective camouflage. Such a disguise mechanism is common among hummingbirds. Spider webs held the construction together, another practice common to these birds.

As was the case with the Puerto Rican screech owl, a commonly-held belief among residents of the mountains, and particularly the haystack hills, relates to the use of hummingbird nests as an asthma cure. In some areas the nest is simply hung from a string around the neck of the sufferer. In other quarters the small cup is burned, and the ashes used to brew a remedial tea.

Dominican Republic folklore suggests that hummingbirds and their nests can serve as a cure for hearing loss.

Following our brief but invigorating dawn walk, we returned to the hacienda for breakfast. Being that the dining room staff spoke no English, and I was the only fossil hunter who spoke Spanish, I ordered for the group. We all decided to experiment with a dish "Crema de trigo" (cream of wheat) which, as it turned out, was absolutely scrumptious.

Immediately after breakfast we were off again to visit caves with renewed vigor and enthusiasm. This time, however, we decided to try another tactic. Rather than seek out the caves that Anthony already had excavated, we sought, instead, to discover new grottos. This change in approach immediately proved a very successful one.

Early during our expedition that day, we came upon an ordinary enough looking fissure nearly hidden by vegetation at the base of a precipitous mogote. Though high enough for a person to enter standing erect, one had to turn sideways to squeeze through the narrow entranceway. Once inside, the passage quickly broadened and at the same time became pitch dark. Slightly further on the passage expanded into a chamber followed by a second. Using our head lanterns we negotiated these whereupon we detected a ray of light far ahead. We worked our way towards it and found that it emanated from what turned out to be the largest chamber in the complex. This chamber was well lit since the entire central portion of the roof had collapsed. A large pile of rubble lay beneath the gaping hole. On the far side of the chamber was a shallow wedge of soil, no more than two feet in depth where it contacted the cave wall and petered out entirely only a few feet away. This small fringe of loose soil, which edged only a few yards of the chamber's perimeter, was practically the only earth in the cave. It was here we began to dig.

Scarcely a few shovelsful of soil had been sorted, and it was already apparent that we had stumbled upon a real find. The deposit literally was littered with bones, and well preserved ones at that. Owing to the unusual blackish cast of the fossils, we designated the locality as Blackbone Cave.

Hour after hour we shoveled the loose soil onto large sieves, sifted out the fine soil, and placed the precious bones left behind into labeled collecting bags. It appeared we had many generations of owls to thank for this windfall, as some fossilized owl pellets were present in the deposit. Our collection rapidly grew and we soon had separated thousands of bones for subsequent analysis.

Though I knew little about bones, it was exciting to feel that any one of these well-preserved relics might be from a species previously unknown to humankind. This feeling was strongly reinforced when I suddenly reached down and picked up what clearly was the jaw bone of a large iguana, a lizard unknown from Puerto Rico during historical times. As it turns out, Puerto Rico's fossil iguana belongs to the same species now found solely on Anegada, the easternmost and most arid of the Virgin Islands.

41

While this single case of a xeric or arid habitat dwelling species becoming extirpated from Puerto Rico might easily be attributed to happenstance, it begins to fit a pattern when other fossils of extinct species are examined, including several collected during our expedition. Particularly fascinating is an extinct giant tortoise, a creature typical of arid lands, fossils of which are known from the nearby island of Mona. One of two bird species new to science described from bones we collected was a palm swift, a bird who's living relatives typically inhabit dry savannas. Also known from Puerto Rico's cave deposits, but not extant today except in xeric habitats in other regions, are the Bahama mockingbird, the burrowing owl, and the crested caracara. Taken together, this evidence suggests that unlike the island cloaked in lush forest at the time of its encounter by Christopher Columbus over 500 years ago, if we go back 20 times further into the past, specifically to the late Pleistocene of 10,000-12,000 years ago, Puerto Rico probably was characterized by open savannas with scattered palms.

An explanation that might account for such a difference in Puerto Rico 10,000 years ago centers on the global effects of the Pleistocene glaciation in full swing at that time. Various studies indicate sea surface temperatures were probably 3 to 4 centigrade lower than at present. Such conditions would lead to reduced evaporation and consequently a reduction in rainfall and a more arid climate.

A related and very interesting consequence of the glacial period is that at its peak enough water was bound up in the polar ice caps to lower sea level approximately 400 feet. This would have united Puerto Rico and all of the Virgin Islands, with the sole exception of St. Croix, into a single landmass. Such a circumstance would explain the former distribution of the Anegada rock iguana and should be considered when looking at the geographical distributions of any species among the islands.

We dug all morning in Blackbone Cave in high spirits until a fair portion of the deposit had been sorted through and piles of specimen bags lay ready to be toted back to our vehicles and packed for shipment to the museum where they would be identified and catalogued. Regrettably, pressing business awaited me in San Juan, and I had to return there that afternoon. Though remorseful about having to leave the group after the discovery of Blackbone Cave, I was glad I had at least been in on what proved to be the highlight of the expedition. In addition to the palm swift that Storrs later described from the Blackbone Cave deposits, we also collected bones of an unusual new genus of finch with a peculiar flattened bill. Unrelated to any living form, Storrs gave this the lofty scientific name of *Pedinorhis stripsarcana* which, translated to the vernacular, means the "flat bill of mysterious stock."

My departure left the expedition without a translator, but no problems were anticipated considering English is spoken widely throughout the island. Having no creeks to ford to get back on the road, I was soon in my car wending my way through the incessant curves characteristic of all mogote roads. After a short stint of driving, and still deep among the haystack hills, I stopped for a quick lunch in one of the small colmados or general stores that dot every roadway the length and breadth of the island. Standing at the counter awaiting my jamon y queso (ham and cheese) sandwich to be grilled (this is the island's staple sandwich prepared in the standard way), a wizened old man entered and stood near me at the narrow serving bar. He clearly was not in transit, but rather was a local fellow who, following a common practice, had come to the colmado to hang out, to catch up on local gossip, and just to pass the time of day. Unfortunately for the elderly patron, fast-breaking news was in short supply at that moment, thus he spent more time stroking his scraggly white beard than in conversation with the store's proprietor. Under most circumstances I would have minded my own business, gulped down my sandwich, and been on my way. Circumstances, however, were a bit askew from typical. I had recently developed a casual interest in the ethnozoology of the island and, on top of that, I was now in that portion of Puerto Rico where traditional folkloric uses of animals were most likely to survive. Therefore, I leveled a question.

"Excuse me, but can you tell me whether the wild animals in

this region are used medicinally or in any other way?"

The old man turned to me appearing somewhat surprised. "Eh?" he grunted. I repeated the question.

Apparently taken aback by the unusual query, he sat in deep thought for a moment while his mind shifted gears. Then he relayed to me the universally accepted belief, on the island at least, of the numerous remedial properties of boa constrictor oil.

The Puerto Rican boa, a species endemic to the island, is a relatively small member of its family. The largest specimens have reputedly grown to about ten feet, but five to seven is a more typical length. The destruction of forests islandwide, the introduction of the Indian mongoose over 100 years ago, and the taking of boas for medicinal purposes all, no doubt, have contributed to the decline of the species. Yet, thanks to the nooks and crannies of the haystack hills and the snake's retiring and nocturnal habits, it appears this heavily persecuted creature is at least sustaining itself in numbers ample enough that it is not threatened.

Not all ground-dwelling creatures managed to survive the mongoose quite as effectively as did the Puerto Rican boa. Several ground nesting birds were nearly wiped out once the mongoose was introduced. The Indian or Javan mongoose as it is commonly called was brought to Puerto Rico in the late 1870's via Jamaica apparently to control the previously introduced rats which were decimating the introduced sugar cane, the heart of the island's economy at the time. The Indian mongoose is a sleek, agile creature with a long body and short legs, reminding one of a squirrel with a long snout. So, the Spanish attached to it a name which reminded them of a similar-looking mammal familiar to them in their native land – Spain. They called it the "ardilla" the Spanish word for squirrel.

But the mongoose is hardly fond of nuts. Though it does periodically eat fruits and other vegetation, it is primarily a voracious predator on a variety of wildlife including poisonous snakes. The story of Rikki-Tikki-Tavi by the renown writer Rudyard Kipling familiarized the world with the exploits of a mongoose which defeated a deadly king cobra. Doubtless respected and beloved in India for its predation on snakes, the powers of the Spanish crown in Puerto Rico during the late19th century decided that they too should reap the benefits of this appealing little animal.

Environmental impact assessments were hardly popular in that day so a few mongoose were brought from Jamaica to Puerto Rico with the hope they would prey on the abundant rat population. This they did, doubtless wrecking havoc on these pesky, ubiquitous rodents. Early studies of the feeding habits of the mongoose in cane fields found that in some cases nearly 90 percent of mongoose pellets showed signs of rats while over half of the mongooses appeared to be feeding exclusively on rodents.

That was all well and good, but early on it became evident that the mongoose was having a much broader impact. For one thing, rats were primarily nocturnal while the mongoose tended to hunt by day. Nothing was confining the mongoose to the vicinity of sugar cane fields where rats were prevalent. The adaptable mongoose found easy prey in many other habitats on the island and thus quickly spread to the island's furthest reaches – from the highest mountains to the seashore and from the rainforest to the arid scrublands. No area was immune to its onslaught.

And just what else did the mongoose feed on? It fed on virtually every animal that dwelled on or near the ground on which it could get its sharp teeth. This included such morsels as ground-dwelling birds, nestlings, eggs, snakes, lizards, frogs, toads, insects, hatchling sea turtles, you name it. And most of these were a no-brainer to catch.

I have made several references earlier to the fact that Puerto Rico is basically a volcanic island which arose out of the sea. The implications of this were discussed with regard to the absence of poisonous snakes and of indigenous terrestrial mammals. Another implication of this geological history is that Puerto Rico's native plants and animals evolved without being exposed to predation by mammalian predators. Yes, there were a handful of hawks, and

45

very few snakes, but there were none of the myriad of smart, wily mammals which harass and prey across every continent of the globe except Antarctica. This absence of mammalian predators resulted in Puerto Rico's fauna evolving without having to cope with such predation and thus not developing adaptations to do so. The introduction of such predators has made native species extremely vulnerable, a recurring scenario which we shall come up against time and again as we delve into the status of the island's unique fauna.

Through the late nineteenth century and into the twentieth the mongoose population exploded while, at the same time, many native species of wildlife doubtless crashed. Among these were all of Puerto Rico's birds which nested on the ground. All three species of quail-doves nearly disappeared. The Puerto Rican short-eared owl went virtually unseen for decades. And the Puerto Rican whip-poor-will, well, we'll get to that later. Lizards, snakes frogs and toads doubtless were seriously affected as well, but this is poorly documented on Puerto Rico. So let's quickly look at some well-documented cases on other Caribbean islands.

The case of the St. Croix ground lizard on nearby St. Croix in the Virgin Islands is a dramatic example of the mongoose's potential impact. Formerly common along St. Croix's coast before the introduction of the mongoose on the island in 1884, the ground lizard declined dramatically, a few surviving individuals being seen as late as 1968. Now virtually extinct on St. Croix itself, apparently due to mongoose predation, small populations of the ground lizard survive only on three small offshore cays all of which are mongoose free.

Even more definitive is the story of the whiptail lizard of St. Lucia. Known from only two satellite islands off St. Lucia's shores, there was interest in establishing a population at a third site, Praslin Island. Twenty-five whiptail lizards were released on Praslin, but all were quickly dispatched. Apparently a single mongoose on the island found them to be tasty morsels and wiped out the entire experimental population. Subsequent to removal of the mongoose another release was tried and this has proven successful. What a difference even a single mongoose can make!

Just imagine the threat to native faunas when more than one mongoose is prowling around. A female mongoose may breed two or three times per year and give birth to three young per cycle. And it is reported that a young female mongoose may begin to breed as early as ten weeks of age!

Returning to the issue at hand, boa constrictor oil is considered an excellent cure for practically all skin and joint ailments. In some cases the snakes are not slain, but rather their bellies are slit open, fat bodies removed, the belly resewn, and the snake sent on its not-so-merry way! That this oil extraction technique is supposed to work was attested to by this fellow who reputedly recaptured a healthy snake with stitch marks on its underside.

Be that as it may, we passed on through several other familiar cures and then moved on to lizards.

"If you have a bad thorn in your hand and you can't get it out, lizards are a great cure," he extolled, touching on a topic new to me.

Needless to say, I was at a loss to grasp how lizards might be associated with thorn extraction. "How is that?" I asked, anxious to fathom the mystery.

Apparently not only my interest had been piqued, but also that of the proprietor and another elderly man, nearly as old as the first, who had entered the store just moments before. We all stood in a tight group by the counter as the white-bearded gentleman continued.

"It's simple," he went on. "If you have a deep thorn that you cannot extract, you take the head of a lizard, open the mouth wide, and sink its teeth into the skin around the wound."

Puerto Rican common anole

Before going on I should clarify that the lizards of which the gentleman spoke are not six foot Komodo dragons, but rather six inch anoles. Many species abound on the island from sea level to the peaks of the highest mountains. The heads of most species are only about one half inch in length with teeth like the finest of needles.

"What then?" I queried, not at all anticipating the answer that followed.

"Well," the old gentleman went on. "The thorn is then pushed out the side opposite the wound."

"What do you mean?" I stammered. "Are you saying that if you have a thorn in your palm and put the lizard's head on it, the thorn will come out the back of your hand?"

"Yes," he responded carefully, no doubt wondering why I had suddenly become so animated.

Visions were sweeping through my brain of just how terribly serious a thorn wound would have to be before I would consider tolerating that a splinter be extracted from the opposite side of my hand. My hand nearly ached just thinking of it. But I must have heard him wrong. The conversation was in Spanish, and I must have misunderstood. Not only would the damage to your body be exorbitant as a result of the splinter proceeding the rest of the way through, say, a hand, but how could a lizard's head have such powers?

I opened my mouth to speak, but the second elderly fellow, who to this moment had been silent, entered the conversation. "It is true," he said, "that you place the lizard head over the wound, but the splinter is sucked out, not pushed through the hand."

I breathed a sigh of relief, both that my Spanish had been up to snuff and that a more acceptable interpretation of the power of lizard heads had been proposed. I waited for the first gentleman to admit his error and concede that he had accidentally stated the case in reverse.

He did no such thing. To the contrary, he staunchly reiterated his position, and in no time the two elderly protagonists were locked in a heated debate. Perhaps fortuitously, there was no poor soul available with a deeply embedded splinter on whom we might test both hypotheses at the sacrifice of a lizard. Having downed my sandwich and seeing no resolution to the conflict in sight, I reluctantly took leave of the group and exited the colmado leaving behind its occupants embroiled in a torrid discussion of what must have been one of the most unusual topics of debate to stir that locality in quite some time.

It was several days later when the fossil collecting expedition, its collecting bags bulging with specimens, finally returned to San Juan. A number of new caves had been explored, several of which had contained fossils, but none comparable to Blackbone Cave. Logistics also had gone reasonably well except for one detail. The morning subsequent to my departure the group had again sat down to breakfast at the hacienda anticipating another fabulous local rendition of cream of wheat. As things turned out, however, their local guide books, "How to Get By in Spanish With 50 Basic Words," or "Fluent Spanish in 24 Hours," did not do the trick. Apparently something was lost in the translation of "cream of wheat" for when the concoction served hit their eager palates, an immediate transformation occurred. This was from a state of expectant bliss to a condition of stark reality and utter distaste. Rather than being served the delicious cereal of the day before, the group managed to communicate to the cook that what they really wanted was flour and water. No doubt considering these Americans to be quite bizarre, the chef met their request and served the expedition a paste that almost sealed their mouths shut for the duration of the day. Considering that sign language was a weak suit of all the breakfasters, they considered themselves lucky to regain the use of their tongues and simply escape from the table hungry. Some cookies and other nourishment were purchased later on the way to the field, but despite the intrepids in the group, veterans of the raging torrent crossing, none would again dare attempt to procure a bowl of delicious, local cream of wheat.

A month after the fossil expedition, Noel received a letter from Storrs, back at the Museum, who had already begun the tedious task of sorting the thousands of bones we had collected. Apparently the Blackbone Cave deposit represented such an outstanding diversity of organisms Storrs wondered whether we might be able to return there and collect some additional material. Delighted to oblige, we recruited Peter and two of Noel's assistants and within the week were off again to enjoy, for one more day, the excitement of fossil hunting.

Back at Blackbone Cave once more we began to excavate, but this time we sunk our trench shovels into the opposite edge of the deposit, a few yards away from our previous diggings. Cautiously we excavated one thin layer at a time, so as not to damage the delicate fossils. We had been at our task for only a short while when we came upon what every explorer hopes for – the big discovery.

Noel's shovel had clinked against a hard object, something not encountered previously in these sediments. The use of our clumsy tools was immediately abandoned, and we carefully worked away the soil with our fingers. To our amazement the shank of a large bone was gradually exposed to view. None of us was particularly adept in vertebrate anatomy, but as more and more of the bone became visible it seemed clear we had something at least the size of the largest fossil species known from Puerto Rico to date, that being the heavily boned ground sloth. The fossil gradually emerging before us was infinitely larger than anything we had found with Storrs and certainly could pertain to nothing smaller than a sloth. What about something larger? Anxiously, we excavated around the bone, but our progress was severely hampered by the extreme fragility of the specimen. Each time the bone was touched with any hard instrument, regardless how gently, a portion of its structure would crumble away. This ultimately resulted in our entire team of five meticulously dusting away the soil from around the prize for the better part of an hour until our priceless find could be worked free. It was then carefully wrapped in tissue paper and stored so that no manner of molestation could possibly cause it damage. At this point the composite wisdom of the group, derived from ceaseless discussion during excavation, concluded two things. One, this was a limb bone. And two, it was a heck of a large one at that.

Astoundingly, to our great good fortune, it was still as-sociated with the next limb segment. So, we set to extract-ing this second bone while in a state of excruciating ecstasy that only such an extraordinary trophy could arouse. Another hour of tedious excavation provided ample opportunity for contemplation and discussion of just what our discovery might represent. The more complete fossil record from Cuba suggested some possibilities.

As was the case with Puerto Rico, Cuba was a much larger island during the Pleistocene than it is at present, due to sea level having been substantially lower. Also like Puerto Rico, Cuba sustained a mammalian fauna which, in addition to bats, included various herbivorous rodents and insectivores uniquely distinct to that island. The island's previously greater size facilitated the survival of a more diverse fauna. Nevertheless, neither Cuba nor Puerto Rico supported any mammalian carnivores to prey upon this array of potential food items. To fill the void resulting from the absence of carnivorous mammals on Cuba, other animals became adapted to substitute in the role of top predators in the food chain. These other organisms were birds.

One group of birds that adapted impressively to Cuba's unique environment was the owls. Basically, the owls of the world are divided into two families, the so-called typical owls, which boast well over 100 species, and the barn owls, which contain fewer than a dozen. Living barn owls all are medium sized, but such was not the case in the past. Not surprisingly, Cuba presently supports the ubiquitous barn owl common throughout North and South America as well as much of the rest of the world. But, it also formerly harbored a gigantic relative of the present species that was so large as to exceed the size of any owl alive today. Furthermore, Cuba supported a third barn owl species, four to five times the size of the living barn owl, which even exceeded its gigantic cousin in size. Not to be outdone in the size department, an enormous representative of the family of typical owls, a bird the size of a bald eagle, also evolved on Cuba. As if three tremendous owls were not enough to gorge on Cuba's ample sloth and rodent populations unchecked by mammalian predators, a titanic eagle, larger than the bald eagle, also evolved.

Given the array of extraordinarily large predatory birds which formerly occupied Cuba, one might expect, in this earlier epoch, that the dry savannas of that island were littered with sloth carcasses putrefying in the tropical sun. Not so. To ensure a clean environment on the island, a huge species of condor with a ten-foot wingspan formerly patrolled Cuba's airspace. The California condor, now confined very locally to the southwestern United States and on the brink of extinction, at one time spanned much of the country occurring east into Florida. A population of this species in Cuba, or a closely-related form, was a conspicuous component of nature's version of environmental pollution control several thousand years before the present.

Though it appears Cuba's extraordinary Pleistocene owl population apparently became extinct prior to human habitation of the island, by either Europeans or Amerindians, the neighboring Bahamas offer a somewhat different story. Those islands, formerly much larger, and many of them connected during the Pleistocene, housed at least one of the giant barn owls present on Cuba. And that owl roamed what is now Andros Island at least until Amerindian colonization around the year 800 A.D. and perhaps into the era of European colonization as well. The result, besides the presence of fossil bones of the bird and its prey, is the legend of the Chickcharnie. The Chickcharnie, according to local lore, was a small human-like creature with feathers, red eyes, and three toes per foot on which it hopped through the forest. That must have been quite the creature to scare the wits out of some unsuspecting wanderer!

While Puerto Rico had a scaled down version of Cuba's Pleistocene mammalian herbivores, meaning similar species but fewer of them, not a single large predator fossil, neither bird nor mammal, had ever been discovered on the island. Could the bones we were digging represent the first known specimen? It was thoughts such as these that whetted our appetites to discover exactly what it was we were so meticulously exposing to sight for the first time in human history. Was it one of the huge owls or a titanic eagle? The bones seemed too stocky and massive for that. How about some large mammal that had not yet been discovered? One of our group recalled that fossils of a nearly bear-sized rodent were known from Anguilla and St. Martin in the nearby Lesser Antilles. The bones we dug seemed like excellent candidates for belonging to such a creature. Yes, that we likely had a large mammal rather than a bird was the consensus. But what?

Two and a half hours of painstaking labor had gone into the extraction of the first two fossilized bones, both of which we had carefully packed away. Now, the moment of truth was at hand. Having removed what were clearly two limb bones, we knew the foot of our mystery animal was next to be uncovered, and this would be the clue that resolved our doubts. While none of us possessed the expertise to identify the animal to which the limb bones belonged, we felt comfortable distinguishing the talons of a large bird of prey from the heavy claws of a sloth or the nubby toes of a rodent. In but a few minutes the great riddle would be solved.

And so it was. A short spurt of feverishly intensive effort exposed enough of the foot that we could clearly discern its form. It was a cloven hoof!

What in the dickens was a hoof doing on our creature? This foot looked like that of a cow! Who ever heard of a fossilized cow in the West Indies? What in the world was going on?

We never did figure out what had happened. Alas, Storrs indeed confirmed that we had dug up a cow. How a cow could have gotten into Blackbone Cave with its narrow entranceway was certainly a mystery. It may have fallen in through the hole in the ceiling of the main chamber. But how, then, did it get buried among the smaller fossils in the shallow scrape of earth off in a corner of the cave far from the collapsed roof? Who knew. There was no practical explanation, no rhyme nor reason at all to the buried cow.

Yet, did it matter? What it came down to was that we had dug up a cow. And to add insult to injury, it had taken the five of us three full hours to complete our embarrassment.

Enough was enough. My fossil hunting days were over. It was out of the dingy caves and back to wild animals in the forests.

⌐‿⌐

Reflections

It took me a while to recognize how much folklore serves to dictate the attitudes of local people. And much of this folklore may not be favorable towards local wildlife. The case regarding the Puerto Rican screech owl is but one example. The situation is substantially more serious on some other Caribbean islands such as Jamaica and Hispaniola.

Natural resource agencies tend to pooh-pooh such "fantasies" – big mistake! People's attitudes mean everything. We ignored such sentiments at our own peril. We ignored the island's few hunters because they were always mad at us and some had strange ideas about the birds they were hunting. So what. Work with them.

If not, where was our constituency? Who was there to support us when we wanted to change a regulation or propose a new law? Who was there to advocate an increase in the budget for natural resources conservation? No one. And then we would sit and wonder why our agency never got budget increases. It was due to our own blindness.

It took time, but finally the message came through to me loud and clear. Natural resource management is not just about the resource. This was our big mistake. It is much more about the people who might use or abuse the resource. Since people are invariably the cause of the problem, they must also be part of the solution.

⌐‿⌐

It seems a natural tendency for people to believe that uninhabited areas are relatively pristine. Wrong. Our fossil hunting expeditions and Monito's cave brought home strongly just how off-base such thinking is. The massive guano extraction which had taken place in some of the caves we visited could easily have been overlooked by the inexperienced. Beyond that, who knows how much those caves in which we had toiled for but a few hours had been homes for indigenous peoples or refuges of escaped slaves for perhaps years, decades, or even centuries. How such habitation might have altered such sites is a matter for speculation and study. What is important is to be aware that such use undoubtedly had its concomitant impacts with regard to alteration and degradation of the natural environment.

This experience with caves is used to serve only as an example. The situation is hardly unique. Mangroves, which are usually uninhabited, may seem pristine until we learn to what extent they are visited for oyster harvesting, fishing, or to cut wood for charcoal or fence posts. Mangroves are also altered dramatically by increased siltation and the alteration of fresh water inputs resulting from human manipulations of surrounding areas.

Yes. When we talk about pristine habitats, we need to be careful. It is much safer to presume that a habitat has been altered until we can document otherwise, than to presume the reverse.

The Crow That Returned
From Extinction

There were times in the course of my work when I couldn't just pick up my binoculars, scope, and field notebook and head for exciting new areas to explore. One of the principal roadblocks to such a carefree existence was the need to evaluate "consultas." Consultas were solicitations from other government agencies requesting our opinion on some proposed project. Early on consultas generally came from the Planning Board, an absurdly powerful agency responsible for zoning development of the island. Providing input into that agency's regional planning schemes could potentially prove highly beneficial regarding the protection of areas important for conservation. The Area of Natural Resources received dozens of consultas a week. Few ever requested our opinion on major zoning decisions. Rather, the typical consulta dealt with a request for the construction of a gas station, grocery store, beauty parlor, or whatever in an abandoned sugar cane field or vacant lot on the outskirts of some town. Only a small minority of consultas pertained to localities of any ecological consequence.

This being the case, one might have expected the understaffed and underfunded Area of Natural Resources to routinely review only the consultas which portended significant environmental damage. Not so. In one authoritative stroke, the head of the Area mandated that every consulta be personally verified by someone on the staff. This meant about half of the technical personnel in our tiny, fledgling agency would commit the majority of their time to driving back and forth across the island relentlessly checking that indeed there was an abandoned sugar cane field where the consulta proposed a gas station be built, or that an overgrazed pasture was in fact at the site suggested for a new grocery store. To make matters worse, it was not enough that a single natural resources specialist check most of these consultas, rather personnel with different expertise would travel together wasting day after day and week after week in consulta reviewing.

Fortuitously, Ruben Freyre, initially my immediate boss in the Division of Flora and Fauna, protected me from becoming mired in this exercise. At the same time, another biologist in our division contentedly filled the void. He apparently believed that consultas were his calling, for he seemed to prefer confirming consulta veracity than taking on more substantive projects. His enthusiasm in this regard helped free me to concentrate on more significant threats jeopardizing Puerto Rico's impressive natural resources.

Ironically, it was the indirect result of reviewing a consulta by which I ultimately became head of the Division of Flora and Fauna of the Area of Natural Resources. This derived from the circumstance that every now and then a major consulta of true consequence came to our attention and our entire division would become involved in its review. Such was the case for a proposal to construct a nuclear power plant in the magnificent mangrove swamp and estuarine system of Jobos Bay on the island's southern shore.

By the time the proposal reached our agency it did not come as a surprise that its proponents not only had spent perhaps millions of dollars in analyzing the characteristics of the site and in developing plans, but also in performing some preliminary land clearing and construction. Why should they already be clearing mangrove forests when they did not yet have a permit to construct the reactor? Who knew? Some powerful industries likely felt that formal project approval was just a formality. Others may have believed that once money had been invested in a site there would be a tendency not to want to see it wasted.

On the positive side, the environmental review submitted to the Planning Board to obtain a building permit was uncharacteristically thorough. Comprehensive lists had been prepared of the birdlife, vegetation, fishes, and other marinelife as well as data collected on geology, soils, marine sediments, water quality, currents, and so on. It seemed ridiculous, however, as our team of five specialists boarded a jeep for the trip to Jobos Bay, that this small brigade, with its total equipment inventory of one 12 foot motor boat and a pair of binoculars, could, in one field day, effectively verify the reams of data compiled over the course of months, often using highly sophisticated equipment.

Regardless, reviewing the consulta was our mission, and we set off at the crack of dawn one morning to give it our best shot. Making up the specialist team were Mitch and myself plus two other members of our division who were the human antithesis of one another. Alvaro was a highly competent marine biologist, as outspoken as he was bright, the product of an unusual Lebanese-Colombian heritage. The other specialist, Charles, studied terrestrial plants and never set foot in the water. For every ounce of Alvaro's boisterousness, Charles was quiet. And Alvaro's challenging, iconoclastic approach was countered by Charles' polite manner and dutifulness. The fifth member of our team was John, a planner, appropriately enough from the Area's planning office.

By mid-morning we had crossed the island from San Juan to Jobos, launched our boat, and uneventfully putt-putted out of the entrance of Jobos Bay. Our initial objective was to assess the quality of the mangrove communities west of the bay. We had nearly reached the area when fate came into play in the form of a faulty spark plug. Result – the motor coughed and expired. Under most circumstances such an event is no big deal. A spare plug is a routine accessory in most boats – but not in this one. Absent a spare spark plug, Alvaro, not unfamiliar with motors, did all he could to restart our defunct engine, but his efforts were to no avail. The motor was not to be revived. Our predicament reached the dimensions of a plight due to our having just left Jobos Bay and being now in the open Caribbean. Though we were only 50 yards offshore, the heavier wave action, coupled with our tiny boat being overcrowded, created a real potential that we might be swamped. Furthermore, our plight was heightened by the presence of a brisk offshore wind that had already blown us 25 yards further from land before we were able to drop anchor and consider our limited options. It did not take much deliberation to recognize that we had only one option: get to shore by any means possible before the wind got stronger and the sea got rougher. With that, Alvaro and I each grabbed an oar, the only auxiliary equipment in the boat, and got in position to row. It was a relief that we at least had oars. But it was painful then to discover that the boat had no oar locks! This meant we would have to paddle, and paddling with oars in a boatful of people against a strong wind can be equated with trying to run up a "down" escalator – on your knees. It was at this point that a pet phrase of the head of the Area of Natural Resources popped to mind. "Anyone can do things with money," he would emphatically pronounce. "The challenge is to accomplish things without money!"

So here we were, anchored in the Caribbean only 75 yards from land, trying to do our job without money – money for one spark plug, two oar locks, and, heaven forbid, a small auxiliary engine. In the balance for these trinkets were, possibly, the lives of several people – for Charles and John could not swim.

Awkwardly, Alvaro and I began to paddle as others of the crew hauled in the anchor. Not surprisingly, we lost ground, drifting a bit further from shore. We knew, however, that this dash was our only opportunity, since the chances of a boat happening by and assisting us were practically nil. So with this sobering thought Alvaro and I laid our backs into paddling even harder. Little by little we stopped losing ground, seemed to break even for a spell, and then begun to make headway. Buoyed by this observation we flailed away until some 15 exhausting minutes later someone dropped over the side of the boat and touched bottom. We were safe.

With our survival ensured, our next obstacle was to get the boat back to the dock and to our trailer. We had covered about three miles in the boat before the motor broke down; it would be a long haul back. Sending someone back by land for help was impractical as the entire shoreline from where we were to the dock was densely forested and practically uninhabited. Our only recourse was to tow the boat by hand.

Enthusiastically Charles lowered himself into the water, waist deep at this point, grabbed the anchor line, and began to drag the boat and its crew parallel to the shore, in the direction of the pier. Towing a boat with four people aboard through three-foot deep water with each footfall sinking an additional six inches into mangrove muck is tedious work. Consequently, at intervals all crew members took turns until John had the line in hand. Despite being the biggest and burliest member of our contingent, John seemed to make little headway in our dogged assault on the pier. Not that the rest of us had done much better. A half mile per hour pace was about all we could hope for and at such a rate the pier was six hours distant. But with John towing the line, we were talking one quarter of a mile per hour and 12 hours in transit. Finding this unsatisfactory, the rest of us in the boat cajoled and taunted John for his lack of effort. But all our admonitions fell on deaf ears. I attributed this to John having "planner's disease" or "programmer's syndrome," a common ailment I had noticed among many of the planners and programmers with whom I had come in contact. The disease's symptoms are: *1)* an acute zealousness to produce written documents, yet an aversion to seeing them implemented; *2)* to consider all plans out of date, even plans they had just completed; *3)* to always appear busy and have a critical deadline to meet; *4)* to never produce anything that yielded concrete results; and *5)* an inability to recognize a truly important and worthwhile task.

Or maybe lethargy was John's middle name. Regardless, nothing could induce John to pick up his pace so he was dropped out of the rotation. He spent the remainder of the trip reclining in the boat gulping down countless oysters which Alvaro had taken the pains to harvest from the bountiful red mangrove roots lining the shore parallel to our route.

Under most circumstances mangroves are a special place.

Though I cannot say that this day was one of them. Four types of mangrove trees occur in Puerto Rico, each adapted to particular ranges of salinity and water depth. Certainly the most distinctive is the red mangrove readily identified by its cluster of prop-roots which support the main trunk well above water level. Reds are the most seaward of mangrove species, typically growing in the sea where the waters are calm. Such areas vary from protected bays and estuaries to shallow waters out at sea that are protected by fringing reefs. The network of intermingled prop-roots created by a forest of red mangroves is about as impassible an environment as anyone could want to transit. Fortuitously though, such forests are frequently cross-cut by meandering channels and dotted with hidden lagoons. The borders of such lagoons, because of their inaccessibility frequently serve as roosting places for herons, egrets, and other colonial waterbirds.

Prop-roots generally are but two or three inches thick. If, however, you are able to pull one up from along the edge of a channel, the submerged portion can sometimes span nearly a foot. This is because of the myriad organisms attached to these roots. Sponges, algae, marine worms, tunicates, bryozoans, barnacles, mussels, and of course oysters like the ones John was savoring, which make these prop-roots their home are jointly referred to as epibiota. They congregate on the roots so as to benefit from the nutrient rich waters flowing through the mangrove. This high nutrient richness derives both from topsoil run-off trapped by the roots as well as from decay of the numerous mangrove leaves which fall to the ground and are trapped by the roots. Not only do sessile organisms, organisms which attach to some firm base, benefit from the richness of the mangrove, but so do mobile creatures such as crabs, anemones, shrimp and small fishes. Red mangroves, due to the nutrients they provide as well as the protective nature of their roots, serve as important nurseries for many marine organisms including shrimp and various fishes. One of the tiny fishes two or three inches long which can be found among these roots, when full-grown, becomes a five or six foot barracuda.

The high nutrient levels of the mangroves serve not only the organisms which reside there. Actions of tides, currents and storms spread these nutrients widely through adjacent waters to the ultimate benefit of many other marine organisms.

Mangroves have further values for humans. They serve as a major buffer to storm surges and they are a sink for flood waters. They capture sediment adding soil to the landmass. They provide a valuable wood for construction and, formerly, for charcoal. Perhaps most importantly they are just a very special environment of great esthetic beauty and richness. Regrettably, this beauty was entirely lost on us as we trudged relentlessly through the muck so typical of mangrove fringes.

It was late afternoon when our motley and exhausted crew, except for John who suffered from nothing more than abraded fingers from all the oysters he had handled, slogged up to the dock. The boat was quickly loaded onto the trailer, and we hastened off for a well-deserved meal. The stars were already resplendent by the time we started our long, winding journey back over the mountains to San Juan.

The next day in the office we were paid a visit by the head of the Area of Natural Resources. This was quite unusual considering it was rare to ever see him outside his office, much less in ours. We presumed he had heard of our near demise of the day before and had come to express his sympathies. Such was not the case.

"Where were you yesterday?" he demanded. His scowl moved from one to the other of us, leaving the option to respond to whomsoever might muster the nerve.

"We went down to Jobos Bay on a consulta," retorted Alvaro undaunted.

"How dare you not be here for yesterday's office party! Don't let it happen again!." He turned to leave.

I was incredulous. Doubtless we were all incredulous. How could he not support that our office had chosen to work instead of party? How could he not care about the trials and tribulations we had suffered?

"Do you realize what nearly happened to us and why?" inserted Alvaro, saying the unthinkable and stopping the cacique in his tracks. He spun around, his perpetually red face now turning crimson. Not missing a beat Alvaro went on to recount our harrowing experience and how it was ludicrous that the office did not supply the basic necessities field workers need to do their jobs effectively and safely.

Despite Alvaro's impassioned and eloquent plea, the cacique remained unmoved. "Anyone can get things done with money," he retorted. "The challenge is to accomplish things without money," and with that he turned and left.

After a protracted debate, the plans for the Jobos nuclear power plant were shelved. This was not due to any input we provided, but rather a consequence of an extinct geological fault being found virtually beneath the proposed reactor site. Ultimately our involvement in the Jobos Bay case had a greater impact on our internal office structure than it did in determining whether the reactor would be built. Purely coincidentally, within a few months of our maritime disaster, Ruben, our chief, was transferred to head a different office, and Charles went to work for another agency. That left Alvaro and myself as the only biologists in the office, with Mitch as our assistant. The head of the Area of Natural Resources now had a tough decision facing him – who should act as Chief of the Division of Flora and Fauna until he could find a replacement with whom he was comfortable. Should he promote Alvaro, a well-trained Latin American biologist with a master's degree in marine sciences, a person completely fluent in Spanish and English who expressed his views rather strongly, but always talked sense; or, should he go with a gringo with degrees in geology and teaching, who spoke in the most broken Spanish imaginable, but who hadn't raised a stir?

The decision was easy. The next day I was designated Interim Chief of the Division of Flora and Fauna.

Prior to becoming a Chief my contact with the head of the Area of Natural Resources had practically been limited to my job interview. Now that he was my direct boss I expected this to change. It didn't. All communications with him were passed through one of his aides or his domineering secretary with whom conversing was pretty much like dealing with the head honcho himself. One day, however, an issue arose about which I just had to see the Area head and, remarkably, I was granted an audience.

The issue concerned a proposed highway, the right-of-way of which reputedly would pass directly through Cambalache, one of the Commonwealth forests. In a preliminary meeting the cacique had requested that I produce an exact map of the proposed route. This I had done following much hoop jumping with the Highway Authority. Entering the Area head's office, I laid the map proudly on his desk and pointed to the section of the road proposed to pass directly through the center of the forest.

"I see," he said seriously, his brow furrowed.

I waited for him to continue.

Silence.

I waited some more, but had he made any remarks beyond "I see," they were inaudible to me. I glanced up from the map we had been studying and looked him in the eye.

"Thank you," he said with a decisive finality that indicated our meeting had come to a close.

"But, but…. Aren't we going to take any action on this?"

"No," he responded, apparently taken aback at my suggestion. "I just wanted to know what was being proposed."

I was at a loss for words resulting from my state of shock and rising anger. How could he take no action on a case like this? Why not at least send a letter to the Highway Authority? If he had never intended to act, why have me waste several days tracking down this detailed map? Judging by the firmness of his response, I knew there was no hope of changing his opinion. I therefore capitulated. "Well, if we are not taking action on this case, I may as well send the map over to the Environmental Quality Board. I believe they are interested, and it will save them the effort of tangling with the Highway Authority." I turned to leave.

"Don't do that!" ordered the ANR head.

"Why not?" I responded, looking back over my shoulder, incredulous for the second time in five minutes.

"If the EQB wants the map, they can get their own!" he intoned with an authority not to be questioned.

⁓

The Area of Natural Resources did not have a monopoly on poor leadership. Early in my employ a newspaper article appeared highlighting that a local institution involved in the maintenance of potable water supplies had come up with a novel idea for ridding reservoirs of the noxious water hyacinth.

The water hyacinth is a beautiful floating aquatic plant with glossy green leaves and a spike of radiant violet-blue flowers which appear not unlike its terrestrial counterpart. Yet, despite its fine appearance, the plant is the bane of fresh water ecosystems throughout the warmer portions of the globe. It has major effects on sunlight penetration, levels of dissolved oxygen, evapotransporation, rates of water flow, and many other factors that matter to water managers, fish, and fowl. Its beauty notwithstanding, the water hyacinth might well be considered the "rat" of the plant world when it comes to the ecology of warm water lakes and slow moving rivers. Control of this pesky plant costs millions of dollars a year in many regions of the world, generally in a losing cause, because the plant seems uncontrollable. Consequently, any reasonable suggestion that might alleviate the problems caused by the "jacinto de agua" generally attracts significant attention. The head of the water resources institution thought he had just such an idea.

What we can do, he suggested in his article, is to bring to the island a creature which loves to eat water hyacinths and can eat lots of them.

So far so good.

Things went downhill from there. His proposal was to import the 6,000 pound behemoth of Africa's river systems, the docile looking hippopotamus. One of these creatures, he suggested, could be placed experimentally in Cartagena Lagoon, a picturesque, shallow lake in the southwestern corner of the island. Cartagena could then be encircled with electric fencing to keep the hippo in its place and voila! We would see if it could accomplish naturally what small fortunes had been unable to achieve mechanically and chemically – the elimination of the water hyacinth.

The idea struck a resonant chord in some. Immediately a well-known newspaper writer hopped on a plane to Washington, D.C. with a suitcase full of water hyacinths. She was ecstatic to report upon her return that the National Zoo's resident hippo had immediately munched down the hyacinths, and indeed the plants appeared to have been relished. Things were looking good for a hippo introduction.

Considering the large number of detrimental introductions Puerto Rico already had experienced, I was bothered by the blasé approach being taken with respect to the hippo. Rats had been introduced centuries before, of course unintentionally, and had caused their typical destruction of agricultural crops and grain supplies. To combat this pest the mongoose was introduced late in the nineteenth century and rather than control rats, it went on to attack domestic chickens and to bring several native species of ground-nesting birds and harmless snakes to the brink of extinction. In another case, Tilapia, a hardy fish from Africa, was imported to serve as an alternate food source and instead was never widely accepted into the local cuisine and only served to churn up channel bottoms, modifying those aquatic environments so that they became uninhabitable for species of native fishes.

Apparently concern for the impacts of the hippo was limited due to the expectation that only one animal was to be involved. This was a naive approach.

Had any thought been given to keeping the hippo within the confines of the lake? Would it want to stray? And if so, how large a shock by the electric fence would be necessary for the animal to get the message that lands beyond the enclosure were off limits? Would the electric current necessary to discourage a hippopotamus electrocute a human being? And one could bet there would be lots of sightseers that would have to be kept away from the fence and the animal.

The plan's proponents apparently had not delved very deeply into the behavior of hippos in their natural environment or they might not have been so quick to promote their new proposal. In actuality, hippos remain in the water much of the day, but during this period they primarily sleep. On the other hand, it is at night that they are active and feed. At this time they regularly wander substantial distances from the water in search of food and as often as not feed in the uplands. It is during these feeding forays that hippos have been found many miles from the nearest water. Furthermore, this massive creature is known to have a palate which finds sugar cane particularly attractive. It was the hippo's depredations of this crop which caused the last herd to be eliminated from the country of Natal. A quick survey around Cartagena Lagoon would indicate that sugar cane was virtually the only agricultural crop grown in the vicinity.

The question of whether hippos would eat water hyacinths in the wild when they had other vegetation to choose from was never addressed. It is well documented that behaviors and apparent feeding preferences exhibited by an animal in captivity do not necessarily represent how the animal will act in the wild. Returning to the mongoose, a mongoose certainly may feed on a rat thrown into its cage, but rats, even where they are abundant, may not become a major component of the mongoose's diet in the wild. For one thing, there may be a more tasty or less combative alternative food item available. For another, the mongoose is a daytime predator while the rat is nocturnal, thus their paths rarely cross, doubtless to the great benefit of the rat.

"Plan Hippo" ultimately was discarded, for what reason I am not aware. I hope a letter I wrote to a local newspaper concerning inadequacies of the plan played some part.

Had Plan Hippo been implemented, I expect that there was a better than even chance that a disaster might have resulted. That the water hyacinth problem would have been controlled without other negative consequences is highly improbable. My greatest concern was the potential future headline: "Enraged Hippo Demolishes Half of Lajas Valley." It would go on to read something like, "On the night of June 14, a believed-to-be tranquil hippo, introduced to Cartagena Lagoon in an experiment to control water hyacinths, became enraged from the shock of an electrified fence constructed to keep it restrained. The irritated hippo then proceeded to demolish the fence and all the adjacent countryside in the vicinity, damaging cane fields to a distance of five miles from the lagoon and sending residents from the town of Maguayo into panicked flight. The hippo was last seen heading east ...."

⌒

Though I generally was wary of consultas, sometimes I actively sought to participate in reviewing them when a key wildlife area was at stake. One of my principal objections to the review of consultas was the process itself. By the time my agency saw a consulta, the proposed project often was already well along the approval process if not already under construction. Besides, non-endorsement by our agency carried little weight. It was the permit issuing agencies such as the Planning Board that had the final say and none of these agencies were noted for their environmental consciousness. At one point the Secretary of Planning stated that there was no way his agency would prepare an environmental impact statement while he was still its head. We had to convince such agencies to concur with us. On some occasions, when the Planning Board agreed with our arguments, its concurrence might require the reversal of a partial approval already granted. Such reversals provide good grist for lawsuits, not to mention much embarrassment. Consequently, expecting the reversal of an opinion on a consulta that was already well advanced was a futile endeavor.

The U.S. Congress's 1969 passage of the National Environmental Policy Act was an attempt to upgrade this approach, but it was only moderately successful. NEPA, as the act commonly was called, required that an environmental impact statement (EIS) be prepared for any project involving federal funds or permits and which might significantly affect the quality of the human environment. Among other things, the EIS was to contain not only a review of the natural resources of the area and how they might be affected by the proposed project, but it also was to identify alternatives to the proposed action. The law also required that EIS's be circulated widely for comment.

Since each environmental impact statement has to include possible alternatives, the intent clearly was for the review process to precede any development. But there frequently appeared to be a way for developers to circumvent this component of the process.

With the passage of NEPA, environmental consulting firms sprang up like jackrabbits to provide EIS preparation services. Most of these firms typically were much more interested in satisfying their clients than in the wise use of the environment; thus, many EIS's scarcely went a step beyond what was included in typical consultas.

When it came to the review of wildlife resources, both consultas and environmental impact statements frequently were shoddy. Often the faunal assessment was treated in a brief paragraph, if at all. While we would return such documents for more comprehensive treatment, we rarely knew whether the requested revisions were ever made since they seldom came back to us for a second look.

After years of playing by everyone else's rules, I decided to try an innovative approach. The Area of Natural Resources by this time had expanded into a full-fledged Department, coupled with a simultaneous increase in the size of its bureaucracy. A special office handled the review of environmental impact statements and consultas, and the office chief was none other than my old boss and friend Ruben Freyre. As in the past, Ruben would only involve me in the most important reviews, and this particular case was no different.

The issue at hand was a proposal by the island's industrial development agency to locate a large 10,000-acre industrial complex in the extreme southwestern corner of the island near Punta Pitahaya. The selection of this locality probably was based on the area around Punta Pitahaya being one of the least inhabited portions of the coastal plain. Also, winds would sweep most of the atmospheric pollution out to sea and finally, to the casual observer, much of the region looked like a lifeless desert. In actuality, Punta Pitahaya and its vicinity are very rich biologically.

Occupying a portion of Puerto Rico's southwestern corner,

these lands lie at the opposite end of the island from the prevailing trade winds which bathe Puerto Rico from the northeast. Approaching from over the ocean, these winds initially contain clouds laden with substantial amounts of moisture. Much of this is precipitated as the clouds bump against the Sierra de Luquillo and the central mountain chain, both sierras possessing peaks over 3,000 feet in height. By the time the clouds have risen above these barriers and passed to their southern side, limited moisture remains and rain becomes increasingly scarce the further one moves toward the southwest. The drier portion of the island south of the sierras is generally referred to as being in the rain shadow. The dramatic role played by the mountains in influencing rainfall is illustrated by the fact that East Peak in the Sierra de Luquillo, the first tall peak to stand in the path of the northeast trades, receives approximately 200 inches of rain per year, while the Cabo Rojo lighthouse, no more than 90 miles away at the island's extreme southwestern tip, may not receive any rain at all during a given year.

Though Punta Pitahaya is an arid area, it should not be presumed that the region is lifeless. Not at all. The dry scrub forests of Guanica, a few miles east of Punta Pitahaya, are known to support a greater array of birds than the lush rain forest of El Yunque in the east. Punta Pitahaya is particularly attractive due to its diversity of habitats. Besides desert scrubland, it contains some of the most extensive mudflats anywhere on the coast, an expansive mangrove forest, numerous offshore cays, and impressive sea cliffs. Each of these habitats in turn serves as host to a peculiar diversity of organisms adapted to its unique conditions.

The sea cliffs are home to the fairy-like yellow-billed tropicbird, an elegant, white seabird with long, streaming tail feathers which the male lowers over the female during their courtship flights. Tropicbirds are so narrowly adapted to nesting on windy, ocean cliffs, and basically falling off them into the air to take flight, that they have lost the ability to walk on land. Like many other seabirds this species can also drink sea water, a substance toxic to humans in anything but small doses.

Mudflats in the vicinity serve as a major resting area and wintering ground for many thousands of migratory shorebirds. Most of these breed far north in the arctic tundra and fly many thousands of miles south to wintering quarters, some as far away as Tierra del Fuego at the southern tip of South America. The threatened piping plover is among these migrants. The Cabo Rojo mudflats near Punta Pitahaya sustain Puerto Rico's only breeding population of the snowy plover.

The mangrove forests provide nesting habitat for the seriously endangered yellow-shouldered blackbird, among other species. Conspicuous birds such as pelicans and herons roost in the trees and feed in the channels. Ubiquitous termites, small in size, yet the builders of immense, complex, communal nests are more abundant in mangroves than in any other ecosystem.

The offshore islands, often forested with mangroves, have a distinct quality all their own by virtue of their isolation from the mainland. Those that are just small sand bars, or aggregates of coral rubble, often serve as breeding sites for terns, such as the least and roseate. Larger cays supporting trees may host heron or pelican rookeries, pigeon colonies, frigatebird roosts, or even roosts of landbirds such as the yellow-shouldered blackbird. It is not far to the east of Punta Pitahaya that I had found the largest known roost of this now endangered bird, on a mangrove cay about one-half mile off shore.

Familiar with the Pitahaya area from previous surveys and concerned about the declining yellow-shouldered blackbird population which had its stronghold near Pitahaya, I was anxious to review the environmental impact statement for the proposed development.

A careful study of the wildlife component of the document took well under thirty seconds. That's right, a half minute because all that was listed in the way of wildlife from this outstanding area were four species! And what four species they were! The first three were birds that could be found virtually anywhere on the island and if someone left their window open, might well occur in one's living room. The fourth was the white-necked crow.

The white-necked crow was an impressive addition to the list.

Formerly a woodland bird confined to the islands of Hispaniola and Puerto Rico, the species had declined in Puerto Rico to the point that it was nearly extirpated by the beginning of the 19th century. Further, the few sightings made in the 1900's were all from the northeast in the vicinity of the Luquillo Mountains. Even there the species had not been seen for over a decade, despite active fieldwork in the Sierra de Luquillo during that time. The bottom line – the white-necked crow was believed extinct in Puerto Rico.

That the white-necked crow had been rediscovered in the scrubland of the southwest was absurd. This was not so much because such a discovery was impossible; on the contrary, unusual discoveries occurred fairly regularly on the island. What made such a rediscovery so implausible was that the bird in question was large, conspicuous, and not easily overlooked. Also, the site from which it was reported was regularly visited by capable biologists who would not have missed such a species. And most significantly, the wildlife section of the environmental impact statement clearly was the work of someone with no knowledge of the island's avifauna. Its author did not so much as recognize that he had listed an extirpated bird! The only note accompanying the unusual record was a comment on the bird's status: "COMMON."

Out of curiosity I paid an early morning visit to the proposed development site and within an hour observed more than 30 species of birds – but no white-necked crows. The environmental impact statement prepared for the project was decidedly inadequate for effective review of potential wildlife impacts. It made no mention of the endangered yellow-shouldered blackbird, a resident in the area, which could lose an important segment of its limited breeding and feeding range if this project were to be implemented. Where was the discussion of how any effluent discharged by the numerous industries would affect the thousands of shorebirds nearby? What about at least making reference to the endemic *Anolis cooki*, a small lizard nearly the entire world population of which is confined to Puerto Rico's extreme southwest coast, including Punta Pitahaya.

My typical response to an EIS such as this was to draft a

73

memorandum noting that the information presented by the project proponents was incomplete, and I would usually indicate a few items in particular that needed further attention. This fairly standard approach generally yielded fairly standard results. If we received a revised document at all, the modifications were usually little better than the original. Ultimately we had to submit comments on the proposal based on what we personally knew of the area.

It was at this juncture that I put a new twist into the procedure. Despite the fact that the EIS had omitted everything of consequence about the locality's wildlife, I believed that the claim regarding the existence of the white-necked crow might prove a more effective single issue to support protection of the site than arguments based upon the actual fauna of the area. It seemed only reasonable that any consulting firm with the nerve to foist such a poorly prepared document upon the public under the pretext of a thorough environmental review deserved to have to stand by its work. Since the project was being proposed by a governmental agency, taxpayer dollars had no doubt paid for this slipshod effort. I chose, therefore, to interpret the EIS documentation as valid and wrote a memo accordingly.

My memo to Ruben was very emphatic. It pointed out the great significance of the rediscovery of the white-necked crow and emphasized the dire need for not disturbing the site until the status and habits of the crow could be discerned and its conservation ensured.

Not surprisingly the supposed rediscovery of the crow proved to be the most significant argument presented within the Department against development of the site as an industrial complex. As luck would have it, Ruben would be unable to attend the public hearings on the project. The Department, therefore, would have to select another spokesperson other than the soft-spoken, mild-mannered Ruben to represent its views before the public forum.

I was summoned to the office of the second highest ranking official in the entire Department. I entered and sat before a round-faced man who was noted more for his dress than his administrative abilities. He did not disillusion me. My attention was immediately drawn away from his ruddy complexion and puffy cheeks by the celebration of color in his broad tie and the even broader lapels of his flashy and impeccable suit.

"Raffaele," he began succinctly. "I have been informed that you prepared the most substantive comments on the proposed Punta Pitahaya project." I was silent. He went on. "Ruben Freyre can't attend the public hearings, so we are considering sending you, but I need to know what you plan to say."

I explained how the EIS reported the occurrence of the white-necked crow in the scrublands of the project site and how this represented the rediscovery of what had been believed an extinct species. The official was apparently distressed at what my comments implied.

"What about just catching the birds in the scrubland and moving them to the adjacent mangroves away from the proposed project site?" he queried apprehensively.

He caught me off guard with that remark. How could a man in his position be so naive as to think that birds arbitrarily could be shifted from habitat to habitat regardless of how different those habitats might be from one another? Did he expect that the birds could survive, or that they would not fly back in an instant to the habitat of their choice?

Improvising, I began to explain how such an approach was impossible. To illustrate I used the example of how truly fresh water fishes could not survive in the sea and how marine fishes could not typically tolerate conditions in a lake. But as I was coming to the end of my explanation it struck me that my example was poor and my message was not reaching its target. If the official could not perceive the no-no's of moving birds from scrubland to mangroves, it was even less likely he would grasp the corresponding analogy when applied to fishes. Through with my explanation, I awaited the official's response.

"Okay Raffaele," he muttered. "You go to the hearings, but try not to make anything more out of this issue than you have to."

A few days later I drove to the town of Cabo Rojo in south-western Puerto Rico where the public hearings were to be held.

Entering the hearing hall I was impressed by the substantial turnout of local townspeople from this small community interested in the fate of the industrial park proposal and their beautiful coastal lands. I sat in the back as the hearings began, listening intently as person after person testified in favor of or in opposition to the project.

The better part of the morning had passed when my turn to speak finally arrived. Taking the podium before the crowd of nearly 200 I dispensed the formal courtesies and then immediately launched into the essence of my message which went something like:

"Dear Mr. chairman, review committee and citizens of Cabo Rojo. I appreciate the opportunity to speak to you today on behalf of the Department of Natural Resources concerning the proposed industrial park bordering Punta Pitahaya. It is only on rare occasions that environmental assessments such as the one prepared for this project contribute significantly to our knowledge of the fauna of Puerto Rico. This is exactly what has occurred, however, with respect to the environmental impact statement regarding this site. The biological consultants performing the ornithological survey of the site have miraculously discovered a remnant population of the white-necked crow, a bird believed extinct on the island for over a decade."

I paused. Simultaneously a wave of "ohhhhs" flooded the hall as the astonished citizenry responded to my remarks. What had some time ago become a lethargic crowd, numbed by hours of tedious presentations, had suddenly come to life.

Immediately a representative from the consulting firm which had made the blooper in the EIS burst from his chair, his hand flailing the air wildly in an effort to get the floor.

"There will be no questions at this time," the chairman remarked firmly to the hysterical consultant. He nodded to me politely, "Please continue."

I then proceeded to relate how such discoveries were few and far between and how the conservation of this lone population of white-necked crows on the island needed careful study and the utmost protection before any decision to alter its habitat could possibly be considered. The gathering listened in silence. Upon completing my presentation, I was dismissed by the panel and everyone broke for lunch. As I made my way from the crowded building to my car, I strongly expected the consultant firm representatives to be in hot pursuit, but they likely got lost in the mass of bodies. I reached the car without incident and in short order was on my way back to San Juan musing on how the consulting firm was going to extricate itself from the deep hole which it had custom-dug.

I never did learn what stopped the Punta Pitahaya industrial park from being constructed. All I know is that the project never went forward and that was good enough for me. However, more remains to the story.

It was not long after the hearing that I was chatting with my fellow workers at the Department and relaying my amazement at how the high official who had involved me in the case could be so ignorant as to think crows could be moved from the scrubland to the mangroves without them simply flying back.

"That's nothing," retorted the head of our geology unit in a blasé tone, unfazed by my outraged ranting. "I was in a meeting with him a week ago," he went on. "We were reviewing geological maps when the official asked me what the "p" on the map stood for. That's not a "p" I told the official. That's a "d." I'm afraid you've got the map upside down."

Reflections

Lots of lessons here. I shall touch on a few.

The consultas taught me a lot of lessons via hard knocks. Most importantly I learned that becoming engaged in the review process for a development project can be the kiss of death. If you are not engaged early, don't bother. Late in the game, too much has been invested by the developers, making the economic stakes too high. Also, a fair amount of habitat alteration may already have taken place.

It is also invaluable to have specific legal authority. One example would be that other entities would have to come to you for a permit. These entities might be other government agencies, the general public, industries, developers, hunters, whatever. The important thing is that a permit must be signed by you before the applicant can begin to carry out a particular action. What action? That depends. It could be sand extraction, timber cutting, land clearing, water diversion or contamination, wetland destruction, negatively impacting an endangered species, you get the picture.

Providing comments to another agency which has such authority is not even a distant second. Oftentimes such agencies have substantially differing mandates than our own and, consequently, look askance at the perspectives we present.

Yet, legal authority means little if it is not backed by political will. This requires that the agency, and the administration which appointed its leadership, has the desire to see the law enforced. There are many laws on the books which may as well have never been passed. Whether for lack of interest on the part of the agency, or lack of funding, it is not uncommon for important legal mandates to go unaddressed.

This leads us to the matter of checks and balances. By this I refer not only to the administration, legislature and judiciary, but I include the populace at large, whether they be out-spoken individuals, the press, non-governmental organizations, or the private sector. Engagement of the public in natural resources management and conservation issues is prerequisite to those issues obtaining political prominence and to being effectively addressed.

In this regard it is especially important to recognize that no one sector of society can go it alone. When the government fails to deliver some of us turn to the non-governmental community as the answer. It isn't. If non-governmental organizations are unable to get the job done, some might turn to local communities and municipalities or to the business sector to provide the solution. They can't. All of civil society has to be empowered for an issue as significant as natural resources conservation to be effectively addressed. Engagement and cooperation among these highly disparate groups, as difficult and tangential to the point as it may sometimes seem, is the only sure way to secure long-term success with regard to resource conservation.

The proposed introduction of the hippopotamus to address the problem of water hyacinth infestation is a perfect example of a simple-minded solution to a complex problem. After all, the real reason water hyacinths clog many of Puerto Rico's waterways is not because something won't eat them. Rather, it is because these water bodies have been overloaded with fertilizers turning them into outstanding breeding grounds for such plants. Consequently, we should heed Albert Einstein's advice that, "The world will not evolve past its current state of crisis by using the same thinking that created the situation."

Applying more sophisticated thinking is no simple process. This entails, for starters, retraining many natural resources personnel who possess few of the skills necessary to cope effectively with the rapidly expanding knowledge-base needed by the modern resource manager. Secondly, it means hiring individuals with the strongest possible backgrounds to do the job. You may recall that I was hired to conduct bird surveys even though my college degrees were in entirely different fields. Not good. Suffice it to say that during my tenure with the Department of Natural Resources I never saw someone selected for a position based upon an official candidates list received from the division of personnel, or on any other competitive basis. Every hire with which I was familiar was based upon who you knew. Let's hope this has changed. Finally, but no less important than the other factors, is salaries. I was considered for a $320 per month job with the Department of Agriculture in 1971. That was a terribly low salary by any standards, even at that time. I would have accepted it only because of my interest to enter the conservation field. Agencies can not expect quality work when they pay sub-par salaries.

The DNR not sharing development plans with its sister agency, the Environmental Quality Board – what can you say? These governmental agencies happen to be part of the same administration and deal with similar issues. What's up? I learned that this means nothing. Agencies are run by people, and the people selected to run such agencies envelope them in their own image. More often than not, this is a negative development. All the more reason for the checks and balances to which I referred above.

Planning is a very interesting phenomenon. It can be a very useful tool if implemented properly. It can be a total waste if inappropriately executed. Of the dozen or more planning exercises in which I was involved during my tenure in Puerto Rico, every single one of them, with no exception, was a decided waste of time if not an unmitigated disaster. The worst of the disasters was when we at the DNR drafted a series of over two dozen maps highlighting salient natural resource priority areas around the island. These included important mangroves, fresh water swamps, caves, reefs, archeological sites, even shipwrecks. We shared the draft maps with the Planning Board for that agency to prepare them in final form. We never saw the maps again! We were unable to get them returned!

Without buy-in at various levels, planning is doomed. Even with buy-in, final implementation is an iffy proposition.

I also found that planning can be used as a tool to delay taking action. After all, until a plan is in place, it can be argued that moving forward would be premature.

Does this mean that there is no place for preparing plans? Of course not. But the planning process provides an inordinate number of mechanisms to delay action and all of us who are part of the world of checks and balances should be aware of this.

The Strong-voiced
Cave-mouth

The ability to mismanage responsibilities was not an endowment confined to a single agency. Rather, this aptitude seemed to be dispersed widely among agencies large and small, powerful and weak, Commonwealth and Federal. Little searching usually was necessary for it to become readily apparent. Like cream, it tended to rise to the surface for everyone to see. What I could never understand was why it was not skimmed off, but it never was. If one wanted to work in the system, one just had to become tolerant of bureaucratic shortcomings. However, this was particularly difficult when the survival of Puerto Rico's unique natural areas, including its characteristic plants and animals, were at stake.

One particularly galling sequence of debacles resulted from the narrow-mindedness of a Federal agency with an ample staff of scientists which should have known better. This agency leased several small islands along Puerto Rico's shores as sites to perform research on monkeys. Of course, as is evident from earlier discussions, monkeys are not native to Puerto Rico, thus their introduction could produce potentially grave consequences were the animals to escape onto the mainland. However, when I raised this issue with the monkey experts in charge of the islands, they assured me that there were no problems whatever, and that I was being overly paranoid.

The source of my concern stemmed primarily from two islands right next to Puerto Rico proper. By "right next to" I mean that one was about 100 yards from shore, and the other was actually attached to the mainland. Of course, by definition the latter island was not one. In all likelihood a narrow channel, now sedimented in, had formerly made it a legitimate island. But this misnomer was of no serious consequence except that the term "island" suggests isolation, a condition which did not exist.

To allay my fears about monkeys escaping, the monkeyites cited a number of immutable truths derived from their innumerable years of research. First, an electrified fence across the isthmus between the island and the mainland was permanently charged, preventing the escape of the monkeys by land. Second, any biologist worth his salt knew that monkeys don't swim. Consequently, though the distance around the fence was but a few yards, no monkey would dare attempt the passage. Third, any monkey that did somehow manage to reach the mainland would certainly return to the island in short order to dine on the copious food supply regularly set out by the scientists. Fourth, the only monkeys likely to stray were young individuals not of breeding age and these easily could be rounded up before they caused any damage. Fifth, most of the critters on the islands were rhesus monkeys and these were entirely vegetarian; thus, even if by some absolute fluke they ever strayed to the mainland, they would not harm the birdlife. Sixth – who needs a sixth! Those experts knew for sure that the monkeys would not escape and being interested in animals themselves, why would they jeopardize Puerto Rico's native fauna through carelessness?

Being relatively ignorant about primates myself, I was not anxious to challenge the experts, nor did I have strong reason to doubt them. That is, not until the reports.

I had no interest per se in the relatively barren monkey islands in southwestern Puerto Rico called Cueva and Guayacan. These two islands, both with restricted access, appeared so deforested that little could remain of their original faunas. It was a bit disturbing that this portion of a beautiful Commonwealth forest had been given over to performing monkey experiments, but this was a separate issue. Were it not for the other more pristine islands and spectacular mangrove ecosystem nearby, I rarely would have come to this area. As it happened, the fabulous areas surrounding Cueva and Guayacan attracted me to their vicinity time and time again.

It was during these periodic visits to survey birds that I gradually accumulated a number of anecdotal reports which, even if only partially true, were distressing and cause for alarm.

"I hear a monkey recently got off the islands and tried to swipe the hat off the head of a fisherman passing down one of the mangrove channels in his boat. Do you know of a monkey escaping?" I inquired of a local resident.

"What do you mean one monkey?" he retorted. "Just last week there was a female with a baby hanging around right near my house. People in town saw a large male."

A bit shaken I queried, "How do you think they got ashore?"

Shaking his head in disgust at my apparent ignorance, he went on, "They swim, of course!"

"What do you mean they swim?" I questioned further, concerned about discrepancies between the local's remarks and the immutable truths of the monkey experts. "Have you actually seen them?"

"Of course I have!" the man went on, becoming rather indignant with my naiveté. "Those monkeys swim real well. Once I tried to stop one with an oar, and it swam right under my boat!"

And so the reports accumulated.

It was early on that I first learned that monkeys could swim and that a female with an infant had come ashore. Monkeyite truths numbers two and four immediately bit the dust. Larger and larger numbers of monkeys were being seen on the mainland, but at least truth number three was holding up – the monkeys were not straying far afield. Not for long, that is. A report came in that a monkey crossing the road in Cabo Rojo had caused a traffic jam. Cabo Rojo is ten miles from the monkey islands. At this point the electrified fence meant nothing; but be that as it may, I learned from several people that they had seen monkeys climbing the fence. Apparently the electricity was sometimes off, and the monkeys had a way of knowing. Now truths one through four were shot down. The only thing saving the main island of Puerto Rico itself was the truth, which it might now be best to refer to as a hope, that the monkeys were indeed vegetarian. Whether this hope was just that – a hope – with little basis in fact, was being put to a severe test on another offshore island, Desecheo, which had monkey problems all its own. Developments on that island were all but reassuring. Indications were that all the truths of the monkeyites were false, and something had to be done, or serious consequences were in the offing.

My gravest and most immediate concern was for the potential impact of the stray monkeys on the endemic Puerto Rican whip-poor-will. This nocturnal bird is almost identical in appearance and habits to its North American cousin, but is considered a distinct species based primarily on differing skeletal characteristics and its unique call. The North American bird derives its common name from its clear rendition of "whip-poor-will" which is widely heard throughout the night in the forests of the eastern United States, primarily just after dark and before dawn during the months of spring and early summer. Inactive during the day, the bird typically rests among the leaf litter of the forest floor where its mottled coloration of browns, grays, and blacks cam-ouflages it perfectly. Whip-poor-

Puerto Rican whip-poor-will

wills have a curious habit – when perching on twigs, they generally do so lengthwise rather than crosswise as most birds do. At night the whip-poor-will feeds only in flight, its diet consisting almost exclusively of night flying insects. Unlike owls, which capture their prey in their talons, whip-poor-wills scoop up their flighty meals in their enormous mouths. To enhance the bird's capability as a flying insect trap, the mouth is surrounded by a series of bristles which aid in funneling the bird's elusive prey into its oversized gape. However, despite the whip-poor-will's impressive prey-capturing apparatus, use of the mouth rather than the feet for gathering meals probably severely restricts the size of prey the bird is capable of taking. This may be one reason some of the "mouth-trap" birds, groups such as the whip-poor-wills, nighthawks and their cousins, plus the swifts, which feed on large flying insects, are migratory. Their status may be balanced delicately with the availability of large insects. Such creatures are not abundant the year round in many areas.

Quite apropos, the former scientific name of the whip-poor-will was *Antrostomus vociferus* or, the "strong-voiced cave-mouth." Interestingly, the scientific name has been changed more recently to *Caprimulgus vociferus* or, the "strong-voiced goatsucker." The term goatsucker dates back well over 2,000 years to the days of the Greek City-States. Apparently the large mouths of the European whip-poor-will and its close cousins were believed by shepherds to be used to suckle goats since the birds were frequently seen flying in the vicinity of these animals. The tale was accepted widely enough that no less than the renown Aristotle relayed the story in his writings. It was also believed in some quarters that goats so suckled would subsequently have their mammary glands dry up and the creatures would die. In New England a prevalent superstition was that the landing of a whip-poor-will on one's doorstep forebode sickness or death. As if these myths were not enough to turn country people against the bird, whip-poor-wills and particularly their cousins the nighthawks can be seen abroad at dusk which leads to their being confused with bats. Of course bats hardly have a sterling reputation of their own, despite the fact that their poor reputation also is unjustified. Inappropriately, one of the common names by which the nighthawk is known in the United States is "bull bat." That the bull bat has feathers, a rather puzzling feature for a bat, is of no particular consequence to farmers who have little interest in scientific quibbling over what differentiates a mammal from a bird.

It seems inevitable that nocturnal creatures receive a bad rap from the human species the world over. This is particularly ironic in the case of the goatsuckers and bats because the former prey heavily on insect pests, receiving only ill-will in exchange for their unrecognized services; the latter not only feed heavily on noxious insects, but some species of bats are of critical importance in pollinating many types of trees which would not survive without this unacknowledged service.

Given the similarities between the North American and Puerto Rican whip-poor-wills, it would not be surprising if the Puerto Rican bird had an interesting story all its own and, indeed, such is the case. To begin with, the discovery of the species is unusual in and of itself. This is because the Puerto Rican whip-poor-will was first recognized as a species only from fossil bones. When the scientific description of the bird was published in 1919, it was based upon the uniqueness of these bones and a single, old museum skin previously misidentified as a specimen of the North American form. At the time of the formal description, nothing was known about the bird itself, or even whether it still survived. Other than that single skin taken in 1888, no one had reported a sighting with certainty. Given the introduction and establishment of the mongoose in the late 1870's, it was presumed that this predator was the likely culprit responsible for the extinction of the whip-poor-will on the island. This was a reasonable assumption because the whip-poor-will is an obligate ground nester. With the spread of the mongoose across Puerto Rico, all ground nesting birds and many other terrestrial creatures were seriously decimated by this new predator. By the turn of the 20th century practically all such birds were on the verge of extinction. These species ranged from the forest-dwelling quail-doves and the whip-poor-will to large savanna species such as the short-eared owl.

Fascinating as well is the more recent history of the Puerto Rican whip-poor-will. Scientists had little to report about the bird in the first half of the twentieth century because the species went virtually unrecorded. Then, in 1961 George Reynard visited Puerto Rico to tape the songs of local birds to produce a record of Caribbean bird calls. While inquiring about places to record, he was informed by U.S. Fish and Wildlife Service agent Ricardo Cotte that an unusual creature called at night in Guanica

Commonwealth Forest. Cotte requested that Reynard tape the call so that the identity of the mysterious caller might be determined. Reynard obliged and sent a copy of the tape to a number of renowned ornithologists. However, none of these experts could identify the mysterious caller. The best they could do was guess that the creature seemed more like a bird than a frog, but it would have to be collected if an identification was to be made. With no other alternatives, Reynard and Cotte finally managed to net one of the nocturnal callers. Upon study of the specimen by surprised ornithologists, the creature turned out to be none other than the Puerto Rican whip-poor-will, a bird thought extinct for the better part of a century! Interested in pursuing the status of the Puerto Rican whip-poor-will further, Reynard made inquiries among the townspeople who lived adjacent to Guanica forest. To his astonishment he learned that indeed the birds had long been there and that during the 1930's, when the Civilian Conservation Corps had an installation in the forest, the calls of the birds made such a racket at night that the CCC workers had petitioned that something be done to eliminate the nuisance!

The reason the Puerto Rican whip-poor-will had been so difficult to identify by the tape of its call was that, though extremely similar in appearance to the North American whip-poor-will, its call is quite distinct. Rather than repeat its entire three syllable name, the Puerto Rican bird utters only the "whip" portion, the "poor-will" having been dropped from its repertoire. This is ironic since there is a relative of the North American whip-poor-will which occurs in the western portion of the continent and sings only the "poor-will" component of the call, having dropped the "whip." Not too surprisingly this related form is called the "poor-will."

The naming of the Puerto Rican whip-poor-will from only a few fossil bones and a skin, with no knowledge of the living form, resulted in a severe misnomer. The Puerto Rican whip-poor-will, in keeping with the onomatopoeic naming of its kin, might most properly have been called simply the Puerto Rican whip. Nowadays it is commonly referred to as the Puerto Rican nightjar.

Subsequent to the rediscovery of the Puerto Rican whip-poor-will by Reynard and Cotte, a survey was performed by the Keplers in the late 1960's to determine the status of the species islandwide. The bird was found to be limited to southwestern Puerto Rico where a population of about 200 pairs survived in Guanica Forest with only a few dozen additional pairs occurring nearby in Susua and Guayanilla. The causes for this extremely limited distribution were likely two factors, one of them again being the mongoose. Southwestern Puerto Rico is, as discussed earlier, the most arid portion of the island, and it is probable that the relative scarcity of water around Guanica keeps the mongoose population in check, though the mongoose is not absent from the area altogether. The scarcity of the mongoose has to be a major plus for the Puerto Rican whip. Second, the whip requires thin forest understory so that it can maneuver amidst the trees. Such open understory only occurs in relatively mature forests, a scarce commodity along the southern coast of the island. Until a few decades ago, charcoal burning was the principal source of fuel in Puerto Rico, particularly in the more rural areas. Consequently, little in the way of natural dry forest remained unscathed by the ax. Guanica is unique in that the forest, although previously cut, has gone relatively undisturbed since about the turn of the 20th century, the result being significant regeneration of the natural forest cover. However, Guanica is an island of forest in a sea of pastureland and sugar cane. Relatively little dry forest remains outside of Guanica that could provide appropriate habitat for the whip.

This brings us nearly to the present state of affairs but for one major incident which, had it unfolded differently, might have quickly short-circuited my career with the Puerto Rican government and any possible confrontation with the monkeyites.

Coincidentally, in my first days as a biologist for the Area of Natural Resources, while the idea of a higher level department was only a dream, there came upon my desk a proposal to create a large garbage dump in Guanica Commonwealth Forest. The specific proposal was to consolidate the open burning dumps of three municipalities in the southwest into a single land-fill facility to be located in the Commonwealth forest. Such a land-fill operation would require significant amounts of soil, and soil in large amounts was only available in one of the valleys well within the reserve.

The implications of this seemed obvious. While improving the management of refuse as a whole for this portion of the island, one of the most important natural areas in all of Puerto Rico would be sacrificed. Sacrificed not to the extent of it being completely destroyed, but certainly to the point where it would be seriously degraded, a more insidious type of destruction.

Among the casualties of this degradation would certainly be the Puerto Rican whip-poor-will. Garbage dumps are notorious for attracting scavengers including mice, rats, feral cats, stray dogs and, doubtless, the mongoose. Though these animals may have already existed within the reserve, they did so in very small numbers. The addition of massive amounts of human trash had the potential to multiply their populations manyfold. And as they wandered out from the dump site, whip-poor-will nestlings and eggs would be prime prey items.

My reaction? You can imagine. I gave Ruben Freyre, my boss, quite an earful.

Ruben sat there quietly taking in my tirade with nary a comment. When I had finished he explained, "Herb, it might interest you to know that this is not an external proposal, it is not a consulta. The proposal was drafted internally within the Area of Natural Resources. We should be able to influence it."

Drafted internally? Was Ruben kidding?

No he wasn't! It turns out the second highest person in the entire agency had put the proposal together. As I have indicated, it was intended to improve garbage disposal for that entire portion of the island. And he did not know much ecology. He had no idea the Puerto Rican whip-poor-will even existed, needless to say its ecological requirements.

So, here I was less than a month on the job facing off with the number two man in the agency!

Fortunately for me, the number two man was a wonderful guy – Roberto Cassagnol. When Roberto learned of the potential

problem such an endeavor would create for the whip, he immediately trashed the proposal. On top of that, he did not take it
personally, as if the whole thing was a threat to his manhood.
I respect Roberto for that and I owe him big time. He enabled
my career to survive its first month and lead to a face-off with
the monkey experts.

Now we truly come to the present state of affairs. On the
one hand, there is the remnant population of the endangered
Puerto Rican whip-poor-will with its last remaining foothold
virtually restricted to the boundaries of the none-too-large
Guanica Commonwealth Forest, one of the few remaining
habitats in Puerto Rico where ground predators are scarce
enough that the bird can reproduce effectively. On the other,
there is the ever burgeoning population of escaping rhesus
monkeys spreading from the area of Cueva and Guayacan, with
Guanica Forest a mere 13 miles away. The monkeyites continued
to argue that rhesus monkeys were entirely vegetarian. I was
not so sure. The last thing the poor whip needed was a new,
intelligent, adaptable predator like a monkey to invade its
world. One additional predator on the eggs or young of the
whip-poor-will could certainly destroy the fragile balance in
which this bird hung. As things developed, evidence relating to
the feeding habits of rhesus monkeys in the wild, which could
shed important light on the potential impact on the whip, was
turning up on another front, on the offshore island of Desecheo.
Judging from this accumulating information, the future did not
appear too bright for Puerto Rico's strong-voiced cave-mouth.

Desecheo is a rugged island lying off Puerto Rico's west
coast. The island's ruggedness is reflected not only in its steep
topography, but also in the abundance of cacti and other pesky
plants, not to mention a scarcity of fresh water.

On July 1, 1966 a group of 56 rhesus monkeys was released on
Desecheo to establish a free-ranging colony. The basic objectives of
the release were to study how the animals might adapt to this new,
harsh environment and how any behavior modifications might

reflect on the dynamics of the monkey population as a whole. A report to the American Association for the Advancement of Science elaborates on the observed group interactions and how future plans called for later release of another subgroup of monkeys formerly associated with the originally released animals. This was to be followed by yet a third release of previously associated monkeys in an effort to "continue to study the ecology of adaptation with particular interest in relationship of environment to social organization and behavior."

Conceptually, this was not a bad study and had the potential to produce much interesting information on the plasticity of primate behavior, group dynamics, and other aspects of adaptive responses to a new environment. Unfortunately, the specific details of the study were distressing. For one, Desecheo is a harsh environment in which to throw a group of monkeys accustomed to having their food provided by humans. Starvation and death of naïve animals was a real probability. For another, though the investigators were interested in the effect of the environment on the social organization and behavior of the monkeys, at no point did they ever express even a remote interest in the effect of the monkeys on the environment. This, despite the fact that they were well aware that Desecheo still harbored large colonies of seabirds.

Not surprisingly the released monkeys soon appeared constantly fatigued and extremely indifferent to humans and had lost much weight. By nine months after the introduction, many monkeys had lost additional weight, their arms and legs had become emaciated, and their abdomens were swollen. However, over the remaining two years of the study, the monkeys appeared to survive reasonably well. Fewer than three years after its inception the study was then terminated due to the difficulties faced by investigators in trying to survive on Desecheo while studying the survival of the monkeys.

Turning from how the monkeys fared on Desecheo to how Desecheo fared in the presence of the monkeys, we might ask: what was expected and what was learned about the impact of the monkeys on Desecheo's seabird populations? A 78-page monograph on the release experiment treats the topic in less than a single paragraph: "In all visits we believed that monkeys avoided the seabird nesting areas because of the unpleasant odor from the bird droppings."

Clearly a significant interaction was not expected and none was observed. After all, rhesus monkeys were known to be totally vegetarian based on common knowledge as expressed in monkeyite tenet number five. It therefore must have come as quite a shock to some observers when reports came in during the late 1960's suggesting that seabird populations on Desecheo were declining alarmingly. This was taken by the monkeyites as speculation despite a half day survey in July of 1970, four years after the initial introduction, during which not a single seabird nest was found on Desecheo.

The monkeyites decried this as insignificant claiming that little was known about the breeding seasons of seabirds in the region, and that July simply might have been a non-breeding month. Besides, they countered, the many thousands of seabirds found on Desecheo early in the century should not have been expected in recent times due to perturbations to the island in the 1940's.

Several lines of evidence suggested the arguments of the monkeyites were weak. Reliable sources who had visited Desecheo during the 1950's and 1960's, only slightly prior to the monkey introduction, indicated that seabirds were thriving. Reports from that period by the monkeyites themselves referred to the abundance of birds on the island. Furthermore, though no seabirds were found nesting on Desecheo proper in July of 1970, over 70 active nests were located during the same trip on several islets immediately adjacent to Desecheo. Evidence from nearby Monito and cays elsewhere around Puerto Rico also suggested that Desecheo should have supported many active seabird nests in July of 1970.

It was at this early stage in the debate over the impact of rhesus monkeys on seabirds that I had an opportunity to visit Desecheo and the somewhat more distant island of Mona. The trip led to discovery of a large, active breeding colony of red-footed boobies on Mona, the first colony of its kind reported from that island. In sharp contrast, the red-foots on Desecheo built nests, but these contained neither eggs nor young. Clearly my findings supported the contention that something was amiss on Desecheo. It seemed likely that Mona's new booby colony derived from red-foots abandoning Desecheo, though I could not substantiate this hypothesis. I was unable to demonstrate that monkeys were responsible for the dilemma on Desecheo, despite being the prime suspects.

The monkeyites latched on to this lack of definitive proof like bulldogs and went a step further. They off-handedly pooh-poohed even the suggestion that the monkeys had anything to do with the reproductive problems of the boobies. Disdainfully they proposed any number of alternative hypotheses to account for the absence of seabird reproduction on Desecheo; one hypothesis being more farfetched than the next. Perhaps, they suggested, the waters around Desecheo had been contaminated, and the tainted fish consumed by the boobies affected egg laying. Oh sure. There was a lot of reason to suspect that. Somehow someone had managed to poison the sea around Desecheo in such a way that it totally inhibited the boobies and other seabirds from laying eggs on Desecheo proper, but had no effect on the same species nesting on Desecheo's offshore cays. Substances such as DDT, of course, are well known for affecting reproduction in birds, but this chemical affects the thickness of egg shells. Broken, thin-shelled eggs should have been present at least in some nests. Another suggestion was that hermit crabs might be responsible for egg depredations. Hermit crabs are found on practically every seabird island I have ever visited and on many they are numerous, yet I have never seen any indication that these small creatures prey on the unbroken eggs of seabirds. However, there are records from other islands of the world which indicate that crabs sometimes are significant predators upon seabird chicks. These cases notwithstanding, it is important to note that one of the principal breeding birds on Desecheo, the red-footed booby, is a tree nester, and I am unaware of any proclivity of hermit crabs of the region towards tree climbing! How then could the activity of these shell-dwelling creatures ever be suggested as a potential threat to boobies nesting fifteen feet above the ground?

The only moderately reasonable explanation proposed by the monkeyites was that poachers were ravaging the seabird colonies and taking all the eggs. The eggs of some seabirds in Puerto Rico are considered to be aphrodisiacs and are highly sought after. However, to believe that collectors had scoured the remote reaches of Desecheo was farfetched. This would have required a Herculean effort entailing not only hiking across exceedingly difficult terrain, but doing so with sack after sack of fragile eggs which it would be next to impossible to keep from breaking. Additionally, obtaining red-footed booby eggs would have required climbing out on flimsy tree limbs to extract them from nests. Though such activities might conceivably have been perpetrated upon nests near the landing area, it is difficult to imagine that such was the case for nests in remote quarters, the principal nesting areas of the birds.

Just prior to my involvement in the Desecheo issue, the monkeyites begrudgingly had agreed to trap the monkeys off Desecheo if someone would provide the funds to do so. The estimated cost in equipment for such an operation was approximately $1,500 and this was generously provided the monkeyites by the U.S. Fish and Wildlife Service. In response to my initial inquiries, I was told the money already had been spent to construct traps and removal of the monkeys would begin in a month as soon as a person was hired to bait the traps. This argument became the standard line of the monkey experts until continued pestering made it untenable. At that point the monkeyites changed their stand and conceded that in fact the money had not been spent to construct traps at all, but rather was being held to perform one last survey focusing specifically on monkey-seabird interactions and the feasibility of removing the monkeys by trapping.

Needless to say the survey was an inordinate length of time in coming, and the results were quite revealing. I queried the head of the monkey people concerning what was learned about the monkey-seabird interactions.

"Monkey-seabird interactions?" he responded in total disgust. "Why, there was no time to look into peripheral things like that. The biologists scarcely had time to sort out troop dynamics on that difficult island."

And so that is how the $1,500 apparently was spent, and I went away seething.

But I would not let things die there. Continued pressure on the monkeyites resulted in a meeting at which upper echelon monkeyite officials from off-island ordered the local intransigents to build the necessary monkey traps with their own funds and get started immediately on monkey removal. It looked like things were finally on the move.

Not so! Shortly after the meeting with off-island officials a new factor entered into the picture. Research on the Desecheo monkey colony had become so costly that the agency to which the island belonged was strongly considering giving it away. That was all the local monkeyites needed. They stalled here and they delayed there and, as Desecheo's abandonment appeared more and more likely, it became hopeless to try and generate any action regarding the monkey problem. Finally, around 1975 Desecheo was excessed by the monkey agency, and in 1976 the island was claimed by the U.S. Fish and Wildlife Service and declared a national wildlife refuge.

During the years that the above incidents were transpiring, several new pieces of information came to light. For one, on a subsequent trip to Desecheo, during which red-footed booby nests were inspected more carefully, I made two new discoveries. One was of broken egg shells on the ground beneath most of the nest trees. This indicated the egg poaching hypothesis likely was false. Furthermore, the eggs, though broken, did not appear thin shelled, suggesting that a chemical such as DDT was not at work. The second finding was the presence of monkey droppings in the crotches of many nest trees. This added fuel to the argument that booby breeding failure and monkey presence might be closely related.

I also learned that a university primatologist unassociated with the monkeyite institution had in fact observed heavy monkey depredation of booby nests. At the time I was unable to obtain further details on his observations, but, as usual, the monkeyites labeled the biologist as unreliable and downplayed his report. However, the report did provoke one monkeyite to try an interesting experiment. Taking some chicken eggs to the monkey cays near Puerto Rico, he placed an egg on the ground in front of a group of monkeys on each of a dozen occasions. Of an estimated 40 to 50 animals that touched the eggs, only one ate or licked at the egg contents more than once. Generally the eggs were picked up and handled as novel objects. Sometimes they would be carried into a tree with other monkeys in pursuit. However, once an egg cracked, the shell rather than the egg contents received the attention of the monkeys. This attention came from the juveniles rather than the adults, the latter usually showing indifference.

The monkeyite then performed the same experiment on Desecheo conducting 15 separate trials. All eggs eventually were cracked, and the contents licked at or eaten. Sometimes the monkeys cracked the eggs with their teeth, opened the shell carefully, and drank the contents as a human would drink from a cup. At least five adults went at the job quite skillfully, without spilling the contents on the ground. This in contrast to tests on Cueva and Guayacan where only juveniles handled the eggs. Also contrary to results from Cueva and Guayacan, only egg contents rather than egg shells received attention when the eggs cracked. The reaction of the juveniles on Desecheo could not be tested because the adults invariably went for the eggs first. However, several infants played with the egg shells while their mothers ate the egg's contents.

The researcher concluded there was little doubt that most of the adults tested on Desecheo acted as if they recognized the insides of an egg and that they ate yolk and albumen readily. Nevertheless, he suggested it was a big leap from observing that a monkey will eat an egg placed before it to inferring that Desecheo's monkeys are thoroughly scouring the island for eggs and that they, rather than people or hermit crabs, are decimating the bird population.

Why this investigator refused to consider monkeys as a

potentially serious threat to the boobies based on the data he collected somehow escaped me. Monkeys are very intelligent animals, a fact widely accepted, at least outside of monkeyite circles. If an intelligent animal is placed in an environment where it is regularly subjected to starvation, it appears reasonable to expect behavioral modifications which enhance its chances of survival. Couple this with the monkeys being deposited on an island inhabited by a myriad of seabirds, an excellent food source totally defenseless against nest predators, it then seems anything but unusual that the monkeys would utilize those invaluable resources.

Ultimately I was able to obtain details of the monkey-seabird interactions observed by the university professor and his students. Though this information in no way swayed the tunnel-visioned monkeyites, it gave the proponents of monkey removal the evidence that had been so elusive and yet so crucial to the issue. What was observed in late August and early September of 1969 by the university group were massive raids by the monkeys on ground nests of brown boobies which then were in the process of egg laying. One graduate student recalls two instances in which approximately 30 monkeys destroyed about 300 booby eggs in only 30 minutes. These raids apparently were for protein rather than liquids as at the time there was a pool of fresh water on the island. The monkeys would easily push the boobies off their nests and were observed to hold an egg in both hands, bite off the top, and drink it like a cocktail. Heavy predation by monkeys was observed on both the brown and red-footed boobies.

The university primatologist, in addition to observing monkey predation on booby eggs, also estimated that only about 30 pairs of brown boobies had young that summer. Most of these had nests located in the most inaccessible places. These findings, coupled with the observations by myself and others through the early and mid-1970's, suggested that successful nesting by seabirds on Desecheo was virtually eliminated through the 1970's as a result of monkey interference.

While the whole debacle relating to the predation upon seabird eggs by monkeys on Desecheo was an issue in and of itself, the information gathered concerning that problem was directly related to determining the potential impacts of free ranging monkeys on Puerto Rico proper. The Desecheo findings served to repudiate the fifth and final tenet of the monkeyites; namely, that rhesus monkeys are entirely vegetarian. Consequently, the straying of rhesus monkeys onto Puerto Rico proper from the nearly monkey islets of Cueva and Guayacan raised a much more serious specter than the monkeyites would ever admit.

As with the case of removing the monkeys off Desecheo, I had periodic contact with the monkeyites concerning the curtailment of monkey escapes from Cueva and Guayacan. At one point, when discontinuing of their lease lay in the balance, the monkeyites acceded to instituting a number of improvements in the barriers separating the islands from the mainland. However, agreeing to make such modifications and actually carrying them out were two different things. To my knowledge, the modifications were never made.

During the course of my seven years in Puerto Rico, despite raising the issue periodically and discussing it with several successive monkeyite administrators, I am not aware of a single improvement ever being made in the control of escaping monkeys. Not surprisingly, by the time I left the island in 1977, the verbal reports regarding monkeys having left the islets spoke of larger and larger bands ranging ever greater distances from La Parguera. However, the monkeys had still not yet reached Guanica forest where they could pose a serious threat to the survival of the Puerto Rican whip.

Perhaps the best hope for the whip is its habitat, an environment so dry and hostile that rhesus monkey numbers may never increase to a level where they create serious pressure on the whip. Unfortunately, such a suggestion places me in the unenviable position of proposing a certain amount of inadaptability on the part of the rhesus monkey, a position the monkeyites took countless times and which always failed. For the sake of Puerto

Rico's strong-voiced cave-mouth, we may have to hope that such a proposition proves correct, at least this once.

Reflections

Let me return to the matter of the role of science in conservation discussed earlier at the end of Chapter 1. The "rediscovery" by scientists of the Puerto Rican whip-poor-will in the 1960's, over thirty years subsequent to the bird being considered a pest by Civilian Conservation Corps members, serves to illustrate just how out of touch modern science can be with the reality of local people. The case of the whip is not extreme. It is very representative of how scientists can often view things so differently than do local people. The assertion that science is the backbone of conservation has many consequences – many of them bad.

For one, while it may prove useful, which is debatable, in the United States and other developed countries, this contention becomes increasingly untenable in less-developed nations. The reason for this is fairly obvious. Developing countries and countries in transition possess fewer resources to train scientists, to hire them, to outfit them with the materials they need, and to set them to work on any but the most pressing matters of public health and sustenance. Even in those key areas, substantial amounts of foreign assistance, including the retention of foreign scientists, is necessary to advance local initiatives.

The perception that scientific study must be undertaken before any progress whatsoever can be made towards conservation, establishes an unachievable goal for conservationists in developing countries around the world. The problem is further exacerbated by the fact that the rallying cry of the developed world, that "science is the backbone of conservation," sets off, through a desire in the developing world to mirror our successes, mis-directed efforts to study every animal in need of conservation measures. This, while other much more practical initiatives might go much

99

further towards ensuring an animal's survival.

Let's take an example – the Puerto Rican plain pigeon. Here is another endangered bird in Puerto Rico that was believed extinct only to be rediscovered in the 1960's. During my tenure in Puerto Rico a small population of approximately 100 birds was known to survive around Lake Cidra in the eastern center of the island. The habitat of this pigeon happened to be secondary forest which, in this area survived in the steep ravines and gullies that emptied into the lake. These small forest fragments were scattered hither and yon and none were protected. All of these bits of forest owed their survival to their occupying such steep slopes that development of such areas was not practical, at least at that time. Over time, however, who knew when it would become profitable for some developer to simply fill the ravines with dirt and construct an expansive, new urbanization on this important habitat.

So, what was a conservationist to do?

How about immediately mounting an educational campaign to inform residents of the Lake Cidra area that they were blessed with the presence of the only population of Puerto Rican plain pigeons anywhere in the world and that they should take special pride in conserving them?

How about mapping out the primary forest plots of the pigeon, particularly those most threatened by imminent destruction, and starting a full-scale initiative to have them protected?

How about meeting with the owners of these particular parcels of land and trying to work out an agreement to keep the forest fragments intact?

How about meeting with the hunters of the region and adjacent areas to inform them about the bird, assist them to identify it, and solicit their help to conserve it so that it might one day again be a species abundant enough for them to hunt?

No, none of these measures would do. We had to study the bird first. And then we would study it some more. And then some more. The Puerto Rican plain pigeon is probably still being studied. But I would not bet that its habitat is yet well preserved or that most of the citizens around Lake Cidra have any idea whatsoever that a very special bird resides in their vicinity.

I hope I am wrong.

It is important I add that a very special friend of mine was the first to study the plain pigeon in the 1970's, a very special friend. But that is what we did in those days. We didn't know any better. But I am not sure that our approach to conservation has changed much since, and that is very disheartening.

Let me make one other very fundamental point about the relationship of science to conservation. That has to do with the training of scientists, particularly field biologists who study wildlife. I happen to belong to that breed, having studied for a graduate degree in ecology subsequent to leaving Puerto Rico, so I have a fair sense of what I speak.

Becoming a wildlife biologist takes, among other things, a substantial amount of perseverance and focus. If one carries out his or her research abroad, in a tropical rain forest for example, one has to stay especially dedicated to one's research for a number of reasons, not the least of which are limited funding for field work and limited seasons during which data collection is possible. These constraints make it nearly mandatory that the student ignore nearly every distraction and attend to research priorities.

Great. No problem there.

The problem, however, occurs when this former student, now, perhaps, the world's top expert on some endangered monkey, is tagged for the task of developing a conservation initiative for that animal's protection. Or, as is equally likely, this person is given responsibility for developing a conservation initiative covering an entire region of the tropics under the auspices of some major international conservation organization. Where does our monkey expert turn? Obviously he or she turns to what they know best – determining status and abundance, setting up monitoring protocols, identifying needs for further research, etcetera, etcetera.

Why is engaging the public not high on the list of priority actions? Where in this mix is the role of ownership by local institutions? The reason these critical conservation elements are lacking, or are buried as low priorities, is that they fall completely outside the typical experiences of our research biologist.

Remember, our researcher had to maximize his or her time in the field to complete their studies. This did not allow time for a lot of mingling with local communities. It did not foster contact with local institutions. Heaven forbid. Local governmental agencies were nothing more than an impediment that had to be coped with in order to collect specimens of that precious monkey. Why would anyone now want to work with such bureaucracies?

It turns out that the entire field experience that served our biologist so well in procuring a degree and this new job or assignment, did not teach him or her anything regarding these other important elements of conservation. In fact, such field research actually selects against individuals who desire to interact with everyone around them. Graduate students who get diverted in such ways may never finish their theses.

Is this a tirade against scientists? Not really. I love science. It is under-utilized in many areas – including understanding our daily lives, and getting a grip on who we are as human beings. What I am trying to make clear is that scientists have their place in conservation as in most other areas. It is a commentary specifically on the role of science and scientists in achieving conservation. There is a major distinction here. What I feel it is so important to point out, particularly with regard to lesser developed countries, is that science has to play a much less pivotal role in directing conservation programs. This became extremely evident in Puerto Rico and appears to be the case nearly everywhere else you look around the globe.

That being said what takes its place? It is substituted for at the top of the ladder by influencing the attitudes of people – educating the populace to appreciate the marvelous living resources around them. Everything else is built upon this base.

Exploring Remote Islands

On a clear day one can gaze westward from the cliffs of Aguadilla on Puerto Rico's northwest coast and observe, far out at sea, the hazy yet distinct outline of a shear cone protruding from the otherwise unbroken horizon. The seemingly perfect symmetry of this far distant feature makes one wonder whether the object can be natural. A 15-mile boat or plane ride is all it takes to convince any doubter that the cone is an island, the island of Desecheo.

The islands of Desecheo and Mona off Puerto Rico's west coast were two I visited during the course of the rhesus monkey controversy. While the findings gathered during these trips already have been referred to, I gave no impression of what such expeditions were like. This account does just that.

Desecheo, only 360 acres in size, along with Vieques, Culebra, and its cays, is atypical of Puerto Rico's surrounding islands. Many of these are pieces of uplifted sea floor or reef, varying from two to 200 feet above sea level. Others simply are sandbars, some substantially expanded by subsequent deposition of coral rubble. The remainder are built up through the agency of rapidly colonizing red mangrove trees, the roots of which readily trap sediments, increasing an island's size. Common to these smaller islands, however, is a single feature – they all are flat. Desecheo, to the contrary, is anything but flat. Its best descriptor is precipitous. An extinct volcanic cone, Desecheo protrudes pyramid-like abruptly from the ocean with valleys eroded into one of its flanks. Two of the island's four sides are so steep as to be virtually impassable on foot. Besides having severe slopes, these cliff faces are strewn with loose, weathered rock debris which provides extremely insecure footing. The third side of the island has a narrow "coastline" of black, sharp basalt, speckled its entire length with an array of magnificent tide pools. Finally, the fourth side, the side to which the valleys drain, is easily walkable at points; at others, where the valleys have eroded sharp cuts to the sea, one has to negotiate narrow ledges, 20 feet above a pounding surf, in order to transit further.

It is along the ridges between these valleys that one can make headway with relative ease on Desecheo. The island's three north-south valley bottoms often are thick with vegetation, and their sides generally are quite steep and sometimes dense with undergrowth. The sharpness of the relief and the harshness of the terrain, combined with the absence of permanent water, have resulted in the island being uninhabited during the better part of recent history. Presently it is only visited by fishermen and periodically by hunters who pursue the goats that manage to survive from stock released sometime in the distant past.

Based on this backdrop one can look upon Desecheo as either a useless wasteland of no inherent importance or, conversely, as a precious environ, a habitat distinguished by having been spared the wave of human disturbance that has influenced most other civilized portions of the world. Over the past 100 years, the island has been viewed from both perspectives, and it is from actions on Desecheo that lessons can be learned, relevant to potential problems facing species and ecosystems on Puerto Rico and elsewhere.

Small islands are particularly important in this regard. Being relatively simple systems, cause and effect often can be readily discerned where the same might prove impossible in more complex mainland ecosystems. A simple example illustrates this point. What if we wanted to determine the effect of introduced browsing or grazing animals on native vegetation? To investigate this question, we could start by building an exclosure – an area well fenced on all sides which prohibits the entrance of any animal that may want to graze within – in a portion of the grassland under study. By keeping a record of the vegetation growing inside and outside of the exclosure, the effects of grazing can be documented. However, if this experiment were to be carried out in the plains of the western United States, the problem of determining which particular species or groups of species were responsible for differences between the exclosure and non-exclosure vegetation still would remain. Were the observed differences due to native bison or antelope, hares, prairie dogs, or a variety of ground squirrels, or to the various introduced herbivores, such as cattle, burros, mustangs, and sheep? Sorting out the effects of each of these species would prove a major undertaking requiring substantially more complex studies. A similar study on the plains of Africa with its numerous grazing fauna of bovids, zebras, and various antelopes would further complicate this type of investigation.

On a small island such as Desecheo the project becomes relatively simple. Desecheo, and many other islands, supported no native mammalian grazers or livestock. Introduced goats represent the only vertebrate herbivore ever to affect the local flora. Thus, the difference between vegetative growth within and outside an exclosure clearly represents the direct impact of goats.

While such an experiment has never been carried out on Desecheo, research of this type on similar islands has produced enlightening results. For one thing, even if the species of plants present do not change as a result of grazing and browsing, there usually is a significant shift in the abundance of different species. That is to say, a plant species which formerly was common might become rare or vice versa. Typically this modification in the plant community shifts towards an increase in spiny species, or those highly toxic to warm-blooded animals. Under conditions of severe grazing or browsing, some plant species may disappear altogether while others, which previously could scarcely survive under conditions of denser vegetation, take over. Such shifts in vegetative composition and structure often create conditions ripe for invasion by plant species which, formerly, never even occurred in the area. Such alien plants, introduced intentionally or accidentally, are a common feature of many heavily grazed areas.

One of the most interesting examples of the effect of goat modification comes from the Hawaiian Islands where goats have been established for centuries. In the early 1970's an exclosure was built in a grassland to perform the type of experiment just described. Subsequent visits to the fenced plot revealed a vine growing inside the exclosure that investigators could not recognize. Further checking indicated that the species was not known from the flora of Hawaii nor, as later determined, was the species known from the flora of the entire world. This vine, in actuality, was a species endemic to Hawaii, but which never before had been found by a whole series of botanical explorers. Puzzled, the investigators searched the ground outside the exclosure; their instincts proved correct. The new species of vine occurred virtually throughout the grassland. However, it did so only in the form of seeds. Outside the exclosure the vegetative plant was never located; the seeds had never germinated. In retrospect, the explanation for this peculiar circumstance appears simple. For centuries grazing by introduced goats apparently thinned the vegetative cover to such an extent that the tropical sun rapidly evaporated any moisture from the soil surface. Formerly, such moisture normally was retained through shading by the denser native plant community. Without sufficient humidity in the micro-environment of these seeds, they had lain dormant, possibly for centuries, until conditions were appropriate for them to sprout.

Such experiments shed light not only on the potential impact of goats or other herbivores on particular species of plants, but also on how foraging by these animals sets in motion a whole chain of events. Feeding goats tend to thin vegetation, which leads to reduced soil moisture. This, in turn, benefits plants adapted to arid conditions, and such plants release less water into the air as a result of evapotranspiration from their leaves. On a much larger scale, such a sequence of events could lead to a reduction in the volume of water flowing through the hydrologic cycle, the cycle from which comes the rains that bathe our planet. It is, therefore, not unreasonable to expect, in the long run, that we will find a process not uncommon on islands, namely that of desertification caused by overgrazing, as acting on a continental scale. Our civilized world is not anxious to recognize its disturbance of natural processes, but likely it is only a matter of time before reasonable evidence is gathered from our complex continental ecosystems that indicates overgrazing in particular and abusive land practices in general have led to extremely serious problems of desertification we see in Africa and elsewhere. Creation of the Convention to Combat Desertification which entered into force in 1996 and now has no fewer than 190 signatory countries is a sign that we are now recognizing the serious problem we are causing to the earth. Most natural plant communities are modified by mammalian herbivores in one way or another. What is extraordinary about Desecheo and other oceanic islands such as Puerto Rico itself, is that such herbivores were unknown to the island prior to their introduction by humans. This being the case, it is reasonable to expect that Desecheo's plant community is a poor reflection of what it may have been like in pre-Columbian day.

Though some might say that at the turn of the 20th century Desecheo was relatively pristine except for the goats, it is apparent that this lone exception is a big one indeed. Certainly the goats had perpetrated unknown modifications of Desecheo's flora. Nevertheless, the island had enough other qualities going for it that in 1912 it was declared a United States bird reserve. And, speaking of birds, the island had birds in spades. A study of Desecheo's avifauna undertaken that same year indicated over 15,000 seabirds nested on the island. Principal among these was the brown booby which accounted for 8,000-10,000 breeding individuals. Brown boobies are large, chunky birds conspicuous by their long, sharply-pointed, pale bills. Their primary body color is a deep chocolate brown, except for the belly and lower breast which are white. These birds spend virtually their entire day at sea where they capture fish by plummeting headlong from some considerable distance above the surface. They are quite at home in and out of the water, their fully webbed feet propelling them effectively beneath the surface after a dive. At dusk brown boobies return to a remote island such as Desecheo to roost for the night. During the breeding season, this bird simply nests on the ground, often merely clearing a shallow scrape in the soil or using a natural depression among the rocks. On occasion a pair may become industrious and gather a few sticks and other debris into a loose nest. This nest building is more symbolic than real, but apparently aids in pair bonding. As a rule, two white eggs are laid, though typically only one young bird survives to fledge.

Male brown boobies are decidedly smaller than females, suggesting they feed on prey of a different size. Reputedly, males feed in shallower, more inshore waters.

The red-footed booby, a close relative of the brown, also occurred in the 1912 survey to the tune of 2,000 breeding pairs. Red-footed boobies are almost entirely white except for some black in their wings, though there is a second adult color phase in which only the posterior third of the body is white and the remaining anterior portion is brown. Not surprisingly, both adult color morphs of this booby have red feet. The red-footed booby is very similar to the brown though red-foots build rather large stick nests in trees and bushes. These boobies, like the browns, plunge from considerable heights to catch fish and squid. They also appear to be the most adept of the boobies at catching flying fish as the latter glide through the air.

One of the most fascinating island nesters recorded during the survey was the magnificent frigatebird, or man-o'-war, represented by a colony of 175 pairs. The frigatebird is one of the largest seabirds in the Caribbean, second only to the pelican. With a wingspread spanning a full seven feet, the magnificent frigatebird is unique in that it cannot swim, nor even float on the surface. This might seem like an insurmountable handicap for a bird dependent upon the marine environment for its survival. The frigatebird rather ingeniously circumvents this obstacle, however, by using a technique suggested by its various common names – it pirates food from other birds. Man-o'-wars regularly can be seen floating effortlessly high over the ocean where, using their excellent eyesight, they search not only for morsels of food their long, sharply-hooked beaks might skim off the sea's surface, but also for other smaller seabirds that have successfully secured some prey. Upon sighting a booby or other seabird emerging from the water with a fish, the frigatebird immediately gives chase, nipping at the tail of the fleeing bird. The frigate's pursuit is relentless until the frightened seabird drops its prey, whereupon the man-o'-war often snatches the falling fish out of the air before it even hits the water. This aerial facility is due to several physical attributes of the man-o'-war. One feature in particular is its extraordinary bone structure. The bones of this bird are so interlaced with air sacs as to be practically hollow. This gives the man-o'-war the lightest wingloading – the ratio of body weight to wing surface – of any bird. It is the lightness of the load supported by the

Magnificent frigatebird

frigate's wings that afford it substantial aerodynamic superiority over all other birds it pursues. Despite the man-o'-war's large wingspan, the entire bird weighs scarcely more than two pounds; the skeleton is but one quarter of a pound. This is such a scanty amount that it is even exceeded by the weight of the bird's feathers!

Despite their audacity in the air frigatebirds, like most other seabirds, are quite harmless while on their nests and can readily be approached. Unfortunately, if flushed from their eggs by a reckless intruder, an entire year's reproduction can be destroyed because the exposed, untended eggs will be scavenged by neighboring frigatebirds in the colony, each frigate destroying the eggs of others. Considering that frigates may nest only once every other year, and that there is a single offspring per brood, such losses can prove highly detrimental.

During their courtship display, male frigatebirds are indeed magnificent creatures. While perched by its nest, the entirely black male inflates its normally inconspicuous throat into a huge, red balloon. By throwing its head back and spouting gurgling notes, it exposes the enormous pouch to best advantage, putting on quite a show for unattached females. The courtship display of the male frigatebird certainly is one of the premier shows in the world of seabirds.

Like the red-footed booby, the frigatebird nests in vegetation, but it does so in low bushes and shrubs rather than trees. On its nest, as in the air, the bird appears quite majestic with its erect posture and large, hooked bill waving in the air. Its transition from perching to flight, however, is anything but graceful. Having such weak feet that it can barely walk, the man-o'-war is unable to spring into the air. It depends to some extent, therefore, upon an assisting breeze and its expansive wings to get the job done. With bushes and shrubs of all types surrounding its nest, much thrashing and commotion often accompany these efforts to become airborne.

Several other smaller seabirds were recorded breeding on Desecheo in 1912. These included a colony of 2,000 brown noddies and 1,500 bridled terns. Both of these terns, a fraction the size of a booby, nest on the ground, often on bare rock. Ledges or cavities in the rock are favored sites, and a single egg accounts for the total clutch. Unlike the predominantly white terns typical of the coastlines of the New World, the noddy is almost entirely brown with a white cap. The bridled tern, though white below, is basically dark above. Additionally, these two birds are not inshore feeders, but rather frequent waters far offshore and, except around their breeding colonies, are not readily seen from land.

The noddy's courtship behavior is the apparent source of its name, since the bird bows and nods frequently during match-making. Noddies, despite being seabirds, are infrequently seen on the water. While feeding they snatch their prey from the sea on the wing. And when it comes to resting, as often as not, they settle on a piece of flotsam, or the back of some larger sea creature such as a pelican, sea turtle, or, perhaps, even a whale.

That remote Desecheo had been officially recognized

early on for its importance as a natural area is a very positive statement about the thinking of that era. Continuing in this positive vein, a presidential proclamation in 1937 transferred Desecheo to Puerto Rico to be kept as a forest reserve and preserve for native birds with the conditions that:

> "There is reserved to the United States the right to occupy such areas of Desecheo Island as may be needed for the establishment of aids to navigation, together with rights for landing and ingress and egress to the areas so occupied by the United States.
> In the event Desecheo Island shall cease to be used for forest reserve and native bird preserve purposes, or be devoted to any other than forest reserve and native bird purposes, the same shall revert to the United States."

The effective conservation of Desecheo appeared to be moving along inordinately well. It should come as no surprise, therefore, that in 1940 the United States repossessed Desecheo for use as a bombing and gunnery range.

Subsequent to World War II, and countless thousands of bombs later, Desecheo was retained by the United States as a possible site for a missile tracking station. In 1964, however, the United States Army decided to turn it over to the General Services Administration as excess real property; in 1965 the island was transferred to another Federal agency as a medical experimental facility. How use as a bombing range or medical experimental facility fit into the spirit of the 1937 presidential decree is not particularly clear. Regardless, during the time the island served as a reputed medical experimental facility, I made my first visit in an effort to assess the impact of the introduced rhesus monkeys upon its seabird colonies.

In December of 1971 I boarded a large vessel with a team of scientists from other disciplines for two days of exploration on

Desecheo. The boat trip took only a few hours, but substantial additional time was spent loading supplies into a small dinghy and transporting the gear and ourselves ashore. To my good fortune, while the first transit ashore was in progress and I waited on board with the second contingent, a peregrine falcon came out of nowhere and swooped over a small flock of cattle egrets passing near the boat. The egrets wavered somewhat in their course due to the peregrine's dive, but I do not believe the falcon was serious in its efforts, and the egrets may have sensed this. The peregrine, at this time, was severely endangered in many parts of its range as a result of egg shell thinning due to excessive DDT levels affecting its reproductive system. Fortuitously, the falcon has recovered well since the banning of DDT. Its survival was further jeopardized due to the robbing of nestlings from their aeries to satisfy the falconry trade. Peregrines are among the premier birds sought by falconers because of their large size and swift flight. Their value had soared into the tens of thousands of dollars and many aeries had to be guarded day and night to prevent pilfering of the young. Some peregrines migrate through the West Indies and a few winter, but what this bird was doing around this remote island was a mystery, as was the presence of the cattle egrets. Peregrines are among the most adroit and powerful of flying birds, and the continuous circling and swooping of this individual entertained me immensely until it was my turn to board the dinghy for shore.

Shore, in the case of Desecheo, has a uniqueness all its own. Nearly every point of contact between the island and the sea is precipitous. Nothing about the island is gentle. Standing on the coastline at the sea's edge, where this is at all possible on Desecheo, it is typical to peer down a full 30 feet into a crystal clear, angry sea and see the bottom.

Though landing by boat, even a dinghy, is impossible around most of Desecheo, three cuts dissect the island's cindery edge on its south side where the valleys funnel down to the sea. At the head of one of these islets is a narrow beach of coarse gravel. It is here that our wooden dinghy dropped us ashore, having negotiated a moderate surf.

Tossing my gear under a tree removed from the beach, I grabbed my binoculars and field notebook and set out to explore the island. For starters, I decided to take the path of least resistance along the island's west edge. As I emerged from around a prominence onto the open tide pool studded shoreline of Desecheo's west coast, there was an immediate surge of noise, a clacking sound that rapidly increased in volume and then died away equally as fast. Peering ahead intently to locate the source of such a curious and forceful sound, I could see nothing for a moment. This was because I was expecting a large object to have produced noise of such volume. To the contrary, the freight train-like clacking was the product of rather small organisms. Crabs. The entire coastal strip was overrun with tens of thousands and they all reacted in concert to my appearance from behind the outcrop, simultaneously making a dash for the sea.

The island's western face was an evenly steep and desolate slope, but the narrow tide pool strip fringing its base was anything but desolate. The shallow pools appeared like an endless series of bathtubs of differing sizes and shapes inset into black, volcanic rock. Depending upon the distance of each from the sea and on minor variations in elevation, these pools were differentially bathed by the ocean. As a consequence, communities of organisms varied from pool to pool, or even within a single pool. Furthermore, the flushing action of the surf served to deposit creatures in the pools that, with the lowering of the tide, were stranded until fresh pulses from the sea - during the subsequent high tide - would permit their escape.

It was difficult not to become distracted by the wonderful world within each pool. Practically all the pools had the ubiquitous sea anemones, not unlike inverted, sessile jellyfish stuck on their backs to the floor and wall surfaces. Also common were the black sea urchins with their long, slender spines and the less abundant red urchins with shorter, stubbier spines, reddish-black in color. Nibbling algae from the rock faces of the tide pools, the urchins are well protected from most predators by their coat of spines. Two other algae grazers well represented in the pools and also adequately protected by impenetrable armor were the limpet and the chiton. The limpet is a marine snail with an unusual cone-shaped shell not unlike an extremely miniature version of Desecheo. Protected under its volcano-shaped housing, the limpet moves idly along scraping rock surfaces with its raspy tongue-like organ called a radula. Distantly related to the limpet, but not at all similar in appearance, is the chiton. Like the limpet, the chiton also has a radula and is a member of the same phylum, the Mollusca. The chiton is very distinct, however, in that it possesses a segmented body covering rather than a single inflexible shield. Chitons look like nearly flat, armor-plated oval disks fastened to the rocks. Their segmented body design lets them adjust to the contours of the surfaces upon which they graze, and their protective plates are edged by a tough fleshy fringe that seals them against the rock when the water level is low; thus, they can survive for hours outside the water with no apparent difficulty.

The few creatures flushed into these landlocked basins by the pulsing sea, and from which they had not yet found a means of escape, were as interesting as the typical residents of the pools. One of the most fascinating I observed was a young peacock flounder, little more than two inches in length and practically invisible against the pool's floor. I was fortunate that I ever located this small fellow, because flounders are equivalent to the chameleons of the fish world, able to change their coloration to effectively match almost any substrate whether light, dark, or multicolored. This individual was virtually invisible until it moved and had it not done so, I would not have seen it even from six inches away. My distinct impression was that the fish was transparent. There was no way to readily determine whether this was indeed the case or whether the fish merely matched its background so effectively as only to appear so. Another characteristic of flounders is that they begin life as free-swimming fry, but with age they gradually spend more and more time settled on the bottom. While settled, flounders always rest on their left side. Simultaneous with the development of this bottom-dwelling habit, the body begins to flatten, and the fish's left eye migrates to the right side of its head. By the time a flounder reaches an age younger even than of the individual I was observing, both eyes are on the right side of the face and the body has flattened, its "bottom" actually being the left side of the fish.

I also encountered in one of the pools a goldspotted eel, less than a foot in length, that was frantically searching for an outlet to the sea. Off-white in ground color, its entire body was highlighted by contrasting black doughnut-shaped spots. Each spot was set off by a center the color of gold. Regrettably, the eel was in such a distressed state that it was difficult to view adequately. As I had not come to Desecheo to observe the island's tide pools, I left the eel in its frenzied efforts to escape and returned to the landing to explore the island in an easterly direction.

Just as I approached Desecheo's version of a beach, the dinghy set out once more from the main vessel to shore. This was somewhat unexpected since all of the expedition's scientists and their gear had arrived in the course of two previous landings and to our knowledge nothing remained to be brought ashore. Also, in the interval that had elapsed since the earlier trips, the sea had picked up slightly and this translated into a significantly more hazardous landing. This was because the cut through which the dinghy had to pass to reach the beach was narrowest at its mouth. As a result, the ocean swells coming through that narrow gap were amplified into impressively large waves. The large swells and the narrow mouth of the cut, not to mention the effects of any currents and wind, made landing on Desecheo at this time a serious operation.

I delayed my departure eastward to watch the landing. But a landing, at least as we think of one, there was not to be. The dinghy was navigated perfectly into the mouth of the cut and appeared to have mastered the most serious portion of the approach when, just as the small boat cleared the entranceway, it was lifted by a swell of enormous proportions, raised up as effortlessly as a leaf in the breeze. Perched atop the swell, the dinghy was clearly out of human control. Suddenly it flipped into the air and dashed into the surf. Pieces of dinghy, motor, and crew flew in all directions and even though only two remnants of the ill-fated landing ever made it to shore, these two remnants fortuitously turned out to be the two crew members.

The dinghy's occupants happened to be the ship's captain and first mate who had come ashore to deliver a very important message. Very apropos was the message: the sea was getting rougher and if we didn't leave the island soon, it might not be possible for the boat to pick us up tomorrow as planned.

Having delivered the message in the most forceful manner possible, there was now a new problem facing the expedition. The vessel to which we were to board was lying a hundred or so yards off shore without its two principal officers nor a dinghy to evacuate anyone. After a brief deliberation, it was agreed that the first mate would attempt to brave the hazardous currents and swim to the ship, return to Puerto Rico, pick up a more effective rubber dinghy, and return to Desecheo the following day to pick us up, if possible. If disembarking the next day were impossible, we would just have to hold on until the weather cleared.

Considering that few other alternatives remained and that as a precaution we had brought extra water and supplies, we found the plan acceptable. Clearly everyone's primary concern was the danger the first mate faced in swimming out to the ship. Desecheo was famous for its currents and no one wanted this venture to escalate into a full-blown tragedy. We all stood nervously as the first mate dove into the sea and headed for the ship. His progress was agonizingly slow, but continuous; thus, after what appeared to be an inordinate amount of time, the mate finally reached the ship and was assisted aboard.

By the time the vessel had lifted anchor and was on its way back to Puerto Rico, I was already up the western-most valley and crossing it to the ridge which divides it from the central valley. It was the central and particularly the eastern valleys which appeared to support substantial numbers of boobies, judging by our earlier observations from aboard the ship.

Despite the presence of goats on Desecheo, the undergrowth at this time was particularly thick, substantially slowing my advance. I did not appreciate this impediment in the least as I had left my canteen behind so that I could travel light and take maximum advantage of the few remaining hours before dark. Any excessive exertion, therefore, was something I hoped to avoid if at all possible.

Passing over into the upper reaches of the central valley, I suddenly paused and became attentive. I had heard a strange rustling in the trees some distance away that clearly was not produced by a bird. Scanning the area from which the sound had come, I saw a single rhesus macaque as it moved off through a thick coppice of trees. This was the only monkey I was to see during the trip, but I had little time, and my principal interest was the bird colonies.

Heading down into the central valley, I noticed red-footed boobies perched in trees on the far eastern side. Upon reaching this area, the birds became alarmed and took flight before I could approach within 50 yards. Flushing several hundred birds from the trees they occupied did not reveal a single nest. Apparently this area was only used for roosting.

Having suffered the ravages of crossing the central valley, I decided to take a shortcut around the seaward side of the ridge which divides the central from the eastern valley, where, from the boat, I had observed the greatest number of boobies. In short order I realized that there is no such thing as a shortcut on Desecheo. Though this new route was shorter in distance and did not require much climbing, the face of the ridge fronting the ocean was particularly steep and littered with loose stones which made every step a precarious one. These constraints were exacerbated by the fact that all nine species of cacti known to grow on Desecheo seemed to be thriving on this cliff face. This made the grabbing of bushes for support a dangerous proposition; one not quite as dangerous, however, as that of tumbling down the cliff and over the ledge to the sea or rocks another 30 feet below.

It was while negotiating one of the more precarious portions of the cliff that I glanced for a moment out to sea and noticed what appeared to be a massive, black rock protruding from the water not a great distance offshore. Preoccupied with my survival while crossing the cliff face, I paid the boulder little mind. After

117

completing the crossing, however, I peered out to sea once more only to find that the rock had disappeared.

This might have been attributable to the changing tide had the outcrop protruded only a foot or so above the surface, but the missing rock had earlier projected a full five feet above sea level. Perplexed, I sat on a safe overlook and studied the sea. Nothing. I looked some more. Then, well off beyond where the rock had earlier appeared something broke the surface, not at all like a rock itself, yet an object which immediately explained what I had seen. Rolling gently across the surface, I spotted the back of a whale. Visible for scant seconds, the whale was gone as quickly as it had appeared. But, moments later the back again emerged, and the creature's small dorsal fin passed in an arc across the surface before the animal again submerged. Studying the whale as it swam effortlessly parallel to shore, I soon noticed that it had a companion, and then two.

Most likely the whales were humpbacks. The waters between Desecheo and the large island of Hispaniola to the west are one of the principal wintering and calving grounds in the entire world for this behemoth. What I had originally thought was a huge, pointed rock sticking out of the water was in fact one of the whales performing a fairly characteristic behavior known as spyhopping. When whales spyhop they poke their entire heads out of the sea reputedly to look around with their extremely small, beady eyes. Just what a whale would be looking for is beyond me, especially since their sight is quite poor. The explanation that spyhopping is indeed for this purpose seems rather anthropocentric. It will be interesting to see whether a more functional purpose, from a whale's perspective, becomes known.

These whales off Desecheo were the first I had ever seen, and I could not help but sit and watch as they so effortlessly lolled off shore. It was difficult to believe that these creatures, so perfectly adapted for life in the sea, except that they must breath air, were derived from entirely terrestrial ancestors. What makes this so difficult to grasp is our poor perception of time. The millions of years which it took for whales to evolve are simply incomprehensible to the human mind. Nevertheless, there is virtually no doubt that the ancestors of whales were land-dwelling mammals. All the characteristics typical of mammals, a class of animals which evolved on land, can readily be found in whales. Hair, a physical feature unique to mammals, though sparse on whales, dolphins and porpoises, is present. Most dramatically, if one examines the bones of a whale's fins or forelimbs, they are extremely similar in structure to those of a terrestrial mammal, so much so that the five digits or fingers are distinctly evident. Even vestigial bones of what were once the whale's hind limbs are present under the skin. Whales also suckle their young in a manner identical to terrestrial mammals.

It is the extreme modification of the whale's body to an aquatic life that makes it appear so un-mammal-like. It has adapted far beyond the beaver, the otter, and even the seal, in its ability to be at home in a marine environment. The most conspicuous adaptations include the loss of the hind limbs, modification of the forelimbs into flippers and the evolution of a fish-like tail. There are other equally fascinating adaptations. For one, the whale's nose has migrated from the front of its face to the top of its head. Some fossil whales from tens of millions of years ago exhibit an intermediate stage in this process wherein the nose is halfway up the face. The nose of the whale is its blowhole from which is emitted a characteristic spout. Contrary to popular belief, the spout is not sea water the whale has taken in, but rather results from the condensing of the whale's hot breath in the cool sea air. Some whales actually have evolved a partition separating the passage between the nose and lungs from the food passage between the mouth and the stomach. The sperm whale, for example, which possesses this partition cannot possibly breathe through its mouth, since the only place air in the mouth can go is into the stomach.

The humpbacks I was watching were typical of most whales in lacking teeth. Rather, they possess an unusual sieve-like structure made of a horny material called baleen, or more commonly, whalebone. Despite their massive size, baleen whales feed on some of the smallest marine organisms, particularly shrimp-like crustaceans called krill. Krill often occur in extraordinary concentrations; it is through these masses that the whale swims, mouth open, until its gape is full of both krill and water. The baleen screen is then dropped from the upper jaw, and the whale's massive tongue presses out the water, the krill being retained by the baleen.

Sometimes a humpback, or even groups of humpbacks working in tandem, makes a bubble net around the krill by circling beneath them while blowing bubbles from its nostrils. Once the krill are surrounded by the bubbles, which they apparently are reluctant to pass through, the whale rises beneath them and feeds to its satisfaction. Needless to say, humpbacks have to do a lot of feeding to sustain their up to forty-five tons of weight.

Many species of whales, the humpback included, have been actively hunted by man for centuries. As a result, the largest of all creatures to ever live on earth, the enormous 150-ton blue whale, is now on the verge of extinction. The same goes for the right whale and the bowhead, as well as for the humpbacks before me. The utility of their body parts – for human and pet foods, bone meal, edible and industrial oil, pharmaceuticals, and stays for women's corsets – have placed these harmless and defenseless creatures in the throes of a last hurrah. Thus, I felt privileged to watch these few, remnant behemoths languishing peacefully nearby. Simultaneously, I experienced both satisfaction and irritation at how, in the face of all the uncertainty in their future, these magnificent beasts could be so distant from it all and continue on in the ways of their ancestors come what may. The rapidly-changing world around them would have to do the adjusting for they were not about to adjust to it. Either they would survive on the terms to which they had adapted over eons, or they would not survive at all.

It was with regret that I pulled myself away from the humpbacks and proceeded into Desecheo's easternmost valley with its large complement of boobies. It was now becoming late afternoon and red-footed boobies were flying in from the sea in increasing numbers to perch in the trees. Advancing toward these birds, they again dispersed well prior to my approach. Nonetheless, I persisted in checking out the perch of every booby possible and, finally, in the midst of this rapidly growing roost, I encountered my first nest. Ultimately I located several other nests, but interestingly not one of them contained a single egg.

Set on investigating this situation further, I was continuing my search for nests when above the guttural "ga-ga-ga"ing and squawking of the red-foots I detected the distinctive whirring of an engine. Suddenly in a torrent of noise, a helicopter burst low over the ridge top and circled in front of the valley mouth. Suspecting that something was amiss, I rushed to an opening on the ridge and took a closer look at the helicopter hovering before me. Sure enough, it belonged to the Coast Guard and though I could not see the crew clearly and we could not communicate, I thought it best to head back to camp.

It was just as well that the helicopter had started me on my return, for by now the sun was getting low and transiting Desecheo after dark without a flashlight would have been absolutely impossible. I traveled quickly across the eastern valley and over the ridge into the central cut. At this point I would have liked to rest for I had no water and was becoming quite tired. However, I knew I was probably the person furthest from camp when the helicopter had arrived and thus would likely be the last one back. It was necessary, therefore, to move on as quickly as possible. Pushing myself I proceeded across the central valley and into the most western of the island's three major ravines. Knowing that this was the last valley spurred me on, but I was pooped. By the time I crossed the third valley and descended into camp, I was exhausted. I felt sick and nauseous and greatly desired some time to recuperate. Unfortunately, as I had surmised, I had been furthest from camp and was the last to return. The helicopter, in fact, had come for us. There it sat on the island's only flat piece of ground - a concrete heliport apparently built by the armed forces during Desecheo's days as a bombing target. All the remainder of our party and nearly all of our equipment were already on board, so there was no time for me to do anything but to jump aboard and join the group.

In an instant we were whisked away, prematurely abandoning Desecheo and the studies we had come to perform. Apparently our ship, upon contacting the Coast Guard, had stimulated that agency to consider our situation something of an emergency. As a result, the helicopter was dispatched, and our expedition to Desecheo was aborted.

Circling above the island before heading back to Puerto Rico, I tried to take in the view as my body savored the most delicious draughts of water that had ever touched my palette. From the vantage point of the helicopter, I experienced Desecheo from a totally different perspective. For one thing, the treacherousness of the island was dissipated. This allowed me to appreciate the island's relief in a more aesthetic manner without considering what those precipitous contours might mean were I on the ground traversing them. The steep slopes played with the evening light that tinted the mottled browns and dull greens of Desecheo by casting some areas into shadow while featuring others with flashing gold highlights. Superimposed upon this were numerous white flecks, each representing a red-foot on its way to roost, and each a reminder of a mystery I had not yet unraveled. Cast against a royal blue ocean, Desecheo appeared an impressive image I would not soon forget.

Though I was unable to learn much about the status of booby breeding on Desecheo, the island certainly taught me a lesson in outdoorsmanship. While traveling light might have its benefits, it was brought home that one thing simply cannot be underestimated - the body's need for water. Particularly in more tropical climates one can become dehydrated or suffer from heat exhaustion extremely easily. This lesson was to pay dividends in the surprisingly near future.

———

Having spent the night on Puerto Rico, we left the next day, this time voyaging to Mona, an island midway between Puerto Rico and Hispaniola in the 90-mile wide Mona Passage. Apparently the rough seas predicted the day before never materialized, for the ocean was relatively calm and the sky clear. Equipped this trip with a rubberized landing craft, we were all set to begin our explorations of this second island. During the voyage to Mona, dolphins played around the bow of our vessel and flying fish flitted through the air alongside. These marine creatures and the periodic pelagic seabirds, such as the bridled tern and brown noddy, kept me on deck and alert during the entire trip.

After several hours at sea, Mona, a pancake flat island, appeared in the distance as a fine line on the horizon, an image totally contrary to that of cone-shaped Desecheo. Though barely noticeable at first due to its low profile, we had been aware of Mona's presence long before it was actually observable. This was due to the large bank of clouds piled up over the island, a phenomenon which occurs even though this former piece of ocean floor is uplifted only a couple of hundred feet above the sea.

As we approached Mona, we soon discerned the most conspicuous human landmark embellishing the island – a lighthouse standing atop the cliff on the island's southeastern corner. Most of Mona's coastline is a two-hundred foot high vertical precipice except for the southern shore along which our boat soon proceeded. Here a coastal plain of varying width fringed the elevated plateau. At its far southeastern end, we cast anchor, boarded our efficient, new dinghy, and landed uneventfully on a sandy shore. It was also here that the few human structures, other than the lighthouse, had been constructed. Principal among these was an airstrip, simply a dirt track cleared in a flat portion of the coastal plain. Some enterprising visitor with an admirable sense of humor had mounted a makeshift sign near the airstrip which read, "Mona International Airport," the "international" apparently referring to the few planes that visit from the Dominican Republic. Besides the airstrip, the Department of Agriculture had constructed five concrete cabins, one of which was used by the police who were there apparently to inhibit smuggling. Smuggling and piracy account for a fascinating and colorful component of Mona's early colonial history. Most notably, the notorious Captain Kidd reputedly bargained for his life with a New England judge promising to share his treasure if Kidd were permitted to return to Mona to dig it up. Apparently the judge was unimpressed, and Kidd was hung. However, Kidd's statement was taken seriously by many gold seekers who to this day visit Mona in search of buried treasure. A second cabin was used by maintenance personnel attached to the Agriculture Department's Division of Fish and Wildlife, the agency with which I had earlier applied for a job. Mona would have been one of my field stations. The three remaining cabins were occupied by our expedition.

Except for the two policemen, several maintenance workers, and a few Coast Guardsmen in the lighthouse at the far end of the island, Mona was uninhabited by any permanent residents. Actually all of the above personnel were on temporary duty making none of them true residents. The unused state of the island at this time was in sharp contrast to the hustle and bustle which occurred late in the nineteenth century when Mona supported a thriving guano industry. I was later to see some remnants of that industrious era at the other end of the coastal plain. Here, old rail tracks were still in place which had carried cars full of guano from the caves to the shore for loading aboard ships.

Certainly it was to the benefit of the island's wildlife that humans had pretty much abandoned Mona. It was during the period of guano exploitation that Mona's endemic parakeet became extinct. That the extinction of this bird was closely tied to the presence of so many humans on this small island is almost certain.

Parakeets, when common, can be notorious raiders of crops. Given Mona's poor soil and growing conditions, the loss of produce to pesky parakeets most certainly would not have been tolerated. Their capture as a cage bird, a pleasant treat on a remote and inhospitable island such as Mona would also have lead to their decline. And finally, the cutting of the island's limited forests for either dwellings or charcoal would have virtually eliminated the cavities which this bird depended upon for nesting. The chain of circumstances which likely befell Mona's parakeet is not too difficult to surmise. This is because the same scenario has befallen all too many of its brethren from all over the Caribbean and beyond.

Fortunately, most of Mona's other unique creatures survived this intrusion and live, even though in some cases precariously, to the present day.

The remaining daylight hours were spent exploring the coastal plain. During our brief exploration, we had the good fortune to encounter the most unusual and distinctive of Mona's surviving endemic species. This was the prehistoric-looking Mona rock iguana. The rock iguana is a magnificent animal measuring over five feet in length from snout to tip of tail. A husky lizard, its most dominant feature is its head which is highlighted by a most impressive set of jaw muscles. One can readily believe that a bite from this animal might easily sever a hand; however, I am unaware of any case in which this creature has ever attacked a human being. As impressive as the jaws of the rock iguana might be, they are only used on fruits, leaves, and other plant matter since this lizard is entirely vegetarian. Among the many plants eaten by the Mona rock iguana is the manchineel, or poison apple, one of the most infamously poisonous plants in the American tropics. Deadly to humans, the fruits of this tree, when in season, are fed on heavily by iguanas without ill effects.

Mona rock iguana

The Mona rock iguana is particularly unique by virtue of being one of but a few surviving species from among a group of iguanas now confined primarily to the Greater Antilles, specifically the islands of Cuba, Hispaniola, Jamaica, Mona, and the small island of Anegada in the Virgin Islands. Though each of these islands supports its own distinct species, it is believed that millions of years ago rock iguanas were distributed much more widely including throughout Central America. Evidently, as a result of unknown factors, possibly increased competition on the continent from a substantially greater number of coexisting and interacting species, the rock iguanas were one of the groups to succumb to the process of natural selection. Nonetheless,

125

though unable to survive conditions on the continent, the group apparently benefited from possessing a superior dispersal ability than many of its competitors or a greater adaptability to island ecosystems and, as a result, populations gradually spread to and through the Antilles. Here they evolved into unique species on each island due to the extremely limited interchange of genes between the distinct island populations. Consequently, the Mona rock iguana represents a relic iguana of a type that formerly existed on the continent possibly tens of millions of years ago.

Humans have posed various threats to this iguana, some intentional and others not. For several hundred years iguanas were hunted with dogs and eaten, though this practice is now obsolete, at least on Mona. Introduced pigs, relatively common on Mona, can be a serious threat to the eggs. Iguanas lay their eggs at the end of two- to five-foot burrows in chambers one to two feet beneath the ground surface. We passed by one of these nesting areas during our walk, but this was not the breeding season, and no nesting activity was observed. The female excavates her nest burrow in the soil digging a tunnel sloping downward about three feet long to one to two feet beneath the surface. Here she lays from 5-19 eggs and then refills the tunnel with sand and sometimes guards the nest for several days to protect it from destruction by other females. The eggs go unincubated, being warmed by the heat of the sun on the sand. Only one percent of the entire island provides adequate soil for nest digging. In dry years when food is scarce for many organisms, pigs, sniffing for underground tubers and other morsels, discover the nest chambers and may destroy every single iguana egg. Doubtless pigs, as well as stray cats, will also feed on small, immature iguanas when the opportunity arises. Goats have a more indirect impact on iguanas. By foraging selectively on certain favored plant species, goats, as we saw with Desecheo, can totally modify the vegetation cover of an area. This has an impact, often negative, on the iguana's food plants. Also, the potential nesting sites for iguanas on Mona are extremely limited due to the rockiness of the island. The principal adequate sites are on the coastal plain and, if these become overly infiltrated by roots or are cleared as a result of over-browsing, there is the potential that what was once a suitable nest site will be no more.

Though humans presently may have no bad intentions against iguanas, they continue to provoke other negative impacts. Simply walking through a nesting site may result in nests being caved in causing ultimate desiccation or predation of the eggs. Riding off-road vehicles through nest sites produces the same deleterious results. Furthermore, the coastal plain of Mona was formerly farmed and much of it later converted into a mahogany plantation. Though the dryness of the island has resulted in the very slow and uneven growth of these trees, the extensive mahogany root systems have probably modified former nest sites to the point that they are no longer of potential use for nesting.

Given all of these real and potential threats, it is impressive that the Mona rock iguana survives at all. Surely the loss of a species such as this would be a tragic setback, for not only is this lizard a spectacular creature to behold, but it is also an outstanding reminder of the Antilles' unusual role in evolutionary history.

All told there are eight species of rock iguanas in the Caribbean and, believe it or not, a few others are more threatened than Mona's. The Jamaican rock iguana was actually believed extinct for nearly 50 years before being rediscovered by a hunter's dog among Jamaica's arid Hellshire Hills. Presently it is estimated that between 50 and 200 individuals survive, but just barely. Charcoal burning of the vegetation is a threat, but the most important factor endangering these animals is introduced predators – with no less than the mongoose leading the list. Juvenile iguanas are an appealing meal to a mongoose and it is believed that if predation by the mongoose is not reduced, the Jamaican rock iguana may well go extinct in the wild.

After our brief reconnaissance of the coast, we ate supper and then gathered around to discuss tomorrow's activities. Our plan for the next day was simple. Five of us, led by Frank Wadsworth, a renown forester, and Roy Woodbury, an extraordinary botanist, would circle the north coast around to the lighthouse on Mona's opposite side. Such a route would take us to Mona's most remote reaches and give those of us who were newcomers a good feel for the island. Though Frank and Roy had visited Mona many times before, this excursion was a first for me as well as for Pete Weaver and Les Whitmore, two young foresters interested in Mona's natural history.

We decided to make the entire 15-mile hike around Mona's rugged fringe in a single day. Though this would require substantial effort, it would allow us to leave behind our camping gear and travel light. It would enable us also to sleep in the comfortable lighthouse rather than on the island's inhospitable, rocky terrain. Frank knew the island well; he had been here about 20 times. If he said the hike was perfectly doable, I certainly had no reason to doubt his judgment, especially since it was Frank and Roy, both about 60 years old, though in excellent shape, who would probably suffer most from the rigors of such a journey. Our plans firmed up, I quickly packed. This took little preparation since the only equipment I chose to bring was my notebook, binoculars and camera; for eats I packed peanut butter, jelly, bread, and water. After my experience on Desecheo two days earlier, I was most concerned about water. To negate any chance of a repeat performance, I packed a full five quarts of the precious commodity. Being thirsty is one thing, but becoming dehydrated is something else. My Desecheo experience had made me extremely cautious, so much so that the following morning I learned I was carrying two and one half times more water than anyone else on the expedition!

Up before dawn, we were out on the trail ascending the face of the plateau just as the sun was breaking through the darkness. Once upon the tableland, we sought the island's edge with its vertical cliffs, not for the view, which was totally breath-taking, but because the vegetation on Mona's lip is significantly sparser due to incessant battering by the wind. Thus, we could wend our way along the edge with fewer impediments. After the initial climb from the coastal plain to the tableland, our hike on Mona was over flat ground. This was certainly a plus. Other benefits were the magnificent scenery and a soothing breeze blowing in from the sea. On the negative side of the ledger, the island's surface was composed of limestone and dolomite, two closely related and easily eroded rocks, which had weathered over the years to appear like a moonscape. While flat overall, the surface was like a pin cushion consisting of sharp pinnacles and ridges of rock, only a few inches high, but more than significant enough to make walking difficult and a fall treacherous. Furthermore, though the vegetation was thinner within a few feet of the precipice, it was far from absent. Due to the incessant winds, the vegetation growing on the island's lip was severely stunted, many bushes being only one or two feet high. While this provided great relief for one's face and arms, after a while our shins became increasingly sore until we began to look for every possible means to avoid battering them against the hardy scrub.

Initially, we progressed very smoothly. Following the cliff edge we had no need to consult our map. And, of course, the view of the sea was spectacular. Down below us the ocean hammered the seemingly indestructible cliffs. Yet, from time to time, we would encounter limestone stacks and boulders separated from the island itself by the incessant pounding and other mechanisms of weathering. It was structures such as these which reminded us that as massive and indestructible as Mona might seem, the island's battle against the sea was inexorably moving in a single direction – towards returning the island to the briny depths – the source from which it had come. The stacks we observed were simply indicators of how that process was taking place.

The stacks also provided a distinct habitat all their own for certain of Mona's avifauna. In particular, they were the only sites on the island where sooty terns were found to nest. A few small colonies of these pelagic terns apparently benefited from the extraordinary protection the stacks provided from terrestrial predators.

After several hours of hiking, Mona's sister island, Monito, came into view. Approximately three miles distant, Monito appeared as an unreal apparition in the early morning haze. Too far away to observe any indication of Monito's bountiful seabird colonies, it was exciting simply to be so near to that spectacular island. Like Mona, a mass of uplifted ocean floor, one had to wonder whether in former eons the two sister islands had once been connected and whether what remained of each was now only a shadow of a previously much more extensive landmass.

In addition to geological formations, we observed also from Mona's cliffs a few elements of marinelife. The most impressive of these was no more than a dozen feet from shore, though hundreds of feet below us, in one of the few small, semi-protected lagoons along the coast. The lagoon's occupant was none other than a large shark which probably had not yet retreated from the island's shallows following the night's hunt. In localities such as Mona, where crosscurrents are strong and shallow areas rapidly give way to deep water, sharks are notoriously abundant. It was fascinating to watch this great marine predator in such a natural environment and yet from so much safer a vantage point than was the case with the creature I pursued off Cayo Ratones. Certainly had the shark below me been the beast Mitch reported on that eventful day, I surely would not have entered the water. The shark here in the lagoon clearly did not have the telltale rusty coloration of a nurse shark, and I would not have dared to mess around with any other kind.

Another marine creature which caught our attention was not a fish at all, but rather a reptile. It was a sea turtle paddling in the waters below us. No fewer than five species of these unusual creatures inhabit the seas around Puerto Rico or nest on its beaches. The animal we were observing was either a hawksbill or green sea turtle. The former species breeds more commonly on Mona than probably anywhere else in the Caribbean. Though greens do not presently breed on Puerto Rico or its adjacent islands, it is believed that they formerly did. While adults are now rarely found, subadults are common in the surrounding waters.

In just what activity the sea turtle was occupied was not clear, but it could have been feeding on the numerous sessile organisms - sponges, corals, anemones, fanworms - which fasten to the submerged portion of Mona's cliffs. Were this the case, the turtle was likely a hawksbill as such immobile invertebrates are standard fare for this omnivore. Contrarily, the green sea turtle is almost entire herbivorous, with its diet centering on marine plants. Had the turtle been somewhat larger with a disproportionately oversized head, it might have been a loggerhead. The enlarged head and jaws of this turtle enable it to crush its prey which includes mollusks and crustaceans. So powerful are its jaws that even the thick shells of giant clams and the queen conch are not immune to being shattered.

One sea turtle which this clearly was not was the leatherback. Leatherbacks are massive creatures, the largest of all living sea turtles, possessing a more tapered shell crowned by conspicuous longitudinal ridges. Unlike the plated shells of hawksbill, green, and other sea turtles, that of the leatherback is soft and skin-like, a characteristic from which it derives its name. The leatherback is certainly not a turtle we would expect to encounter foraging at the surface along a sea cliff. Leatherbacks are highly marine and deep diving. Apparently their principal food is jellyfish, and they possess imposingly jagged jaws with which to grasp this slippery prey. As if this apparatus were not enough, leatherbacks also have a series of two- to three-inch long spines lining the mouth and the entire surface of the esophagus to facilitate swallowing its jello-like diet.

After watching for a while as the turtle fought the rough water near the cliff, we proceeded on our way. We took periodic short breaks throughout the morning and by midday when we stopped for lunch, Monito was far to the rear. It appeared we were making good progress.

As I sat down to make short work of some peanut butter and jelly, my eye caught sight of a peculiar gray mass the size of a tennis ball, lying within a cavity on the ground. Picking it up I noticed immediately that it was the shed skin of a snake. This was particularly exciting because one of Mona's endemic species is a boa constrictor not recorded for many decades. That the skin was probably a boa's was indicated by it being in a wad, a characteristic of boa sheds. My rediscovery by shear happenstance of evidence indicating that this endangered species still survived was an exciting bonus of the trip – the kind of discovery much more prone to occur in out of the way places such as Mona. It so happened that investigators, a few years later, specifically searching for the Mona boa at night with powerful lanterns, located three

131

or four individuals in a matter of hours. Their discovery suggested that the Mona boa was not necessarily endangered. Rather, this species of nocturnal habits and retiring demeanor may have simply gone unobserved by Mona's casual visitors and non-herpetologists. The boa's endangered status could have resulted from the unique habits of the snake and may not have reflected the true abundance of the species.

While gobbling our lunches we had the good fortune to rest where a yellow-shouldered blackbird was involved in its most distinctive behavior. Flying into the forceful wind coming off the ocean, this small landbird would struggle out past the cliff face and plummet over the side, disappearing below. After some time the bird would reemerge and fly into the scrub, only to later repeat its dive over the precipice. This activity is pursued in an effort to use the nooks and crannies of the cliff and sea caves as protected sites in which to nest. Such unusual behavior may prove very critical to the yellow-shouldered blackbird for this species is undergoing a rapid decline, its survival being threatened by factors affecting nest success.

As its name suggests, the yellow-shouldered blackbird is entirely black with a brilliant yellow patch or epaulet at the bend of its wing. Though its closest relative in North America, the well-known red-winged blackbird, has a distribution spanning the greater portion of the continent, the yellow-shouldered is confined solely to Puerto Rico and Mona. Differing subspecies occupy each of the two islands. As recently as the turn of the 20th century, the yellow-shouldered blackbird on Puerto Rico proper was common around the entire coastal plain from mangrove and freshwater swamps to arid scrublands and foothills. However, probably as a result of major land use modifications on the coast, the species declined significantly in the early 1900's until by mid-century it was uncommon and fairly local in distribution. At this point a major new threat to the species' survival came upon the scene.

The new threat was in the form of another bird, and a rather fascinating one at that. The interloper looked innocuous enough. Only about eight inches in length, approximately the same size as a yellow-shouldered blackbird, the bird even appeared very much like a yellow-shouldered, but without its yellow epaulet. Entirely glossy black with a purplish tint, the species goes by the common name of the glossy or shiny cowbird.

Unknown to Puerto Rico proper prior to the 1950's, the shiny cowbird population exploded across Puerto Rico in the 1960's and 1970's. Native to tropical and subtropical regions of South America, the shiny cowbird has extended its range northward through the Lesser Antilles since its first arrival among the islands in 1891. Though it is not entirely clear what initiated this rapid range expansion, it is likely that movement northward was facilitated by deforestation which transformed these formerly well-forested islands into a checkerboard of habitats including fields and open scrublands, habitats much more suitable to the shiny cowbird. Human destruction of the forest cover occurred on all of the islands to varying degrees, for basically the same reasons – to promote farming, to produce charcoal, to graze cattle, and to build homes. It was not only the shiny cowbird that benefited from the conversion. In Puerto Rico alone the mourning dove and white-winged dove naturally invaded the island and colonized these newly-created open habitats. Among the Virgin Islands the mockingbird and Lesser Antillean bullfinch have done the same. Nonetheless, it is the shiny cowbird which has become a serious pest because of a particular trait. It is a nest parasite. Rather than manifest the typical approach to breeding of most avian species, the shiny cowbird has the quite unusual habit of not building a nest of its own.

Instead, it simply lays its eggs in the nests of other birds. This is accomplished when the host's nest is at some moment left unattended. To enhance the chances of survival of the cowbird's eggs, the female cowbird often punctures or removes the eggs of the host, guaranteeing their failure. The cowbird egg also requires a relatively short incubation period of only about 11 days, several less than most other songbirds. By hatching prior to the young of the host, the nestling cowbird has a head start in growth and consequently an advantage in competition for food brought to the nest by its foster parents. While the above trait bodes well for

133

the survival of cowbird offspring, such parasitism has been highly detrimental to the reproductive success of many songbirds.

An obvious question we might ask is why the parasitized, or host species, tolerates this type of intrusion at the expense of its own young. The answer is not a simple one. Basically, birds are creatures of instinct with limited innate flexibility to respond effectively to highly unique circumstances. This is certainly not a condemnation of birds. Instinct has served the group well for nearly 200 million years. Where parasitism is common, birds, in fact, do evolve a response. A dramatic example is found in the diminutive yellow warbler, a species common through much of the United States. Overlapping the distribution of this mite in many areas is the brown-headed cowbird, a close relative of the shiny cowbird and also a nest parasite. When the brown-headed cowbird lays an egg in the nest of a yellow warbler, the latter often recognizes the alien object and responds by building a new nest on top of the old one, abandoning its own eggs in the process and laying a new clutch. If the new nest is also parasitized, the yellow warbler once again builds a new nest. In the course of a summer where parasitism rates are high, yellow warblers may construct apartment complexes with several nests, one on top of the other, all abandoned. The yellow-browed tyrant, a flycatcher of South America, has evolved this same response to shiny cowbird eggs found in its nest.

As the shiny cowbird has rapidly colonized the West Indies, one of the species it has encountered, interestingly enough, is the yellow warbler. Unfortunately for the latter, the West Indian races of the yellow warbler, unlike those in North America, have evolved for thousands of years in the absence of nest parasites. As a result, they have never acquired or they have lost the capacity to identify, or at least respond to the presence of, unusual eggs in their nests. This inability to cope with the threat of the cowbird appears to have resulted in the dramatic decline of the yellow warbler on some islands, such as Barbados.

The plight faced by the yellow warbler has, regrettably, also befallen other species, including the yellow-shouldered blackbird. Yellow-shouldered blackbird numbers in Puerto Rico have now declined below 500 birds with nearly 100 percent of nests that are unprotected by humans being parasitized in some areas. Though young yellow-shoulders sometimes fledge from parasitized nests, this recruitment to the population is inadequate to offset natural losses, thus the continuing decline. Reducing cowbird numbers by trapping in the vicinity of remaining blackbird nesting areas and removing cowbird eggs from active nests are the only mechanisms presently available to foster effective blackbird reproduction.

It was hoped that Mona's small population of about 400 birds would remain isolated for a while from the cowbird's range expansion, but scarcely a year after my visit a flock of a dozen cowbirds was observed on the island. Considering the plight of the yellow-shouldered blackbird on Puerto Rico, the best remaining chance for the survival of the species is that the Mona population has idiosyncrasies in its reproductive behavior of which the shiny cowbird cannot take advantage. The habit of diving over the cliffs to nest in crevices might be just such a survival mechanism. It can only be hoped that such is the case.

While the yellow-shouldered blackbird is being driven towards extinction, the shiny cowbird has not stalled in the least in its dramatic population expansion. This is because the bird is a generalist in terms of the species it will parasitize. The loss of one host species has little effect on cowbird reproduction overall. Vireos, flycatchers, warblers, and orioles are all subject to cowbird parasitism, though of course with varying degrees of success.

A major reason why the yellow-shouldered blackbird is so highly susceptible to shiny cowbird parasitism is that, in addition to not rejecting foreign eggs, it is a poor nest attendant. Even having laid a clutch of eggs, adult yellow-shoulders may be away from the nest as much as 12 percent of the day. This provides ample opportunity for a female cowbird to quickly sneak to the nest and deposit an egg. With the continued increase in shiny cowbirds and the decrease in yellow-shoulders, the latter are taken advantage of to such an extent that in one study of 35 nests, all were parasitized with each nest containing an average of over five cowbird eggs. The maximum number of cowbird eggs found in a yellow-shoulder nest to date is eight.

The significance of the yellow-shoulder's poor nest attendance is brought home when one compares it to the Puerto Rican flycatcher, an endemic bird to Puerto Rico and the Virgin Islands, which often nests in conditions similar to those of the yellow-shoulder. Both the yellow-shoulder and the Puerto Rican flycatcher are aggressive to cowbird intruders, but unlike the yellow-shoulder, the flycatcher forages for food in close proximity to its nest. This allows it to be readily at hand to fend off intruders and consequently its nests are only lightly parasitized. Such behavior is often referred to as preadaptive – an attribute evolved under one set of conditions that fortuitously is of benefit to the species when new circumstances arise. That the Puerto Rican flycatcher is not entirely preadapted to parasitism is demonstrated by the fact that should a shiny cowbird sneak an egg into its nest, the flycatcher does not recognize it as alien and thus incubates the egg and raises the chick as one of its own.

The number of host species parasitized by the cowbird throughout its large range numbers approximately two hundred. Unfortunately, because the shiny cowbird is the first nest parasitizing species to occur in the West Indies, it has proved highly successful due to the native birds' inabilities to cope with its tactics. Which birds on other islands will suffer a similar fate can only be surmised at present. Certainly, the tawny-shouldered blackbird of Cuba and Hispaniola, islands which have been recently invaded by the shiny cowbird, merits careful scrutiny. So does the extremely unique palm chat of Hispaniola. The impacts of the shiny cowbird's invasion on the avifauna of the West Indies is only in the initial stages of being brought to light and could ultimately prove a severe blow to a significant number of endemic West Indian forms.

While deforestation in the West Indies probably resulted in opening up the islands to colonization by the shiny cowbird, the same process in North America promoted the expansion of the brown-headed cowbird. Not surprisingly, the expansion of the brown-headed cowbird had consequences similar to those of its cousin. Kirtland's warbler, like the yellow-shouldered blackbird, only recently exposed to nest parasitism, had no defenses. As a result, heavy parasitism within this bird's limited breeding range in central Michigan is one of the principal causes of its endangerment. All told, cowbird invasions in both North America and the West Indies have had identical results.

The potential threat of the shiny cowbird dampened somewhat my enjoyment of the unusual cliffside behavior of the yellow-shoulder, but the bird's antics were still delightful. We soon finished lunch and continued our way along the precipice of Mona's coastline. Through the afternoon we trudged onward; the bushes buffeting our legs became increasingly annoying. From time to time we were forced to turn inland to by-pass some obstacle or other, and here we were immediately overwhelmed by the oppressive heat, absence of a breeze, swarms of mosquitoes, and innumerable cactus spines. Unfortunately, as we headed eastward Mona's terrain appeared to be a bit more broken, requiring more frequent circumventions of fissures and cracks. Our water supplies, even my seemingly inexhaustible one, were dwindling ever more quickly. It was getting towards late afternoon when Frank motioned for us to halt. Gathering us around he broke the news.

"I am stopping here," he remarked matter-of-factly.

I couldn't believe my ears. I glanced around. I was not looking at my companions, but at the landscape. The ground was a bed of sharp rock that had already torn my new hiking boots to shreds. In the few spots where there was even a modicum of soil, cacti and scrawny bushes grew. How could anyone possibly sleep out here? On top of that, we had left behind all of our camping gear, so it was just us and the rocks!

"I am stopping too," chimed in Roy. "I have bad ankles, and I can't go on."

For Roy to say this, it is probable that his feet were literally falling off for Roy was never one to complain, even under the most dire of circumstances.

I was aghast. As usual in such circumstances, I was momentarily at a loss for words. While trying to compose myself, Pete, who was never caught flatfooted, although his feet were killing him now, immediately offered his opinion. "There's no way in hell I'm stopping here!" he countered.

Frank looked at Les and myself for our opinions. Les responded first. He'd go on.

I felt very bad at this point, not wanting to leave Frank and Roy to suffer alone through a night on Mona without any bedding and virtually nowhere to sleep. But I could not see how my suffering along with them was going to do them much good, and I knew what it would do to me. "I'll go with Pete and Les," I put in embarrassedly.

And so the decision was made. Leaving Frank and Roy behind, Pete, Les, and I set off at a more brisk pace to try and reach the lighthouse before dark.

About a half hour after leaving Frank and Roy, with thirst and pain foremost in our minds, my mood suddenly changed to one of elation for before us emerged an enormous colony of red-footed boobies. Pete and Les, being plant men, did not share in my enraptured state though for a while they waited patiently for me as I zoomed through the colony checking nests. Unlike the nests I had observed two days earlier on Desecheo, every single one of these had either eggs or a chick. Clearly something about the Desecheo colony was amiss, and this colony on Mona proved it. Furthermore, this colony was new. Red-footed boobies had never before been recorded breeding on this island. The likely explanation was that some of the red-foots on Desecheo had shifted breeding sites as a result of disturbances by the monkeys. One could only hope that all of Desecheo's red-foots would at some point make a similar adjustment and move to Mona. Though this new, thriving colony suggested things were severely awry with the birds on Desecheo, and despite the reasonableness of the explanation for the formation of the new Mona colony, the discovery did not provide certain proof that it was in fact Desecheo's monkeys that were the cause of problems on that island.

Having scampered through the booby colony to get at least some idea of its size and the stage of the nesting cycle, I hurried to rejoin Pete and Les who had continued on enroute to the lighthouse. Hiking onward over the flat plateau, we kept expecting the lighthouse to appear at any moment upon the horizon, but we were continually frustrated in this regard. All that emerged before us was boundless scrubland.

The long hike was really starting to bother me. I had finished my water some time back and was becoming quite thirsty. Furthermore, the constant battering of the stunted bushes against my legs and arms had made them bruised and sore. This resulted in my maneuvering on every step to find the path of least resistance through the vegetation, yet each foot of forward progress invariably involved being struck by a branch on one tender portion of my body or another.

Despite my problems I knew they paled compared to those of Pete. For one thing, Pete wore a very old and beat-up pair of boots. At this stage of our hike, one of the boots had been significantly torn open and the other was scarcely in better shape. As a result, Pete's feet had paid the price, and he was limping badly. Even more serious, Pete had brought along only a single quart of water and was really suffering from thirst. From time to time we would stop to eat fruits from *Harisia*, a cactus endemic to Mona, Monito, and Desecheo, which yields tangerine-sized yellow fruits containing a white edible pulp. I found the fruits rather unappetizing, but Pete savored them as though they were the main course at a king's banquet. Besides Pete having brought only a single quart of water, the vessel housing this elixir happened to be a former plastic soap bottle. To Pete's great misfortune, all of the soap had never quite been cleaned from the container, thus the water had taken on a strong soapy taste, so much so that it was hardly drinkable. So bad was the contamination, I later learned, that a single swig made one feel almost nauseous – as though upon opening your mouth no words would come out, only soap bubbles.

Les's condition fell somewhere between that of Pete's and my own. An experienced hiker, Les had no serious foot problems, but the lack of water was making him, like Pete, something of a connoisseur of cactus fruits.

Struggling on in our exhausted states, evening was beginning to set in, and we were becoming concerned that once it was dark we would have to halt for the day and resign ourselves to a miserable night on the open rocks a la Frank and Roy. It was at this point, as our morale was seriously waning, that the lighthouse suddenly emerged before us, closer than we ever expected. Somehow, despite the flatness of the plateau, this tall structure had remained hidden until we were nearly upon it. By what mechanism the lighthouse had skirted detection from a greater distance was puzzling, but hardly of concern to us as we rejoiced at its timely appearance. Recharged with new energy, we hastened forward to within a mere 75 yards of the edifice when we were stopped in our tracks. Between us and the lighthouse, which was scarcely beyond hearing range, the vegetation changed completely. Rather than the low brush through which we had fought during our entire circumvention of the island, we now had before us a dense field of cacti. This field, composed entirely of towering pipe-organ cacti about 15 feet tall, was so densely packed that it appeared an ant, not to mention a human being, would have difficulty traversing its short width.

Resigning myself to the extra three quarters of a mile it would take to circle the cactus field and reach the lighthouse via the coastal plain road, I suggested that we get started on our detour. Pete, however, had other ideas.

"There's no way in hell I'm going to walk around this field!" Peter asserted with determination and anger, applying a phrase not unlike that he had leveled at Frank and Roy. The island had pushed him far enough, and he wasn't about to take one step further than he had to. While I admired Pete's determination, it appeared his efforts would be destined to failure. Nonetheless, brandishing a machete Pete launched himself at the cactus barrier with a vigor I had not seen in him since early that morning.

About to strike a cactus with the impressive blade, Pete noticed an opening between two plants and skirted through it. Raising the weapon once more to smote the thorny barrier, he again spotted a fissure through which to sally, and did so. And so we continued on in this way, Pete invariably on the verge of slashing a cactus when, the blade about to fall, one of us would find an opening in the seemingly impenetrable, bristly forest, and we would proceed forward.

Fifteen minutes after our initial assault on the cactus barricade, we were through to the other side and this, miraculously, without a single stroke of the machete. By now it was completely dark, but this no longer mattered. We plodded the last few steps to the door of the lighthouse and entered to the most welcome comforts of cold drinks, hot showers, and irresistible beds anyone could possibly hope to experience.

The following morning we had expected the relatively early arrival of Frank and Roy. Since sleeping out on the plateau had to be anything but comfortable, we surmised that they would rise early and hike to the lighthouse in short order. We were therefore surprised when by late morning neither Frank nor Roy had appeared. When they did not show up by mid-day, our surprise turned to alarm. By 12:30 we were convinced something was wrong, and a Coast Guardsman prepared to radio the main island to have a helicopter dispatched to search for the missing hikers. At the moment the call was being put through, a shout from the tower indicated that the two stray biologists had been sighted; the vigil was over.

When Frank and Roy arrived, we anxiously awaited their story. As things turned out they did have difficulty sleeping on the plateau as we had surmised. What we had not anticipated was that in the morning, after hiking part of the way to the lighthouse, they would decide to hole up for a while in the shelter of a cave and take a nap. Despite the floor of the cave being coated with goat droppings, they were able to snooze, and it was the nap which had caused the delay.

The remainder of our stay on Mona was uneventful. I had the opportunity to revisit the booby colony to collect more data, and our group later returned by way of the road along the southern shore to the cabins on the coastal strip.

The following day we were off again by ship to return to Puerto Rico. For my part, the Mona trip enabled me to gather some valuable information relevant to the booby problem on Desecheo. What the others of the group learned I can only guess. However, I do know this. My good friend, Pete, upon returning to Puerto

Rico, carried out some interesting research on Pico del Este in the Luquillo Mountains. It may not be pure coincidence that he chose Pico del Este on which to work. This peak happens to be the wettest spot in all of Puerto Rico. Two hundred inches of rain fall here per year. Certainly this would be the last place on the island where Pete would have to worry about being thirsty - a place where a soapy water container could remain the furthest thing from his mind.

Reflections

The difficulties of access with regard to remote islands are more than made up for by their special qualities. Among these is the tendency, particularly by the most inaccessible of their kind, to harbor animal and plant life unable to survive on larger land masses. Most conspicuous of the birdlife on Puerto Rico's satellite islands are their seabirds. In other cases, particularly with regard to lizards, they serve as isolated natural refuges for numbers of species, the Mona rock iguana being the most notable.

Then there is the matter of the simplicity of island ecosystems. The smaller the island, the fewer the number of species likely to inhabit it.

Also, the finite size of small islands sets sharp limits on the ranges of their inhabitants.

These factors in particular serve to make islands extraordinary natural laboratories for studying wildlife, not to mention conserving it. As a consequence, off shore islands should always be evaluated for their potential to serve any of many conservation functions. Use as field research sites, as areas to understand basic ecological principles, for experimentation with eradication of invasive species so as to restore the islands to their more natural condition, to serve as isolated refuges for species unable to survive on larger landmasses due to irreversible alterations in their habitat – these are but a few of the great potential islands have as tools for understanding ecology and delivering conservation.

Coupled with an understanding of the ecological and conservation values of remote islands, I learned a fair amount about their downsides. One is the great potential for abuses to take place. This is primarily the result of the "out of sight out of mind" mentality. The decimation of Desecho's seabirds, for example, would have been less likely to take place in an area experiencing regular visitation. Remote islands also require more time, effort, and resources to visit, thus oversight of activities transpiring on them often goes unattended. This can result in substantial degradation of an island before a problem is noticed, and sometimes detection occurs too late. The demise of Mona Island's parakeet is a case in point.

Another downside of islands is their fragility. What might appear as a minor perturbation can have resounding effects. One of the most infamous cases demonstrating island fragility is that of the Stephen Island wren. This nearly flightless bird was endemic to a small island off New Zealand, which housed little more than a lighthouse and its keeper. It so happens that the lighthouse keeper acquired a cat which, in 1894 brought to him fifteen specimens of this unique bird. It turns out that these fifteen individuals are the only specimens of the Stephen Island wren ever known. One single cat wiped out every last wren.

The Mermaid of
the Caribbean

O ne of my more exciting and unusual adventures resulted from the passage in the United States of the Endangered Species Act in 1973. Subsequent to its enactment, the federal government prepared a list designating animal species considered either threatened or endangered. Among the animals on this list, and one in which the U.S. government showed particular interest, was a very peculiar marine mammal native to the Caribbean including the West Indies, the east coast of Central America, and the north coast of South America, as well as Florida in the United States. This particular mammal goes by the names of manatee, West Indian manatee, or sea cow.

The manatee is a most extraordinary-looking creature, appearing very much like a partially inflated balloon. Generally ten to 13 feet long and 300 to 800 pounds, behemoths have been recorded nearly 15 feet in length and weighing over a ton. Manatees have no hind legs and their forelimbs appear as two sausage-like appendages which seem to serve for precise maneuvering and underwater "strolling". Locomotion is performed by the animal's large, horizontally flattened tail which can propel the creature through the water at speeds up to 14 miles per hour, though normally manatees move lethargically at rates closer to two to four miles an hour. Entirely aquatic, manatees appear weightless in the water, seeming equally comfortable upside down as rightside up. Lounging peaceably, sea cows spend between six and eight hours a day feeding on a wide variety of aquatic plants. Consuming 10 to 15 percent of their body weight per day, an average manatee will put away a full 100 pounds of green leaves and sundry plant parts in the course of twenty four hours. This immense feeding capacity is testimony to the appropriateness of the name sea cow.

An animal primarily of estuaries, river mouths, and shallow, calm coastal waters, manatees inhabit the types of areas also frequented by humans for fishing and recreation. The inshore preferences of this animal, the tastiness of its flesh, and almost total unwariness have combined to cause its severe range-wide decline – a result of over-hunting, or over-fishing, as the case may be. Not only was the manatee favored for the delicacy and flavor of its flesh, but also for the ability of the meat to keep well when preserved in salt or the animal's own fat. The utility of the sea cow went even further when one considers that the skin could be processed into

West Indian Manatee

tough leather, the blubber into a pleasant-flavored oil, and the rib bones polished to yield an adequate ivory substitute. All in all, 85 percent of a manatee carcass could be effectively utilized. In the Brazilian state of Amazonas alone, as recently as 1950, it is reported that more than 38,000 manatees of a species similar to that in the Caribbean were killed for commercial purposes. This kind of commercial pressure, coupled with increasingly intensive subsistence use as human populations have burgeoned, has placed substantial stress on the manatee.

The West Indian manatee was first described by no less a personage than Christopher Columbus who observed it while undertaking his most historic voyage. His diary of January 9, 1493 relates, "On the previous day, when the Admiral went to the Rio del Oro, he saw three mermaids, which rose well out of the sea; but they are not so beautiful as they are painted, though to some extent they have the form of a human face...." From this description one might suppose that Columbus, though a great explorer, was not much of a scientist, but then, science in the 1400's was scarcely in its heyday.

Actually, three species of manatees exist. The West Indian manatee has a close cousin confined to the Amazon and a second relative distributed among the coastal waters and rivers of Africa from Senegal to Angola. The latter two species are appropriately referred to as the Amazonian and West African manatees respectively. The only other mammalian family joining the manatees in the order Sireni, a name derived from their somewhat farfetched similarities to mermaids as depicted in Columbus' description, is that of the dugongs. Dugongs resemble manatees in general appearance, but are somewhat more marine in habit. Though only one species of dugong presently survives, occurring sparingly through much of the Old World tropics, a large form of dugong, known as Steller's sea cow, historically inhabited portions of the western Bering Sea off Alaska. The sad story of the Steller's sea cow may provide some insight into what could be in store for the surviving manatees and dugong.

The Steller's sea cow was first discovered in 1741 when an expedition led by the Russian captain Vitus Bering was stranded on the island that now bears his name. Steller's sea cows were enormous animals weighing between four and five tons and measuring approximately 25 feet in length. Yet, despite their size, these animals inhabited the inshore waters among the Commander Islands where they fed on kelp and other marine algae. The waters where they grazed were so shallow that the sea cows often exposed the better part of their backs above water as they half swam, half walked with their forelimbs across the sea floor. Entirely trusting, the Steller's sea cows were easily slaughtered by Bering's starving sailors and later by other expeditions that visited the area. The slaughter of these animals for food and leather was so intensive that within a mere 27 years of its discovery, the Steller's sea cow was extinct. It is also interesting that though only one or two thousand Steller's sea cows apparently existed at the time the animal was discovered, skeletal remains from the late Pleistocene indicate Steller's sea cow and a related species formerly rimmed the entire northern Pacific from

Monterey Bay in California to Japan. It is surmised that the substantial reduction in the distribution of Steller's sea cow, limiting the species to its remote northern refuge, and the extinction of its close relative, were the result of heavy hunting pressure exerted by aboriginal peoples spreading through these coastal areas. The Steller's sea cow population, exterminated in the eighteenth century, was simply a small remnant of what was once a widespread species. Nevertheless, it appears that pressures exerted by humans, possibly thousands of years apart, were responsible for the extinction of this extraordinary beast.

The human pressures which wiped out Steller's sea cow are very similar to those faced by all of its surviving relatives. In the particular case of the West Indian manatee, the species is clearly experiencing a decline, which, if not stemmed, could rapidly lead this creature to a fate identical to that of its larger cousin to the north.

In Puerto Rico manatee meat was commonly sold in local markets until well into the twentieth century. Over-fishing of this slow reproducing species, however, has made the manatee a rare commodity in recent decades. By the time the Endangered Species Act was passed in 1973, manatees probably were taken only incidentally by fishermen due to their already rare status. Regardless, the Act now made it illegal to "take" a manatee at all, meaning to "harass, harm, pursue, hunt, shoot, wound, kill, trap, capture, or collect, or to attempt to engage in any such conduct" in Puerto Rico and the United States. Though this new legislation provided comprehensive protection for the manatee, supported by strong penalties for violators, there was no one to implement the law. Locally, it was a law confined to paper.

One problem with the Act was that, though passed with all good intentions, it created hardships for people already struggling under heavy burdens. In the case of the manatee, and even more so the protection of sea turtles, Puerto Rico's subsistence fishermen would suffer from the law's impact on their allowed catch. Concern for the fishermen, coupled with a substantial dose of inefficiency, inhibited the implementation of the Endangered Species Act on the island as it related to manatees and sea turtles for a substantial number of years.

Despite the difficulties in implementing enforcement of the Act, there was interest in learning more about the status of the sea cow in Puerto Rico. This curiosity initially derived from U.S. Fish and Wildlife Service biologists in Florida responsible for conservation of manatees in the southeastern United States. Through the course of correspondence, I communicated to them anecdotal information indicating that, though extremely rare, the manatee still occurred, at least sporadically, along much of Puerto Rico's coast. This was enough for the Service biologists to want to perform some surveys, including one by plane.

On a beautiful August morning, as virtually all mornings are in Puerto Rico, James Powell and I drove to the small Humacao airport in extreme eastern Puerto Rico to perform the island's first aerial manatee survey. James was a biologist working for the U.S. Fish and Wildlife Service and sent down on this assignment. He certainly was as excited about this event as I because, in addition to performing the first survey of its kind on the island, this was James' first visit here, so everything he saw was new.

Taking off at 8:00 A.M. we were over the coastline in an instant and the survey was underway. Our plane, a small Cesna 172, held only James, our friendly pilot Tony, and myself. Tony was a middle-aged fellow, a flyer for many years, who earned his living piloting for a small plane rental operation. Though Tony had heard of manatees, he really had little idea what they were or how they might look. Notwithstanding this hiatus in his knowledge, he was genuinely interested in the world around him and anxious to learn what this unusual flight was all about.

Whether we would observe any manatees at all was a concern of both James and myself. While I had heard of a few records here and there, I had never seen a manatee despite having visited excellent sea cow habitat. A variety of factors can make manatees difficult to observe. They frequently inhabit murky waters where they are easily overlooked. Since they graze on aquatic vegetation, much of which is rooted to the sea bottom, manatees often remain submerged for considerable lengths of time. Average periods underwater usually last four or five minutes, though a well-documented submergence of over 16 minutes is on record. Manatees are also quite solitary, thus they can easily pass unobserved. Small groups of courting bulls sometimes follow females in estrous, but this period only lasts between a week and one month per breeding cycle. Large congregations of manatees occur in Florida during the winter around nuclear power plant water discharge pipes and at a few natural springs, but these concentrations are apparently associated with the animal's attraction to warm water, an important feature in northern Florida which appears the northern boundary of the species' range. Approximately 21 degrees centigrade is the minimum water temperature favored by manatees and large die-offs have been known in Florida in years when water temperatures have become too cold for this tropical creature. Since Puerto Rico's waters are generally warmer than those of Florida, there is no need for manatees to seek our warm water discharges and congregate there. This may explain why concentrations of sea cows have not been recorded on the island. Considering all of these factors, not to mention the rare status of the animal, my not having seen a manatee hardly qualified as a gauge of its abundance. At the same time, never having seen one after much time in the field did little to bolster my expectation that we would be successful on this particular outing.

Tony leveled off our plane at 400 feet following James' instructions, and we cruised at 70 to 80 miles per hour. We had not traveled more than ten miles when James pointed excitedly out the window.

"Look!" he exclaimed. "Manatees!"

I peered intently into the waters of Algodones Bay and immediately picked out two manatees swimming at the surface. That was one exciting moment. Besides seeing a manatee for the first time, here we were setting out on the first survey of its kind ever performed in Puerto Rico documenting the status of this endangered species and scarcely out of the blocks we had already found two animals. We circled the sea cows at a lower elevation to get a better look and then proceeded on towards Roosevelt Roads Naval Reserve.

Most of Puerto Rico's manatee records were from Roosevelt Roads, and we were charged with expectation as we entered the limits of the base. The base contained extensive coastal wetlands including numerous bays and coves. Most of these were unaltered and still surrounded by unbroken mangrove forests. These areas were also off-limits to local fishermen whose nets presented the most serious threat to the manatee. Another attractive aspect of the base was that the fresh water effluent of the base's sewage treatment plant attracted manatees. This was apparently due to the desire or possibly the need of the animals to drink fresh water. Recent reports indicated that at least one or two manatees hung out at the discharge pipes on a regular basis.

As things turned out, while we saw no sea cows at the sewage outflow, we spotted a cow with a calf half her length in clear water by Punta Cascajo, just south of Ensenada Honda, the base's largest bay. Observing a cow and her calf together apparently is not at all unusual since female manatees suckle their young from one to two years. Considering that the gestation period is an additional 13 months, females can only bare a single calf at a minimum internal of two and one half years. This slow reproductive rate makes the manatee all the more susceptible to over-harvesting while the restoration of populations becomes an increasingly complicated task.

Calves, at birth, are pinkish, weigh 40 to 60 pounds, and average over three feet in length. Manatees, along with whales and dolphins, are the only mammals to give birth in the sea. A newborn calf is quickly pushed to the surface by its mother to take its first breath. The young calf then rides on its mother's back for several hours while she conditions it to diving by keeping it submerged for successively longer intervals. Calves suckle at single mammary glands located in the mother's armpits. By as early as one month of age, calves begin feeding upon vegetation.

Male manatees do not mature until eight or nine years of age and follow females only when the latter are in heat. During this brief period, receptive females are promiscuous and are constantly followed by a herd of males numbering as many as seventeen.

The female and her calf were the only manatees we saw at Roosevelt Roads Naval Base, but our total was now up to four animals very early in the trip, and our spirits were high. We were distracted for a moment from our manatee search when we sighted a huge sea turtle right in the middle of Ensenada Honda. This bay happens to be where warships dock and other boat traffic provides for a substantial amount of disturbance. It was therefore quite a surprise to find a sea turtle here. Likely the turtle was foraging among the *Thalassia* beds on the bay bottom. *Thalassia*, commonly called turtle grass, though not a grass, is a favored habitat of some sea turtles. The monster we observed, doubtless hundreds of pounds, was much larger than those usually found offshore, with the sole exception of the huge leatherback which this was not. To what species this impressive specimen belonged, I was not certain, but the combination of its size and presence over *Thalassia* suggested green.

We passed Punta Figueras at the northern boundary of the base. Here cattle egrets were still dispersing from a tree clump roost in which hundreds if not thousands had congregated for the night. This particular roost was unfamiliar to me though I had encountered many others scattered at intervals along Puerto Rico's coast and on several offshore cays. Cattle egrets congregate in these coastal areas. Often they occupy trees overhanging the water such as red mangroves, both to sleep and to nest. Almost entirely white like the island's other two egrets, the snowy and the great, the cattle egret is distinguished more by its habits than by its plumage. The snowy and great egrets, along with all of Puerto Rico's herons, are basically aquatic birds generally found only in wetlands. But the cattle egret is an upland species. As its name implies, this bird typically occurs around cattle and other large herbivores as well as tractors and similar machines – artificial but adequate substitutes for large grazing animals. Dispersing to pastures and fields during the day, cattle egrets follow large animals or their mechanical equivalents and prey upon the insects and other small animals flushed from the grass by the movements of these beasts. Possibly the most common and conspicuous bird on Puerto Rico's coastal plain, the species is well adapted to its island environment. While this may now be the case, it so happens that prior to 1953 cattle egrets were unknown from Puerto Rico and nearly all of the West Indian islands.

The cattle egret represents a special case in the annals of avian range expansion in that it is the first species known to have naturally colonized the New World from its original range once limited to Africa and Eurasia. Unknown in the New World prior to 1877, the cattle egret was first reported in Surinam in that year, subsequently expanding its range rapidly through the remainder of northern South America. How the original founding population reached South America is not clear. A flock of cattle egrets simply may have wandered across the relatively narrow stretch of ocean separating Africa and South America – if over 1,800 miles of ocean can be considered narrow. More likely, the flock's passage across the gap may have been abetted by a storm. Regardless of the details of the dispersal, it is believed that the egrets arrived without human intervention and that they encountered an environment ideal for their mode of survival. Not unlike the case of the shiny cowbird's expansion through the West Indies being made possible by the transformation of island forests into fields, a similar change greatly enhanced the suitability of South America as cattle egret habitat.

In past ages, the near absence of grazing mammals in South America would have made colonization by the cattle egret much more susceptible to failure. The relatively recent introduction of cattle to the plains and cleared lands of South America and the rest of the New World created an environment nearly identical to that in which the bird flourishes in Africa and Asia where elephants, rhinos, buffaloes, and wildebeest serve the purpose of insect flushers. Doubtless feeling perfectly at home around cattle in the Western Hemisphere, this egret spread quickly to North America, occurring in Florida in the early 1940's and now ranging as far north as Canada. First recorded in the southern Lesser Antilles in the early 1950's, the cattle egret colonized virtually the entire West Indian archipelago by the end of that decade.

The folklore that has developed in Puerto Rico concerning the cattle egret is interesting considering the bird's brief presence on the island. For one thing, one of the cattle egret's local names is garrapatero which means tick-eater. This name derives from the belief that cattle egrets primarily eat ticks off of cows. Though cattle egrets often sit upon cows, and possibly take a tick now and then, such food is a negligible portion of the bird's diet. It has also been reported that cattle egrets were specifically introduced for the purpose of eating cattle ticks. From whence this fallacy arose, I am not aware, but it is a belief widely held around the island. At least for the sake of the bird, it is a positive sentiment that can only enhance its chances of survival. And this is all for the good, because cattle egrets effectively serve the beneficial purpose of dispatching numerous noxious insects destructive of pasture grasses. This makes the species a substantial economic asset to ranchers and dairy farmers. At the same time, the cattle egret's presence appears to have in no way upset the ecology of other native organisms. The cattle egret may be a rare example of a species filling a vacant niche thus causing negligible detrimental impacts, while at the same time performing a valuable service for humankind.

Continuing northward out of the base along beautiful coastline, broken periodically by small fishing villages, we rounded the extreme northeast tip of the island known as Las Cabezas de San Juan. Here we had our next manatee sighting, another cow with a half grown calf. Thus far the census had been more productive than we had ever hoped. Six manatees recorded and we had logged only about 20 miles of coastal flight. With well over two hundred miles yet to go it looked like we might have a spectacular day. On the other hand, most of Puerto Rico's north coast shallow water shelf is very narrow and adjacent to dense human populations. Neither factor is particularly propitious for manatee survival. Over the next several hours we scanned this coast in vain, and then turned south to trace the island's west side.

Despite the absence of manatees along the hundred plus miles of the north coast, this leg of the flight was hardly unrewarding. Several small sea turtles were spotted and a number of rays. Two nurse sharks were also observed, the same type of shark with which I had become all too familiar at Cayo Ratones. Actually, I was a bit surprised that no other sharks were viewed; I was particularly hoping to see one of the large hammerheads, reputedly 12 to 15 feet long which patrol the waters off shore.

Besides the marine creatures, we also enjoyed some splendid scenery. First there was the fabulous crescent beach of Luquillo lying in the shadow of the great Luquillo Mountains. Then came the extensive mangroves of Torrecilla-Pinones followed by the city of San Juan with its string of tourist hotels lining the shore and the much more delightful old portion of the city with its restored buildings, the capitol, and, of course, the great fort of El Morro guarding the entrance to San Juan Bay. Later we flew over the extensive sugar cane plantations around Dorado and the pineapple fields in the vicinity of Vega Baja. Most spectacular of all, however, was the coastline further westward in the area of Quebradilla. Here a phalanx of cliffs abuts the sea, rising over 100 feet above the pounding surf. These cliffs, bordering the coast for several miles, are among the only ones on the main island, though Mona is well endowed in this regard. It is here that the fabulous white-tailed tropicbird nests in cliff cavities from which it makes sorties out to sea to dive for fish and squid. White like terns, the tropicbird is easily distinguished by its two long central tail feathers which stream well behind the bird. Though tropicbirds look superficially like terns, they are actually more closely related to a group of birds very different in appearance including the pelicans, frigatebirds and boobies. These families are united into a single order based upon the unique anatomical character of having all four toes on each foot joined by webbing. Interestingly, the duck, which even non-birdwatchers know to have webbed feet, does not have all the toes of each foot webbed together. The duck's thumb, on the rear of the foot, is free of this connection.

There are three species of tropicbirds and all are confined, as their name implies, to the tropics and subtropics. Two of these are known from Puerto Rico. The rarer red-billed only occurs regularly off the east coast among Culebra's cays. The more common white-tailed is generally found anywhere there are cavity-bearing cliffs abutting the ocean. At this very season the birds were completing their nesting cycle at Quebradilla. Though I glanced to admire the cliffs, I did not divert my attention from our task at hand long enough to enjoy these most elegant sea birds.

155

Continuing on around Puerto Rico's northwest shoulder out along the western horn of the island, the cone of Desecheo came into view. My mind wandered there but my eyes remained on the lookout for the elusive manatee which we now had not seen for nearly two hours. No luck. Our good fortune had really petered out. Not a single manatee along Puerto Rico's entire north or northwest coasts.

Finally, three quarters of the way down the island's western coast we again spotted a manatee, a large one off Punta Ostiones. This sighting substantially elevated our enthusiasm once again, and we redoubled our efforts to spot the animals as we flew over the extensive turtle grass flats northwest of the Cabo Rojo lighthouse at Puerto Rico's extreme southwest tip and later at Punta Pitahaya, the site of the famous white-necked crow episode. Our hopes were particularly high for seeing manatees at these localities because the waters were clear, the region was sparsely populated, and shallow turtle grass flats abounded. Considering the manatee's propensity for calm, shallow waters and abundant aquatic vegetation, these areas appeared ideal.

The manatee feeds so relentlessly on coarse aquatic vegetation that it gradually wears out its teeth. There are five or six teeth in a row on each side of the upper and lower jaws, but only the first tooth in each series is actively used in chewing. As the forward-most tooth in each row is worn out, it is replaced by the one behind and so this process provides the manatee with a continuously new set of choppers. This pattern of tooth replacement is quite unusual in mammals; consequently the manatee is considered a close relative of a group with the same tooth replacement mechanism. It so happens that this group is the Proboscidea – the elephants – which clearly are not particularly similar in appearance to the manatee.

Such relationships are suggested because taxonomists use what they refer to as conservative traits to determine whether species are closely or distantly related. This means that they examine characteristics of animals which change very slowly over time, such as the structure of teeth or other skeletal elements. Contrarily, they ignore quickly evolving characteristics such as coloration, or differences in size. Mammalogists consider the other closest surviving relative of the manatee to be the hyraxes of Africa. Hyraxes are small creatures, very rodent-like in appearance. They are extremely agile animals capable of rapid movements on steep and rugged surfaces. Such dexterity is facilitated by extraordinary adaptations of the foot which include special musculature and moisture secreting glands which enable the hyraxes' foot to invaginate in the center and function as a suction cup. Hyraxes shot on near vertical surfaces have been reported to remain clinging there due to the effectiveness of this suction apparatus. Though appearing totally dissimilar to the manatee of today, the relatedness of these two taxa is based on their apparent derivation from a common ancestor.

One reason the closest living relatives of the manatee order seem so unrelated is that the manatees diverged from their four-legged terrestrial ancestors way back in geological history. Fossils of extinct sirenians, the order of which the manatee is a member, have been found dating to the Eocene over 60 million years ago. Evolving these many eons to the conditions of an aquatic existence has left the sirenians with no close living relatives.

Some unique anatomical modifications for an aquatic exis-tence which have evolved in the manatee include the loss of the hind limbs and the transformation of the forelimbs into flippers as mentioned earlier. As these flippers still possess nails, it was formerly believed that manatees crawled onto dry land at night and sometimes plundered crops. Recent studies indicate that in fact manatees never leave the water and if taken from this medium, must be kept constantly moist to avoid desiccation. Another major evolutionary modification is the near elimination of the pelvis. All that remains of this bone, so very important in terrestrial quadrupeds, are one or two pairs of vestigial bones suspended in muscle. Unlike any other mammal, the manatee has but six cervical or neck vertebrae. Practically all other mammals have seven. Manatees also have no external ears, though they have outstanding sensitivity to sound. Squeals, screams, and other cries are important in various social interactions. The upper lip of the manatee is fascinating as it is divided in two, each half functioning independently and with a vertical rather than a horizontal orientation. Like the whales, the manatee has lost nearly all of its hair. Bristles around the mouth and scattered solitary hairs on the body are all that remain of this uniquely mammalian phenomenon.

Despite our perception of the Cabo Rojo and Punta Pitahaya turtle grass flats as being idyllic habitat for manatees, none were seen. But we were not disheartened. We were now approaching the extensive La Parguera mangrove complex with numerous channels, shallow inlets and broad turtle grass beds where our hopes were high once again that we might observe manatees.

By this stage in our trip seven manatees had been sighted, all the observations initially being made by James or myself. Through the course of the flight our pilot, Tony, had become increasingly excited about his involvement in the survey and was expressing ever more adamant regret that he himself had not yet been the first of us to make a manatee sighting. Tony's time was not long in coming. We passed the La Parguera mangrove without event followed by the Phosphorescent Bay, a narrow-necked cove in which, at night, particularly during the darkness of a new moon, disturbance of the water causes it to sparkle brightly. This phosphorescence, or more appropriately bioluminescence, is created by minute microorganisms called dinoflagellates, a type of protozoan, which, when disturbed, emit a self-generated light. The concentration of many millions of these one-celled protozoans in this bay creates enough light to be clearly visible to the human eye. Bioluminescence is not unique to this bay as it occurs elsewhere in the world, including several other bays in Puerto Rico for that matter. The Phosphorescent Bay is better known than many others because of the intensity and regularity of its bioluminescent display. No manatees were seen here either, but as we passed into the next bay to the east, Bahia Montalva, Tony at last was the first to spot a manatee.

"There's one! There's one!" Tony shouted ecstatically.

James and I had been looking sharply as we cruised at an altitude of 400 feet, but the waters over which we were flying were murky, and it was difficult to distinguish any object not fully upon the surface. We could not discern a manatee, but before we could say a word Tony had already taken matters into his own hands to ensure that James and I would corroborate his sighting.

The plane suddenly jerked sideways and plunged into a power dive reminiscent of all the aerial dogfights I had seen in war movies as a kid. In this case, there were two important differences. One, I was in the plane. Television and real life just are not the same thing, a point which had been hammered into me time and time again through my childhood, but which now was being brought home far more forcefully than ever before. Though I had enjoyed seeing dogfights in the movies, I always knew the good guy would win, and even if he didn't, I had nothing at stake. Furthermore, watching a plane banking on television just isn't the same as being in one – as my stomach was making abundantly clear. It had taken me years to become even moderately comfortable with the significant gap between any plane in which I flew and the ground, a gap not easily erasable should the plane have a serious problem. My uneasiness with planes was not buoyed by the fact that the sister flight to the first one on which I had ever flown had sucked a swan into a propeller engine and went down in flames, everyone aboard being lost. It was only over the course of many years and numerous flights that I had by now become, not at ease, but at least not entirely tense either, each time I went up in an airplane. This acceptance of flying was now in jeopardy of being lost all in one fell swoop.

The other important difference between this power dive and those in the movies was that planes in the movies seem to have all the space in the world. Our dive was beginning at an altitude of 400 feet.

Somehow spotting Tony's manatee lost all importance to me. Turning my attention to the pilot it was obvious that he was excited to the point of distraction, expectant of the supreme moment when we would confirm his discovery. Tony was turned halfway in his seat, his bulged eyes gazing out of the window while he flailed emphatically with his left hand, doubtless at the spot where the manatee was to be seen. Contrarily, my conception of the imminent supreme moment had nothing to do with manatees but rather with the grove of coconut palms which we were approaching all too swiftly.

"I see it! I see it!" I yelled to Tony with not an eye on the water but rather the coconut grove just before us. We were now so close to the palms that I could make out the individual fruits and was sure I could reach them had I a long pole.

Fortunately Tony accepted my desperate acknowledgment of his discovery as confirmation enough and coolly leveled off the plane only a few feet above the waving palm fronds. Now in a calmer state Tony circled once more in a much less dramatic loop as my heart retired from my throat and settled back down in my chest. James had still not uttered a word, likely as a result of deep trauma. Glancing at his face I noticed he was at least taking in air even if his respiration was in the form of deep gasps as was mine. Gradually, James and I were once more able to concentrate on the water, but we saw nothing until a large, fan-shaped tail suddenly arose out of the turbid depths indicating that a manatee was in fact present. Tony, it so happened, had located one of the murky water animals so easily bypassed in this type of rapid survey.

Continuing eastward after this trying experience, we soon encountered another surprise, but one of a different sort. Less than 15 miles further down the coast, at the point where Punta Verraco sections off the western half of Guayanilla Bay, I noticed a nurse shark – and then another. Suddenly here and there were nurse sharks until in a tiny pocket of reef just off the point we observed an aggregation of at least 50 sharks. So closely packed were these large fish that had you been among them in a boat, a foot placed overboard would have invariably landed on one of these animal's backs. Just why the nurse sharks had congregated so thickly at this particular locality was not evident, but nurse sharks are known to do so when mating which may well have been the case on this occasion.

Observations of mating sharks are extremely rare. Yet nurse shark matings have been seen and one can understand why any self-respecting shark would not want such machinations to be made public. Females appear to do everything possible to avoid mating such as thrashing around, swimming into shallows, and digging a pectoral fin into the sand to hold themselves sideways. Only the most dominant and relentless males are successful at copulation. This event is achieved only by biting down on the female's free pectoral fin, using this leverage to drag her into deeper water, and then rolling her over and contorting his body so as to wedge his tail under her and perform insemination. Hours of struggle result in only minutes of actual copulation.

Holding on to the pectoral fin is not unique to nurse sharks. Rays and skates, close relatives to the sharks, also display this behavior during mating. Also common to all sharks and rays is that fertilization is internal, a sophisticated evolutionary feature for a marine organism, even a fish.

When it comes to development of the embryo, however, sharks have evolved a wide array of reproductive strategies to successfully bring forth their young. Some sharks are oviparous, meaning they lay eggs. Keep in mind that shark eggs are nothing like chicken eggs in appearance. Shark eggs come in all types of shapes and have ancillary structures for attaching to the sea floor or some other substrate. Other sharks are ovoviviparous which means reproduction begins with a fertilized egg, but the egg hatches within the female's body and the young are born live as well formed sharks. Under this scenario, however, the unborn shark receives no nutrition from the mother other than that provided by the egg yolk. The most advances type of shark reproduction from an evolutionary perspective is viviparity. This has the same result as ovovivipary – a live born shark. The difference, however, is that once the unborn shark runs out of yolk, it is nurtured by other means while in the oviduct. In some species the adult female simply continues to ovulate and the unborn sharks sustain themselves by feeding on these unfertilized eggs. Not a bad approach for a species destined to become a top of the line predator.

The site of the shark gathering was particularly puzzling, because it was immediately adjacent to a shipping channel used by tankers transporting oil to the various refineries of

Tallaboa and Guayanilla. In total, approximately 70 nurse sharks were near the bay entrance, an impressive sight by any standards.

The final leg of our trip included potentially productive coastline around Mar Negro and within Jobos Bay. To our misfortune, however, by the time we reached this area the seas were becoming rough, so we covered the area only superficially, and no manatees were seen. On the other hand, just east of the town of Arroyo where the shallow inshore grass beds are relatively narrow and we had little expectation of seeing a manatee, two feeding adults were sighted. As if these two individuals were not enough, we spotted a third manatee a short distance further east near Punta Guilarte along an equally narrow inshore coastal strip.

The remaining southeast coastline had virtually no shallow inshore flats, and no manatees were either expected or seen during the remainder of the flight back to Humacao. All in all, we observed eleven manatees during our six and one half hours in the air, not to mention the sharks, sea turtles, many rays, and an abundance of beautiful scenery. Puerto Rico's first thorough manatee survey had been completed successfully without mishap, but not without trepidation.

How accurately did the eleven animals we observed represent the remaining manatee population of Puerto Rico? That is difficult to say. Certainly manatees residing in murky water, such as the individual so dramatically pointed out by Tony, must have been overlooked. But how many animals fell into this category? Jobos Bay was poorly covered and we did not get to Vieques Island from which manatee reports were known. Estimating conservatively James and I felt that we could easily have missed from one half to two thirds of the island's manatees. Projecting this out, the minimum number of sea cows inhabiting Puerto Rico's waters would be between 22 to 33 animals. Numbers such as these clearly indicated the endangered status of the manatee locally, yet at the same time it at least gave us hope that, notwithstanding past persecution, the species was still holding on, even if precariously.

Despite passage of the Endangered Species Act and the new knowledge we had gained from the aerial manatee survey, pressures on this species showed no signs of being reduced. For example, the Act required that the potential impact on endangered species be assessed for any project involving the expenditure of federal funds. If it were determined that a significant negative impact to an endangered species might result from such a project, the use of federal funds could be prohibited.

Just such a project came to me for review regarding which our survey data directly applied. The proposal dealt with construction of a dock on the south coast. My draft response for the Secretary's signature read as follows:

> The Department of Natural Resources cannot say with certainty that there are no endangered species in the area of the proposed dry cargo barge dock near Guayama. The endangered manatee *Trichechus manatus* has been observed in Jobos Bay and three were seen at one time near Punta Figuras less than 10 miles to the east. Indeed, most of the shallow coastline in this region, although narrow, is suitable for manatees and probably supports them. A specific survey of the area in question would be necessary to determine whether it is in some way inadequate for the species.

While the letter that ultimately went out contained intact the first two sentences of my draft, the concluding remarks were modified to read:

> Nevertheless, the nature and extent of the work to be carried out by this project will not have any significant adverse effect on endangered species.

Yes, we now possessed more information that could help promote the recovery of the manatee in Puerto Rico. The immediate problem at hand was convincing the institutions with authority and which should care about the manatee and other endangered species to intercede on their behalf before future surveys indicated that there was no need for any conservation effort – that it was now too late.

Reflections

The story of the manatee was a singular adventure related to passage of the Endangered Species Act in 1973. There were other impacts resulting from the Act which were less humorous. Most significant among these was its impact on subsistence fishing of sea turtles.

Fishing of sea turtles had doubtless occurred off Puerto Rico's shores and on its beaches since the first days of human habitation of the island by the Arawaks. For centuries these valuable animals, their eggs, and their shells had been staples as food and, in the case of the latter, raw material for jewelry. But, poorly regulated harvest through the years had resulted, by 1973, in sea turtles becoming a miniscule portion of the island's fishery. Primarily, sea turtles were taken incidentally or opportunistically, there being very few if any fishermen remaining who relied heavily upon the harvest of these magnificent sea creatures.

Decline of the sea turtle fishery relegated it to a subsistence affair, depended upon principally by rural people with limited opportunities for alternate sources of protein or income. Regardless, the Endangered Species Act was quite specific concerning the immediate cessation of turtle harvesting. This strict law caused quite a conundrum within our agency as to just how to administer this new piece of legislation. Were we simply to circulate new regulations prohibiting immediately the taking of sea turtles, we knew we would have a political furor on our hands as well as denying an important resource to subsistence families. Were we to choose any other course, we would not be implementing the letter of the law.

We chose not to implement the letter of the law. Our plan was to initiate an educational campaign to inform fishermen that within a year's time the taking of sea turtles would be banned. The intent here was to give time to affected persons to transition into other activities or occupations that might substitute for the loss of sea turtle products. While implementation of this plan left a lot to be desired, we felt, at least, that it provided a fair shake to those who would suffer the economic burden imposed by the Act.

The lesson here was straight-forward, but a hard one. It is easy to support the protection of endangered species. I believe very strongly in such efforts. At the same time, it is important to take steps towards conservation in such a way that they do not trample unnecessarily upon people's livelihoods, particularly of individuals struggling to survive.

The matter is not black and white, and that creates a challenge. But addressing this issue effectively is, ultimately, in everyone's best interest.

I should add the clarification that I am not suggesting here that the Endangered Species Act should be modified in such a way that it imposes no hardships on anyone. Not so. Most individuals, businesses, developers, and the like in the United States have more than enough resources to satisfy their daily needs yet some are never satisfied with what they have, always needing more. The Endangered Species Act benefits society as a whole. It sometimes does so over the selfishness of a few. It should remain that way.

Adventures on Culebra

Not all of my adventures occurred while I was working in a professional capacity. For one thing, I gradually became active in the Puerto Rico Natural History Society which regularly had field trips to various localities around the island. It was one such trip that was particularly eventful.

The Natural History Society was Puerto Rico's local nature club which held monthly meetings at which Society members or guest speakers gave presentations on one or another of the island's myriad nature subjects. These were then followed by a Saturday field trip to a site illustrating some components of the talk. While the Society also became involved periodically in conservation issues of importance, it was the slide shows and field trips that attracted the greatest membership interest. At the time I became active in the Natural History Society it appeared that field trips had covered virtually every significant location within a day's drive of San Juan. I therefore proposed to lead a rather ambitious weekend excursion to the island of Culebra, a site never before visited on a Society outing.

It is little wonder the Society had not previously visited Culebra. Lying approximately 17 miles east of Puerto Rico, the island is not reached conveniently by either ferry or plane. About eight miles long and four in width at its widest part, Culebra is not a large island. Nor is it particularly high. Monte Resaca, the highest peak, stands to 650 feet, not enough to significantly impede the passage of clouds over the island so that they might dump their moisture. As a result, visitors are immediately struck by Culebra's most salient characteristic – its aridity. No permanent freshwater ponds exist and large catchment structures have been built on several hillsides to channel the limited rainfall into cisterns to sustain Culebra's 600 or so permanent residents at that time. Despite these catchment basins, islanders were often short of water during drier periods, and water had to be rationed. During a number of my earlier stays on Culebra while performing studies for the Department of Natural Resources, public water was available for only one hour per day. During the most severe stages of a drought, water was actually brought in by plane or barge.

Though having no high mountains, Culebra is of volcanic origin, thus, it is hilly over its entire length. Its soils are shallow and laced with boulders making them poor for agriculture. Regardless of these conditions, most of the island's forests were cleared by settlers by the turn of the 20th century and the land planted to sugar cane. It was at this time that the island's unique race of the Puerto Rican parrot was wiped out in retribution for its depredations on local crops. Ultimately, sugar cane proved unprofitable, and the scarred landscape was converted primarily to cattle production. Drought-tolerant Zebu were brought in to cope with Culebra's decidedly harsh environment.

Dewey, Culebra's only town, boasted two hotels and a single restaurant. A few roads led from Dewey to outlying homesteads, but only one of these was paved for any distance. Since there was no public transportation and cars were unavailable for rental, the presence of roads mattered little. Clearly, these were important reasons that argued against going to Culebra.

At the same time, Culebra had some attractions. One was its beaches, some of the most beautiful in the Caribbean. Flamenco Beach, a magnificent crescent of calcareous sand so brilliant that it tortured the eyes, was within a moderate distance from town. This would make for an extraordinary base camp. If participants chose to do nothing else but to bathe in Flamenco's calm, crystal-clear waters, the trip would be a success for many. If we could also get to one of Culebra's more remote beaches, so much the better. Not only did these have unique beauty all their own, but they were also the nesting grounds of several species of sea turtles, extraordinary marine reptiles virtually extirpated as breeding species on Puerto Rico proper, but still maintaining a "flipperhold" on Culebra. Maybe we would be lucky and see one of these beasts emerge from the sea to nest.

Behind two of Culebra's beaches were lagoons, scenic in their own right and important habitats for endangered native waterfowl such as the white-cheeked pintail and the ruddy duck. To the west of Flamenco Beach stretched long and narrow Flamenco Peninsula, a strip of land controlled by the United States Navy for bombing practice. Remarkably, despite the bombing, the peninsula managed to sustain a massive colony of sooty terns well worthy of an afternoon visit by the group.

All in all a field trip to Culebra would offer an exciting change of venue for Natural History Society members. It would also expose them to a number of conservation problems not evident on the main island and to species not readily observed there. I launched into setting up the excursion.

A fundamental detail to be resolved, trivial in most cases, but not in this one, was how to reach the island. To go by ferry would involve driving an hour by car to Fajardo at Puerto Rico's northeastern tip. Here we could leave the vehicles over the weekend and board a ferry for a three-hour crossing to Culebra. The trip would take the better part of a day each way, and time was precious. Alternatively, the trip by air, though somewhat more expensive, was logistically less complicated and considerably quicker. I weighed both options.

What concerned me most about taking a plane was Culebra's airstrip. It was reputedly the worst in the region. Such a reputation was not to be taken lightly considering that some of the local airports were real doozies.

Take Virgin Gorda, for example, in the British Virgin Islands. As you approach the island by plane for the first time, you have no idea you are about to land. One minute you are flying at several hundred feet absorbing a breathtaking view of the magnificent Virgin Islands, and the next you are shuddering as you scarcely clear a peak strewn with large boulders and immediately drop into a power dive to dramatically and breathlessly reach the runway a short distance beyond.

Mona may be worse. Flying low over the island's plateau one bumps and bounces due to the warm thermals rising from the surface of the shimmering terrain. The moment the cliff falls away the aircraft banks precipitously into a sharp U-turn whining back towards the skimpy dirt runway nestled on the island's scanty coastal plain. My first crack at this airstrip might have unnerved me more than it did had I not been accompanied by Noel Snyder who hates planes. Wheeling into our U-turn with the entire world shifting off kilter, I was feeling sick as I turned to ask Noel in the seat behind me how he was doing. He did not respond to my query, nor was it at all necessary that he do so. Noel's state was evident for he had turned a dull shade of green. Ironically, Noel appeared so sick that he made me immediately feel better, and I took the landing like a pro.

Of course, Puerto Rico has many local dirt landing strips which are no more than cleared pasture land. Oftentimes the greatest hazard on such runways is cattle, and these can be frightened away by several low passes of the plane. Contrarily, cattle notwithstanding, Culebra's airstrip is downright treacherous.

For one thing, the hilliness of Culebra provides little flat ground on which to construct a landing strip. As a result, the island's airstrip is bounded by a bay at one end and a small mountain or ample hill, take your pick, at the other. Due to considerations of wind direction, landing from over the bay is usually impossible; consequently, planes must approach the strip from the opposite direction and face an impressive hill in their path. Clearly, this is not very practical either, so to bypass the mountain, aircraft come in at a sharp angle to the airstrip. Once past this obstacle they then swerve immediately onto the strip.

Being in a plane during such maneuvering is quite an experience. Flying low over Culebra's mountainous terrain the aircraft suddenly slows and begins its descent. Out the window one can see we are now below the level of the highest peaks, an experience which always gives me a sinking feeling. This is particularly the case on Culebra, for peering forward it is readily apparent you are headed directly for a V between two rapidly approaching and impressively immovable mountains. Why use the definitive term "mountain" when before I ceded that they might be large hills? Because, in an airplane you know with certainty that they are mountains. The engines are then cut back slowing once more to nearly a stall as the gauntlet is entered. Thermals of rising hot air tilt the plane's wings this way and that. To either side wing clearance between the enveloping mountains appears all too narrow as the boulders and cacti on the cliffs can be seen in excruciatingly fine detail. As we practically float between the precipices, I try to control my fear since the mind has the ability to make things into a lot more than they are. At this point some strikingly unnatural colors appear on the hillside off to the right. These turn out to be nothing less than the gnarled wreck of an aircraft which had failed to be precise enough to negotiate the mountain pass. As if this were not sufficiently unnerving, a similarly mangled plane decorates the hillside to the left. Emerging from the gauntlet, a sigh of relief is in order. However, this is cut short when you notice that though we are well nigh upon the airstrip, it is slanted off at a sharp angle requiring the plane to stoop steeply yet delicately in its final approach. That such a maneuver requires deft handling and should be attempted only by the most experienced pilot is attested to by the presence of no fewer than three additional planes crashed about the airstrip on all sides. Fortuitously, our minds are not permitted to dwell on this matter for our plane immediately accelerates, plunging down into a sweeping turn to the runway and in a moment we are on the ground, a bit worse for wear and quite determined to take the ferry on any subsequent trip to the island.

Reliving a Culebra landing in my mind I immediately came to a decision. We would travel by ferry.

On Saturday morning, the beginning of an extended Labor Day weekend, a band of about 30 enthusiastic Natural History Society members met at the Fajardo ferry landing to embark for Culebra. Despite tremendous hustle and bustle around the pier, the NHSers arrived promptly, picked up their tickets, and boarded the boat with surprising efficiency. Five minutes prior to departure everything seemed totally in order. Suddenly, a car drove up to the gate of the pier where I stood basking in the extraordinary smoothness of our departure. A frantic woman jumped out.

"Is this the boat for the Natural History Society's trip to Culebra?" she inquired urgently.

"It certainly is," I responded, a frown immediately etching itself on my brow as I glanced down at my watch.

"Please hold the boat for me," squealed the woman whom I did not recognize at all from any previous Society activity.

"I'll try." I shouted after her as she leapt back into her vehicle and sped off as best one might among the throng bustling before the pier.

Where the woman might park was a difficult question. Certainly all the spots near the pier had long before been taken and doubtless she would have to go some distance to find a place. With the mulling mass of humanity blocking her way and the problem of carrying her luggage back to the boat, her chances of returning to the pier in time appeared exceedingly slim. After waiting impatiently at the pier gate for several minutes, I yelled to the people on board to hold the boat just a few minutes, then scurried into the crowd to try and find the truant woman to give her a hand with her baggage and expedite her arrival.

Away from the pier for scarcely a minute it became immediately apparent that I would never find her among the hustle and bustle of the waterfront. Resignedly I hastened back to the pier only to find the entrance gate closed! Worse, the crew was already casting off the first hawsers that held the ferry to its moorings. The ferry was too far down the pier for anyone to hear my shouts for assistance, along with those of anguish and disgust. Therefore, I turned my attention to the gate.

The gate before me was about six feet high, but was crowned with several fierce rows of barbed wire that made scaling a dubious venture. It was supported by stanchions on either side of the pier and each of these had a crescent of metal spikes extending out laterally about two feet over the water to inhibit trespassers from climbing around the gate. These spikes looked more ornery than they were; so to make things a bit rougher on potential violators, they were covered with generous gobs of axle grease. With no other choice at hand and the boat with my consort about to pull away from the dock, I made my decision.

Taking as tight a grip as I could of a greased spike, I worked my way out over the water to get around the gate. The grease was doing an excellent job of jeopardizing my balance and, as a result, I had to keep my body as close to the spikes as possible. This was especially so as I turned the corner of the prickly barricade and, as a consequence, my new T-shirt and pants had rapidly become a grimy mess. As I finally set foot upon the pier once more I was able to take little satisfaction in having escaped from a fall into the bay. My clothes were a wreck, my hands solid goo, and I was in a foul mood as I jumped to the ferry, irked at what had started out as an exceedingly smooth departure and had so rapidly degenerated into an abysmal one.

My frame of mind did not change for the better when, upon setting off, who should I see but the woman I thought we had left behind! She flashed me a quick smile and then continued on in a conversation with a friend. How had she gotten aboard? Apparently she had shown up during the brief moment I had gone in search of her. Well, at least everyone had made it on board, and we were now on our way to Culebra.

The Culebra ferry is an ample vessel capable of carrying several hundred people. Some passengers took up positions in the open stern to enjoy the beautiful view of the coastline and quaint customs house, pink of all colors, which dominated the structures in the vicinity of the Fajardo pier. A brisk breeze blew as we smoothly steamed across the bay to begin our three-hour crossing to Culebra. Once outside the protected coastal waters, the magnitude of the swells picked up considerably as did the velocity of the wind. Shortly, virtually all of the stalwarts from the stern had retreated inside to the large interior cabin of the ferry. Here everyone sat, some trying to peer out of the large plastic side windows, a rather hopeless exercise considering the quantity of dried sea salt and grime coating the window exteriors. With gradually increasing frequency, the spray, generated by our vessel cutting through the rough seas, would get caught in the clutches of strong winds and come showering against the ferry's windward side. Though the day had appeared pleasant enough from shore, the sea had not yet recuperated from the heavy rains and near-gale winds of the week before. Those passengers tolerant of rocking vessels and anxious to keep an eye out for flying fish or pelagic seabirds were pretty much thwarted in these efforts. Other less hardy souls had not a moment to contemplate such lofty interests for they became totally preoccupied with the fundamental tasks required by serious bouts of seasickness.

The skimpy concrete pier of Culebra, scarcely two hundred feet in length, was a welcome sight for all of the exhausted passengers after such an unusually grueling voyage. Thanks to the good-naturedness of the bunch, their spirits were already picking up appreciably as they unloaded their camping gear onto the dock and began to prepare for the long walk to Flamenco Lagoon. Amazingly, despite the roughness of the sea, ashore there was scarcely a wind, and it was a typically warm, balmy day.

Watching all the exotic paraphernalia being unloaded ashore I found it hard to believe that some of these participants and I were contemplating the same brief camping trip. All of my equipment, as was my habit for overnight field excursions, was contained in my old, disintegrating Boy Scout pack which I had used since I was twelve. In it were my old stalwarts – air mattress, shower curtain, hammock, peanut butter, and jelly. I was ready for everything; well, almost everything. On the other hand, some of my companions were apparently prepared for everything, plus some. What they apparently had not kept in mind was that we were not certain of any assistance in getting to Flamenco Beach where we would camp. The entire hike there would be out in the open without benefit of shade. With all the coolers, lanterns, and other camping gadgets being piled up on shore, I was anticipating a long and difficult afternoon trek for at least some in the group.

When everyone and everything was ashore, we began to prepare for the long hike to Flamenco. It was at this moment that I got one of the biggest surprises of my years in Puerto Rico. The caravan was near setting off when rumbling down the dusty road came a shiny yellow school bus. This vehicle was a recent acquisition, the only one of its kind on the island, and an object of pride among the townspeople of Dewey. In the vehicle, accompanying the driver, was none other than the island's mayor who greeted us with a big smile and a friendly hello. Feliciano had been mayor of Culebra for some years, and I had enjoyed the pleasure of talking with him on several prior occasions during the course of my field work on the island. Most impressive among the mayor's attributes were his clear sincerity and dedication to the needs of the people of Culebra.

I had made it a point, on my previous visit to Culebra, to inform Feliciano of my intention to lead a visit of the Natural History Society and to seek his approval for use of the beach. At the same time, I asked whether there was any way he might be able to assist in getting the campers to the beach. Of course, it was difficult for him to make an impromptu commitment to my request and though I followed-up on the matter by phone, I knew that requesting transportation assistance from such a small municipality was a tall order, and I had pretty much written off any support. As things turned out, Feliciano not only availed us of the bus for transportation to and from the campground, but also for any other activity for which we might need it during our stay.

Our transportation problems solved, what had been materializing as a long, arduous hike now turned into a quick and easy shuttle. In less than an hour our entourage had arrived, distributed themselves along the radiant sands, and set up what was doubtless the most colorful if not most impressive assemblage of tents and campsites ever established on Flamenco Beach.

The better part of the afternoon was enjoyed by all languishing on the beach and wallowing in Flamenco's crystal clear waters. Some of the more intrepid souls swam about a hundred yards offshore to snorkel upon one of the island's smaller reefs.

Among its most outstanding natural features, Culebra's reefs narrowly fringe many portions of the coastline. This fringing

175

pattern is dictated by the shore's steep slope since most corals must live near the surface to absorb sunlight and grow. Though corals are animals, in fact relatives of the jellyfish, a significant portion of their nutrients appear to derive from a commensal algae called zooxanthellae which lives within the tissues of the coral polyps. Algae, being plants, produce their own starches and sugars through the process of photosynthesis by using carbon dioxide from the air or water and sunlight as raw ingredients. The need for intense light sets limits on the depth at which most corals can effectively grow. The steep slope of Culebra's shoreline provides very limited, but yet very excellent habitat for corals and their associated reef communities.

One particularly important reason for the impressiveness of Culebra's reefs relates to conditions on land. That is, the island's aridity. Being an area of little rain means little runoff; little runoff means little silt in the coastal waters, and clear, warm, shallow coastal waters mean luxuriant reef communities.

Culebra's reefs, though very narrow in width, were quite ample in extent and consequently provided a livelihood for many local inhabitants. The taking of fish and lobsters was a principal occupation; one enterprising individual made a living trapping small reef fish and selling them to aquarium dealers in the States. The principal source of this fellow's income was a tiny jewel of a fish called the fairy basslet or royal gramma. And royal it is. This little beauty, only about two inches in length, has a vibrant violet anterior contrasting with its brilliant golden hindparts. For some curious reason the royal gramma, while not particularly common in the reefs around Puerto Rico, is surprisingly abundant in the vicinity of Culebra.

Not to make the day too tedious, that evening I took those persons interested on a moderate hike to the pier in the hopes of observing an extraordinary nocturnal creature, the identity of which had only been sorted out a few months before. So unusual was this animal that upon my first encounter with it, I could not distinguish whether it was beast or fowl. The animal could fly, a strong hint that it could be a bird, yet it was nocturnal and foraged over the water. Though there are a reasonable number of nocturnal birds, I knew of none which foraged in such an environment. Certainly, if a bird, there would be some interesting new discoveries about this species' ecology. On the other hand, were the animal a bat, it was certainly the dang largest bat I had ever seen. The wingspread appeared to be a good two feet, and the wingbeat was relatively slow and methodical, quite the opposite of all the bats I knew which were characteristically small and fluttered about rapidly and erratically.

To resolve this embarrassing dilemma, Jim Wiley, Noel Snyder, and I had set about on a previous trip to determine its identity. Observing the animal from the pier as it flew beneath the limited illumination of the dock lights was simply not sufficient to resolve the matter. We therefore decided to trap it.

To do this, we first observed the creature's behavior at length. Typically the animal flew low over the open water of the small cove that was Culebra's harbor. Yet, it periodically passed directly under the pier where we sat. It was obvious that our best chance to capture this unusual animal was to extend a net beneath the pier and – we'd be in business.

Jim, a dedicated and talented biologist who worked with me at the Department of Natural Resources, volunteered to do the honors of setting up the net. To do this, he had to wade out from shore, up to his chest, to attach one end of the net. The whole process would have been simple enough were it not for a sting ray which chose to pass beneath the dock just as Jim was in the midst of his labors. As luck would have it, the ray insisted upon making its transit exactly where Jim was working. Noel and I saw the ray coming under the far side of the pier, but our warning to Jim was too late for him to maneuver to one side. Consequently, Jim did the only practical thing possible – he turned toward the ray to see what action this fish had in mind.

The ray stopped dead in the water, no more than three feet in front of Jim – and hovered there. Its only discernable motion was the fine rippling of its fins which buoyed up the creature in its aqueous medium. Face to face, Jim and the ray remained in a standoff. Neither would budge an inch. Jim was well aware that the ray was equipped with a venomous barb in its tail capable of inflicting a serious wound that would take weeks to heal. He did not want to initiate any action that might provoke the animal. At the same time, the ray, a close relative of the shark, both groups virtually unchanged over the past several hundred million years, had something going on in its primitive mind. But who in the world knew what. The standoff, an uneasy one from our perspective, appeared interminable. Yet, Jim held his ground and in the end the ray decided it had better things to do than glare at some large, aberrant creature which in no way resembled food, and so detoured to one side and went calmly on its way.

Jim quickly finished setting up the net and rejoined us on the pier to await the results of his handiwork. After a short while our flying question mark returned, zipping here and there, low over the calm water in the style of a nighthawk. Periodically, a ripple would spread on the placid surface where the animal had dipped to the water for food. From time to time it would pass beneath the pier, but not between the stanchions upon which hung our net. Finally, after some patient waiting, our mystery creature swept under the pier opposite where our fine mesh net covered the exit like a humongous spider web. Expectantly we leaned over the dock to observe the impact – but nothing happened! Instead, it apparently sensed the obstacle and turned an abrupt right angle under the pier and shot out beneath a different portion of the dock!

With that dramatic maneuvering, we scratched our heads and wondered what to do next. Since there was little else we could do, we decided to simply sit, wait, and hope for the better. Our wary creature made two other adroit aerial gyrations to avoid the net, but then, on the fourth pass – wham! – it was caught.

Jim, already wet, hustled into the water to retrieve the prize from the net lest it escape or hurt itself, while Noel and I waited anxiously on the dock to learn its identity. Working quickly and efficiently Jim had the animal free in but a few moments and held it up for Noel and me to see. Not a bird at all, the large creature was none other than a fishing bat, the likes of which none of us had ever seen.

Ugly was as good a word as any to describe it, though not

nearly so gruesome as many other bats. The body color was a uniform brown, the wings nearly black. Its small beady eyes were inserted inconspicuously in front of the large, pointed ears. The massive snout sustained a fold of skin that covered the sides of the mouth as in dogs of boxer ilk. Beneath this flap was doubtless a most impressive chomping apparatus, but none of us felt quite brave enough to try and move this fold for a better view of what was inside. As intriguing as its face was, this was not the bat's salient feature. Rather, what immediately drew one's attention were the bat's extraordinary feet. The feet were no less than ten times the size of what an animal this large should possess. Furthermore, they were tipped by claws with which only an eagle is rightfully endowed. It took no expert to surmise that the bat uses these grappling hooks to rake its prey from the water. The ripples we had seen earlier were no doubt a by-product of this fishing technique. Appropriately, Jim had brought thick gloves anticipating the possibility that a bat might be trapped, and it was plenty lucky he did considering the weaponry with which this animal was endowed.

Once the bat was free of the net, Jim passed it to us and then took down the apparatus. No sooner had he completed this task and was laboring towards shore than Noel and I noticed a movement in the water near the far end of the pier. Staring into the dim light, we observed a medium-sized shark cruising toward shore, apparently to determine what all the commotion was about. It was just as well that Jim was nearly out of the water for we had no interest in having the shark take over where the ray had left off. At that point I made a mental note. Never, ever, enter the water with Jim for any reason – unless it's in a pool!

Excited over our discovery, Jim, Noel, and I headed off to my hotel room to examine our prize more closely. In this confined space we immediately became aware that after its feet, the most outstanding characteristic of this bat was its smell. Boy, did it stink! In no time at all my room smelled like an aberrant pig's sty. I couldn't wait to get this flying stink-bomb out of there. Urgently we took measurements, photographs, and extracted the numerous ectoparasites from the bat's smooth skin to send to some expert who likes that sort of thing. Then we hustled outside with the utmost urgency, taking precautions so that other clientele of the hotel not notice our creature, since their enthusiasm for this discovery might not be equivalent to ours. At the pier we released the bat back into the night.

I could not bring the Society members here to Culebra without exposing them to this extraordinary bat. The small group that accompanied me sat on the pier observing its peculiar behavior. An obvious question was how the bat located its prey. The small eyes of these bats immediately make one suspicious as to whether they are useful for anything at all much less locating small fish beneath the surface. In fact, the bat's eyes are apparently useless for this purpose. Rather, it has been determined that the fishing bat uses its extraordinary sense of echolocation to detect its prey.

Echolocation works pretty much like sonar. The bat emits a rapid series of high-pitched calls which bounce off surrounding objects, varying from trees to potential prey items and echo back into the bat's sophisticated ear structure. These echoes are then immediately in-terpreted so that the bat can avoid an obstruction or attack prey as the case may be. Some bats feed on easily detected items such as fruits hanging motionless from a tree or

Fishing bat

on large mammals from which they suck blood. Such bats emit relatively quiet vocalizations. However, it is believed that fishing bats identify their prey by detecting disturbances on the water surface, not a small feat even if visual cues were used. Consequently, these bats, as well as those that feed upon small insects such as mosquitoes and even smaller fruit flies, issue calls substantially louder than their cousins which feed upon large prey. Some of these loud calling bats emit sounds a thousand times stronger than do their weaker-voiced relatives. These calls, at a distance of two inches from their mouths, or their noses, for some bats call through their snouts, are as loud as the roar of a jet plane. The effectiveness of this echolocation system is vouched for by the abilities of some bats to detect the presence of minute insects from as far away as a yard. The "leaves" and other peculiar structures on the snouts of some bats suggest they are species that call through their noses. It is believed that these fleshy structures help focus the calls so that the bats can direct sound at specific objects.

That bats go roaring through the skies seems a bit suspicious considering that all we ever typically hear from them is a bunch of relatively mild twitters. The reason we do not hear these flying lions is because most of their calls are at ultra-sonic frequencies, well above the range of human hearing. While humans have the capacity to hear sounds as high pitched as 20,000 cycles per second, or 20 kilohertz, bats use sounds ranging at least as high as 85,000 cycles per second. For sure, if it were not for sophisticated experiments, we would know next to nothing about bat aerial guidance systems due to our inability to detect their calls. One of the first individuals to definitively demonstrate that bats rely upon sound and not sight was the Italian biologist Lazzaro Spallanzani who, during the 1790's, plugged their ears and found this to result in total disorientation and an inability to avoid objects in their paths.

Subsequently, a renowned French biologist, without performing any new experiments of his own, managed to reinterpret and severely misinterpret Spallanzani's work to come up with the unfounded notion that bats have extremely sensitive skin and thus use their delicate wing membranes to sense the air during flight enabling them to detect obstacles. Somehow this new explanation succeeded in taking hold, likely because of the fascinating characteristic of human nature whereby we tend to believe what we want to believe regardless of whether it has any foundation in fact. Such was probably the situation during Spallanzani's time because the Frenchman's hypothesis was lauded despite Spallanzani having proven it false by coating bats with as many as three layers of lacquer without affecting the animals' abilities to navigate flawlessly in the dark.

As a consequence of this debacle, Spallanzani's work sank

into obscurity and it was many years before experiments similar to his were performed without any knowledge of his earlier work. Virtually a century and one half was to elapse before our knowledge of echolocation by bats was to advance significantly beyond where Spallanzani had brought us and before his work was to be resurrected and Spallanzani given the credit he was due.

Through the use of echolocation, bats are able to navigate effectively in total darkness, an ability unachievable by organisms which depend upon vision. Even the most nocturnal of owls, such as the barn owl, needs at least some light by which to see. Without small amounts of light, they are grounded. Not so with bats. Blind bats, with the exclusion of certain groups which do depend upon sight, are not impeded in the least by the loss of their vision. The ability to echolocate is so advantageous over sight at night that bats significantly dominate birds in filling the many nocturnal niches which birds so effectively fill during daylight hours.

Just as insects have evolved myriad types of camouflage to avoid predation by birds, recent discoveries indicate that they have also evolved some impressive mechanisms for avoiding bats. Moths have ears, not on their heads where we are accustomed to seeing them in vertebrates, but rather on the lower part of their thorax near their abdomens. With these it has been determined that some moths are able to detect ultrasonic bat calls. Since some moths can detect bat signals before they themselves are detected, a certain advantage is provided the moth. Such moths do not waste this opportunity. Upon hearing a far off bat signal, moths slip out of cruising speed and zoom into overdrive in the direction opposite from which the signal emanates. On the other hand, if the moth picks up the signal when the bat is already upon it, a different tactic is executed. In this case, evasive action consists of making erratic loops, or sharp dives, thus becoming a difficult target for the bat. From this it may appear that bats might as well throw in the towel when it comes to preying upon moths. Not so. With their far more rapid cruising speed, a bat can come upon a moth that is in its escape mode if the bat happens to be flying in the same direction. Additionally, even if a moth is too evasive for a bat to secure in its jaws, many bats have the capacity to scoop up such wary prey with their wings and even the webbing between their feet and tail!

Not to be outdone so easily, a few moths take matters one step further; they emit ultrasonic clicks of their own. Experiments have indicated that bats on the verge of attacking such clicking moths veer away the moment the clicks are heard. It is speculated that these clicks, emitted by a peculiar structure on the moth's side, are issued only by very distasteful moths. As a result, bats that have had a few bad experiences with such moths learn to leave well enough alone. In this case, the ultrasonic signal by the moth may serve the same function as the red, yellow and black of the coral snake, or the brilliant orange and black of the monarch butterfly. They all mean "stay away, I'm bad news"!

Bats are fascinating creatures, not only for their ability to echolocate, but for many other characteristics. They are, in fact, the only mammals capable of true flight. Many of the other supposedly flying species, such as the flying squirrels or the flying lemurs, are capable only of lengthy glides.

For a formerly terrestrial mammal to evolve the capacity to fly required a significant number of anatomical changes. But perhaps the most interesting of these were modifications of the hand. The hand of all bats is enormous, the middle finger of most species being as long as the head, body and legs combined! This finger, as well as the other four, is not conspicuously visible because it is shrouded in the fine skin membranes that make up the wings. Only the thumb and sometimes part of the third digit are partially free from this webbing to serve for grasping. The thumb also plays a significant role in walking, functioning pretty much to pull the animal along. While the hand supports the entire outer portion of the wing, the forearm and upper arm support the interior section. In many species of bats, webbing is also found between the tail and hind legs. This serves both as an aid in flight and in scooping up prey. Evidence that bats have followed successfully an evolutionary strategy of occupying nocturnal aerial niches is attested to by the existence of nearly one thousand bat species, approximately one fourth of the world's mammalian fauna.

The fishing bat we were observing was a relatively large species with a wingspan of approximately two feet. Yet, even these are comparatively small when compared to the large bats known as flying foxes, found primarily on islands of the Old World. This group includes species with wingspans ranging to six feet. On the other hand, since most bats are quite small, they face a predicament afflicting all tiny warm-blooded animals; a substantial proportion of their body mass is directly exposed to the environment. In other words, they have a large surface area. Their large, extremely membranous wings only exacerbate the potential problems these animals might have with heat loss. To sustain the high body temperature required for the survival of a mammal their size, the smallest bats would probably have to eat day and night to consume sufficient energy. To circumvent this dilemma, bats have their fair share of coping mechanisms.

Many species adjust to the potential problem of heat loss by simply living in the tropics where temperatures are relatively warm the year round. Others, though they may well live in the temperate zone during the summer, migrate to warmer latitudes in winter. Still, other temperate species hibernate.

It has been determined that bats are so effective in their ability to hibernate that the use of oxygen is reduced one-hundred fold. Even during their daily sleep, bats can enter into a state of semi-torpor during which their body temperatures drop significantly and oxygen consumption is reduced to one tenth the normal level. Whether the fishing bat we were observing used any specific heat retention strategies was unknown to me. Regardless, it was at least satisfying to know something about what makes this mysterious group of animals tick.

Certainly bats have received far more than their fair share of ill will through the ages, due basically to their nocturnal habits and our ignorance of their ecological importance. Not only are these animals of benefit to humankind due to the immense deposits of guano large colonies produce, but bats have also been known for some time to be important predators upon noxious insect pests, continuing into the night the role beneficial birds such as swallows perform during the day.

One example is the Mexican free-tailed bat, the most colonial of all mammals. Twenty million of these bats form a single colony in Bracken Cave located in Texas, the largest congregation of mammals known in the entire world. These bats forage invisibly each night as high as ten-thousand feet above the ground, their presence and activities detected only by radar. Specialists estimate that two hundred and fifty tons of insect pests are consumed on a typical summer night by these natural pest control agents.

More recently, biologists have begun to recognize other major benefits of bats. Foremost among these is pollination. While the activities of bees, moths, and hummingbirds have long been recognized as important in this regard, it is becoming increasingly clear that bats, particularly in tropical forests, also play a major role. Many plants simply cannot be pollinated without assistance from an intervening organism, in some cases bats. No pollination means no offspring, in this case seeds, an unacceptable situation for any sexual organism if it is to survive beyond its own generation.

The mechanisms which plants have evolved to "use" for their own benefit the organisms which feed upon them is a fascinating area of ecology referred to as coevolution. With respect to pollination, the flowers of many plants have evolved to attract specific types of pollinators. For example, flowers adapted to attract bees typically have an aromatic or minty fragrance, open only during the day, and have a protruding lip to serve as a landing platform for these insects. Furthermore, the petals are usually yellow or blue, not red which these insects are incapable of seeing. In fact, some flowers which we consider dull are far more attractive to bees because they can see colors in the flowers which are indiscernible to the human eye. Oftentimes such colors serve to highlight exposed landing pads upon which the bee alights.

Similar floral adaptations, primarily of tropical trees, exist specifically to attract bats. Such trees tend to produce large, dull-colored flowers on exposed leafless branches, the flowers often hanging down from long, sturdy stalks. Not surprisingly the flowers only open at night and usually have a strong unpleasant smell from the perspective of the human nose. Trees which attract small bats usually have flowers with long corolla tubes into which the bats must push their heads. In the process of performing this maneuver, the bats are brushed with pollen which they then transport unintentionally to another flower.

One of the most interesting cases of this type is that of Sanborn's long-nosed bat. It had been reported that this bat fed exclusively on nectar, a resource high in carbohydrates, but virtually devoid of proteins. Proteins are an essential ingredient in the diets of all mammals because no mammals, including humans and bats, can produce their own amino acids, the basic building blocks of proteins. It was subsequently learned that indeed Sanborn's long-nosed bat takes in proteins, but not while feeding. Rather, it does so while it is grooming its fur! The scenario is as follows. Many nectar-feeding bats have specially structured body hairs to which pollen adheres readily. Then, while grooming, the bats ingest the pollen which provides the proteins unavailable in nectar. To take the matter one step further, pollen from such plants has been found to contain substantially higher protein levels than pollen from flowers not fertilized by bats. The discrepancy between protein levels in these two types of pollen is hardly insignificant. Protein levels are as much as five times greater in bat-pollinated flowers. The advantage to the bat is clear. The animal is able to obtain ample protein and carbohydrate food resources from a visit to a single species of plant.

What about the advantages to the plant? Well, by providing such important resources to the bat, the plant tries to guarantee itself a regular customer that will distribute its pollen far and wide to other individuals of its species, something the plant would have difficulty doing by any other means.

To top this off, the story does not quite end here. Pollen grains are not particularly easy to digest, and it is believed that high sugar levels in the bat's stomach caused by the nectar aid in the extraction of the proteins. Finally, it is known that Sanborn's long-nosed bat occasionally ingests its own urine. It is surmised that this plays an additional role with respect to pollen digestion for urea is known to degrade pollen proteins.

There's no getting away from it. Despite their gruesome appearance, bats are amazing creatures. It is truly a shame that we humans dislike them so much. Bats have become so well adapted to their environment that some have scarcely changed since the first known fossil records of the group about sixty-five million years ago. In contrast, if we look at the horse of that era, Oligocene horses had three toes instead of a single hoof and were no larger than a sheep. This point merits consideration from another perspective. Had bats not been well adapted eons ago and had they followed the evolutionary trend of the horse, to increase in size, my companions and I might not have been out on the pier enjoying one of nature's marvels. Rather, we might be huddled in our respective homes afraid to venture out at night for fear of being attacked by a monster bat specialized on relatively large prey like ourselves. Then again, we might have evolved the sensory capacity to detect ultrasonic sounds emitted by bats so that as they were approaching we could zig and zag and....

The following morning before it became too hot, a group of us took another hike beginning with an exploration of Flamenco Lagoon just behind the beach on which we were camped. Flamenco is Spanish for flamingo which suggests that these regal birds once inhabited this water body. Protected from the sea by the berm of Flamenco Beach, the shallow, extensive, hypersaline lagoon – having a salt content well above that of the sea – appeared excellent flamingo habitat. The lagoon's high salinity is of particular importance for the growth of various aquatic algae, tiny crustaceans, and other minute organisms which form the diet of these unusual birds. Primarily pink with extremely long legs and necks, flamingos feed by immersing their heads upside down in the water and use their peculiar bills to strain the bottom ooze for food.

While offshore islands with salt water ponds, like Culebra, were formerly excellent refuges for flamingos, they are no longer so. This is because flamingos nest on the exposed mudflats which border the lagoons where they construct low, conical mounds using muck from the lagoon bottom. Such nests are extremely visible; consequently the birds have depended for millennia upon breeding grounds which are free of natural predators, conditions often provided by islands.

Colonization by humans changed all that. Flamingo eggs and young fell easy prey to new settlers attempting to eke out a living off the land. As a result, Culebra's flamingos, like those of Puerto Rico proper and of the Virgin Islands, had disappeared due to over-harvesting even before the beginning of the 20th century. We, therefore, would have to forego the opportunity of seeing these most extraordinary birds in the wild and muse upon the fact that practically the only places where flamingos now appeared capable of surviving in the region are in ponds at the fanciest hotels, zoos, and racetracks.

Despite the demise of the flamingo, it was another bird we sought during our stop at Flamenco Lagoon. This was the white-cheeked pintail or Bahama duck. Primarily a mottled brown, this duck is distinguished by its white cheek and particularly its bright red bill, distinct from that of every other duck in North America or the West Indies. Like the flamingo, the white-cheeked pintail has suffered significantly since the colonization of these islands, though not as severely as that long-legged, pink wader.

A combination of factors have affected the pintail. As with the flamingo, over-hunting and the poaching of eggs have no doubt had a detrimental effect on the species. Second, the draining of major swamps such as Anegada and Guanica and the channelizing of others have seriously reduced the available habitat for this duck. And, finally, the introduction of the mongoose to Puerto Rico also played an important role. This is because the pintail often nests in uplands some distance from the ponds on which adult birds normally spend their time. Upon hatching, the chicks have to waddle as much as a kilometer or more to reach the safety of water. Prior to the introduction of the mongoose, such a trek was relatively safe since the island was uninhabited by terrestrial mammalian predators. The mongoose and rats changed all that. Of the few pintail nests I managed to locate on Puerto Rico proper, all had been destroyed, apparently by a terrestrial predator. I even found one dead adult, possibly killed defending its nest. Given all the pressures on this duck, it should come as no surprise that the species is extremely rare in Puerto Rico. As the mongoose is not present on Culebra, the white-cheeked pintail is able to survive here in reasonable numbers with reduced persecution.

The openness of Flamenco Lagoon, coupled with the presence of a hill conveniently located on its southern shore, provided a special opportunity for us to view these rare ducks; this without any great effort on our parts or causing the birds undue disturbance. Our group observed the behavior of several dozen foraging pintails. In addition, we also enjoyed the presence of a few black-necked stilts which fed actively and cackled loudly, keeping us all amused. The black-necked stilt is one of our larger shorebirds, unmistakable by its bi-colored body, black above and white below, as well as by its long, bright pink legs. The local name "Viuda," means widow, a reference to the bird appearing to be draped in a black shawl of mourning. Though many shorebirds migrate from the northern reaches of Canada to the West Indies and locations much further south to avoid the cruel northern winters, this stilt represents one of the few shorebirds which actually nests in the Caribbean. The timing of our visit happened to coincide with a period during which the stilts might be breeding, but a search for their nests along the exposed edge of the lagoon proved of no avail.

Having had our fill of pintails and stilts, we turned westward and headed to the base of a rocky ridge jutting far out to sea known as Flamenco Peninsula. Flamenco Peninsula was a military bombing zone. You could not go out on it very far without jeopardizing life and limb, or without violating the "no trespassing" notices placed hither and yon by the U.S. military which controlled the area. Long and narrow, the peninsula had near its center several targets painted on the rocks which were fired upon by either ships or planes. Craters and pulverized rock littered the peninsula from years of blasting, and only cacti and fire resistant grasses and shrubs grew in the zones of moderate impact.

Considering the condition of this bomb-ravaged peninsula, an obvious question was, "Why would we want to come here?" Well, it so happens that totally due to happenstance, the bombing had created ideal conditions for the breeding of a bird difficult to see from land, the pelagic sooty tern. Unlike the common white terns regularly seen along bathing beaches, the sooty tern is entirely black above and forages well offshore. It can only be observed easily on its breeding grounds or from a boat at sea. As fate would have it, the sooty tern nests in relatively open terrain where grass clumps abound – as at the bombing range on Culebra. Of course, no birds nested in the principal impact area. However, in the adjacent zone, fire kept the shrubs down and the fear of stepping on live ammo rounds kept all but the most brazen egg poachers away. The result – a thriving sooty tern colony of over fifty thousand birds at a site where they had never existed before! Though our group could not go out onto the peninsula to see the birds up close, with our binoculars we could make out the swirling mass of adults circling over the colony intent on bringing catches of fish to their hungry, rapidly-growing young. Soon the young would leave their nests and shortly thereafter migrate far out to sea with the older birds.

Outside the breeding season sooties do not return to land each night to roost, apparently spending the night at sea. Since only very infrequently are they ever seen to land on the ocean, some researchers believe sooties sleep while in flight. Sooties are scarce in the region during the non-breeding season. It is reported that some sooty terns range to Africa's west coast during this period where food resources are more abundant. Juvenile birds may remain there until their sixth year, the approximate age at which they first breed. No other species of gull or tern takes as long to reach maturity.

Some members of our party expressed dismay at not being able to observe the tern colony at close range, certainly a very exciting experience. Yet, despite the excitement associated with entering such a restricted area, adventures of this sort can also have their drawbacks. Such was the case when, on a previous trip to a similar bombing area on the nearby island of Vieques, I had become lost deep within the restricted zone.

On that particular occasion, Alvaro, my Jobos Bay rowing companion, and I had roamed to the heart of Vieques' bombing range in search of the Puerto Rican screech owl. The last record of this owl from Vieques had been made around the turn of the 20th century from a forested hill now within the bombing range, and I was anxious to determine whether the owl still survived there. Since this owl, like most of its relatives, is active at night, I had obtained the necessary clearances to remain in the restricted area from before dawn until 9:00 A.M., plenty of time, I thought, for an owl reconnaissance. What I had not properly taken into account was my own zealousness to search for birds where few investigators had gone before and also to consider some peculiarities of the bombing zone. These oversights notwithstanding, Alvaro and I set off before dawn on our owl search with no particular trepidation. Our enthusiasm was bolstered when we encountered small but ample tracts of woodland that could potentially support the owl. To our dismay, however, several hours of searching did not reveal the presence of the bird. Not wanting to abandon this rare opportunity to rediscover the owl, especially knowing that adequate habitat was available and that I might never again have the opportunity to perform a survey in the restricted zone, I waited until the last moment to depart from the area. It was ten minutes to nine when I reluctantly ceded to Alvaro's prodding and switched on the jeep's ignition in order to leave.

As fate would have it, the spot where we had parked was in a gully out of sight of the ocean – which we had counted on for orientation. Using the sea became necessary because the topographic map we were using was obsolete as far as roads, or more appropriately dirt tracks, were concerned. The military had built various new routes since our map had been printed. Unperturbed, I suggested we head for high ground so that we could again view the ocean and regain our bearings. What I had not counted on was though the restricted area on Vieques was a long strip of land, like Flamenco Peninsula on Culebra, it was substantially wider. While it looked narrow enough on a map, this was deceptive. Thus I had to drive for some time to gain the elevation necessary to see the ocean. And what did I learn once we reached high ground? I had been driving in the wrong direction! Not only that, as if my directional blooper were not enough, at the moment I realized my error an ear shattering roar bounced us out of our seats. Glancing out to sea with eyes bulging, we immediately sighted the source of our distraction – a large, gray warship. Whether it was a cruiser or battleship was not of the slightest interest to either of us, especially when red puffs from the ship's guns indicated that another salvo had been fired and was headed our way. It was surprising to see the shots fired without them being accompanied by an associated rumbling. That was to come moments later as the sound waves trailed far behind those of light. This was another fascinating feature of our plight which neither Alvaro nor I were particularly anxious to discuss. Our minds were on other things. How in the heck do we get out of here!

I revved up the jeep and spun it about in a U-turn, dirt flying in all directions. We blazed down the bumpy dirt road as though it were a paved highway, and it might as well have been for we did not even notice being tossed and thrown around in the jeep; our total concentration was on listening for the next barrage of cannon fire and anticipating at any moment the crash of a shell in the vicinity of our vehicle.

As you might have guessed, we did not get blown up. Nor for that matter did a shell land anywhere near us. Nevertheless, the experience did provide me with an everlasting respect and wariness of military bombing zones, not to mention an intensive lesson in some of the fondest explicatives of Colombian Spanish!

No, I did not regret that the Natural History Society group could not get out on the peninsula to get a closer look at sooty terns. Such a site was not a place for a tour, even if by a dedicated group of nature enthusiasts.

Having gotten the best possible view of the terns from our distant vantage point, the hikers lazily wandered back to Flamenco Beach to spend a relaxed afternoon basking in the sun and gearing up for the highlight of the trip. Scheduled to begin that evening was a nighttime hike in an attempt to observe nesting sea turtles.

Sea turtles are a highly distinctive group of marine reptiles represented by seven living species, no fewer than five of which occur in Puerto Rico's waters. So adapted are these creatures to the sea that they virtually never come to land; that is, except for the females which must emerge to lay their eggs. Even this occasion is a very rare one, for most sea turtles apparently breed only every second, third, or even fourth year. Despite the rareness of this event, encountering these creatures on land is not as difficult as it may seem. Most importantly, sea turtles only nest on sandy beaches and in no other habitat. And not just any sandy beach will do. The beach, for example, must rise high enough so that when the nest pit is dug, the chamber will not fill with water during high tides or storms. Furthermore, egress from the ocean is restricted in many areas by impediments such as sand bars, intensity of wave action, and rock outcrops. By severely limiting where sea turtles might emerge from the sea, these factors facilitate locating females. Sea turtles of some species are also extremely consistent in using the same beaches and even the same portion of a particular beach from breeding cycle to breeding cycle. This site fidelity can be relied upon like clockwork in some cases. Finally, during a given breeding season, sea turtle females emerge not once, but twice, or even three or four times, and these emergences too are at quite regular intervals approximately two weeks apart. Detection of a first emergence by performing regular beach patrols allows one to anticipate a subsequent visit by the same individual animal.

Regrettably, for the field trip participants, I had not been able to carry out any intensive beach checking prior to our excursion; nor was August necessarily a good month for sea turtle nesting. The peak of the season had occurred earlier during the spring. Nonetheless, we were going to look for turtles on a hunch or, to be more positive about it, an educated guess.

You see, some months earlier I had been assigned to determine the status of Culebra's sea turtles in response to a request directly

193

from the governor's office that such an assessment be made. Requests of this sort were highly unusual; however, its basis was clear.

At that time there was a substantial amount of friction between the residents of Culebra and the U.S. military which was using the Flamenco Peninsula as a bombing range. In talking with townspeople, I regularly heard horror stories, tales of errant bombs landing in the bay around which the town was nestled, or of bombs even dropping into people's yards. Whether these stories were well founded or not, the people of Culebra, or a vocal portion thereof, were anxious to get the military off the island, and they had won the support of the governor's office. Apparently errant bomb stories were not quite enough to dislodge the military, so the Commonwealth government was looking for other angles from which to launch its attack – and it found, believe it or not, that sea turtles were one of them! The reason for this is that two of the region's sea turtles, namely the hawksbill and the leatherback, were listed as endangered under the federal Endangered Species Act. Consequently, any activity that had a negative impact on these creatures was in violation of a very strict federal law.

The Commonwealth's contention was that bombs and shells which missed their targets on narrow Flamenco Peninsula and landed in the surrounding waters would very likely explode on the fringing reef. Clearly a bomb exploding on the reef would have a negative impact on this habitat, the primary habitat, it so happened, of the endangered hawksbill sea turtle. (There was no concern about the leatherback since it occupies deeper waters.) If the reliance of hawksbills on the reefs of Culebra could be demonstrated, along with the negative impact of the bombs, the U.S. military was in trouble. It was my job to look into the matter.

It did not take long to determine that the military had made at least one major boo-boo with respect to the reefs. In 1970 an immense amount of undetonated ballistics were gathered up, piled on one of Culebra's most impressive reefs, and exploded. The underwater crater from the clean-up operation and the devastation of the reef were readily apparent off the south-central portion of Flamenco Peninsula. Documenting that hawksbills relied on these reefs was a somewhat more difficult task.

Published literature indicated that sea turtles, particularly the hawksbill and the green, were formerly quite common in the waters surrounding Puerto Rico and its offshore islands such as Culebra. Intensive harvesting for the flesh of both species, however, as well as the shell of the hawksbill, had reduced populations substantially so that breeding of the green sea turtle was no longer heard of and nesting of the hawksbill was scarce. The decimation of these turtles was intensive not only

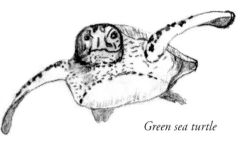

Green sea turtle

as a result of fishing, but also due to taking females off the nesting beaches. A particularly deleterious practice which was all too common involved marking the nest of a female that had just laid. Such nests were located by strolling the beach in the morning to look for tracks of turtles which had lumbered ashore during the night. The nests themselves could easily be located by probing in the soft sand with a pointed stick until an egg was heard to pop in the nest chamber. Like the meat, turtle eggs were highly prized. Approximately two weeks later the beach would again be patrolled, but this time at night so that the female, returning to nest for the second time, could be intercepted. On this occasion her second clutch of eggs would be taken and she herself would be slaughtered – a grand catch for the hunter.

The relentlessness of the sea turtle hunters to the point of extirpating sea turtles from many areas resulted not only from the consummate utility of the animals – meat and eggs for food, offal for soup and fat for cosmetic oils, leather for shoes and handbags, and shell for jewelry – but also from the undocumented but widespread belief that turtle eggs and some body parts are strong aphrodisiacs. At the time of our trip, a large hawksbill was worth nearly $200, its shell alone selling for approximately

$50 per pound on the international market. Hawksbill shell is so valuable that shark fishermen in Japan open the stomachs of their catches to check specifically for turtle shell.

The extent to which sea turtles have been decimated is best illustrated by the case of the Olive ridley sea turtle, a very rare visitor to Puerto Rico's waters. Prior to 1950 it is estimated that over ten million adults occurred off the Pacific coast of Mexico. By 1969 this number had declined to scarcely more than one million and in 1983 possibly as few as 80 thousand individuals survived. A similar situation exists for the related Kemp's ridley sea turtle, a species famous for nesting on only a few beaches but doing so simultaneously in massive waves known as "arribadas." In 1947 a single arribada at Rancho Nuevo in Mexico contained 40 thousand turtles. Only about five thousand females came ashore on average through the 1960's, one thousand per year in the 1970's and, by 1982, 621 individuals were recorded on the beach.

Despite the dramatic decline of sea turtles worldwide, as well as around Puerto Rico proper, the survival of these marine reptiles has greater potential in remote, lightly inhabited areas like Culebra.

Discussions with Culebra's residents indicated that such was the case. Not many years before, sea turtles had been so abundant in Culebra's waters one could make a living strictly off harvesting them. Now, though significantly less common, these creatures reputedly continued to occur in moderate numbers. To determine just what was meant by "moderate numbers," I initiated a field survey.

It was immediately apparent that I could learn a lot more about the status of Culebra's sea turtles by monitoring the island's beaches where the turtles came to nest than by trying to encounter individual animals out in the water. On several occasions, therefore, I visited Culebra's principal beaches where I managed to locate evidence of turtles having attempted to nest, though unsuccessfully. Following up on my field work, a full-time turtle researcher determined that what I had observed was not an unusual case, but rather the rule. The startling result was that of 19 turtle nests found during the course of a two-week study, every one of them had been dug up and the eggs taken, apparently by humans!

This astounding finding suggested that whatever negative impact the U.S. military might be having on Culebra's sea turtles, the effect must be minimal when compared to that of the local islanders.

Needless to say, the politicians were not interested in this "irrelevant detail" and used the sea turtle "conservation" issue to maximum effect against the military. Such shenanigans were at levels far above mine and about which I had no control. So much for the government "interest" in sea turtles.

The turtle field work on Culebra had demonstrated that sea turtles were substantially more abundant here than on Puerto Rico proper. It was based on these findings that a turtle hike seemed worthwhile. Besides, the beaches of Culebra are so spectacular, a visit to them would be a winning proposition even if no sea turtles were found.

The nearest turtle nesting beach to our Flamenco campground was beautiful Playa Resaca. Access to this beach was the most difficult of any on the island. For that matter, Playa Resaca is probably the most remote beach anywhere in Puerto Rican territory. One has to climb over a small, but rugged mountain to get there. Approaching by sea sounds doable were it not for a curious peculiarity of that coastal area. Though Flamenco Beach, where we were camped, was bathed by gentle one foot waves, adjacent Resaca was plastered by heavy surf. Why the difference? I don't know. Flamenco Beach is protected from direct wave action by a palisade protruding out to sea which inhibits passage from Flamenco to Resaca by means of the shore except by intrepid mountaineers. Protection of the beach might also be provided by offshore reefs or by one of the many nearby islands. Regardless, reaching Resaca by sea would require anchoring behind the breakers and then swimming through a heavy surf – an activity somewhat beyond the fitness levels of many in our group.

While access to Resaca Beach might be difficult, it was this characteristic that made the beach so attractive. Despite the heavy nest robbing identified by our earlier studies, sea turtles certainly had a better chance of surviving around Culebra and on its beaches than they ever would in the vicinity of Puerto Rico proper. Our work had verified this. Not only was the hawksbill sea turtle still relatively common and attempting to nest at Playa Resaca, but just a few months prior to our visit a giant leatherback had been slaughtered and removed from Resaca Beach.

Now, when we talk about sea turtles, we are not talking about your everyday pond turtle. Nor are we referring to the little critters people have in their homes and over which such a big fuss is made about catching Salmonella. The hawksbill is the smallest sea turtle species to breed in Puerto Rico's territory, and adults weigh between 60 and 90 pounds, with specimens ranging up to 280. The shell length of an average adult hawksbill is approximately three feet. The green sea turtle, a former nester, averages somewhat larger weighing in at around 200 pounds when breeding, the record being an 850 pound adult. Then, there's the loggerhead, about the size of a green and an extremely rare breeder in the region. And finally, we have the leatherback. Thousand pounders are not uncommon, and there are reports of individuals weighing nearly a ton with shells over eight feet in length. Wouldn't that be some animal for the group to see!

As large and impressive as the leatherback might be, even it is dwarfed by the most immense sea turtle of all time, specimens of which come from – Kansas?! Evidently a great interior seaway cut across North America during the Cretaceous era from the Gulf of Mexico to the Arctic and in this water body the granddaddy of all sea turtles formerly swam. It weighed several tons and was 12 to 13 feet long. Why this behemoth became extinct at the end of the Cretaceous, about 65-70 million years ago, along with many other impressive marine reptiles such as the monstrous 50-foot mosasaur, is just beginning to be unraveled. Be that as it may, some impressive sea turtles still survive in the world's seas, and our visit to Culebra provided an unusual opportunity to try and observe them.

Our trek to Resaca Beach would not only entail hiking over

Mount Resaca, but would also require that we do so at night to better synchronize our arrival at the beach with any potential sea turtle emergence. Culebra's mayor generously assisted once again by providing the school bus to take us from Flamenco Beach to the base of Mount Resaca. This passage was made some time after sunset. Upon being dropped off, the twenty of us counted off and each remembered his or her place in sequence so that we could keep track of the group. Well, wouldn't you know it. One of the participants, a retired Army colonel, refused to cooperate. Despite the obvious usefulness and downright importance of being able to keep track of the entire group on a dark and inhospitable mountainside, he simply refused to be regimented by being assigned a number. Apparently he had received more than his fair share of that kind of treatment during his professional career and had had more than his bellyful; or possibly he just was not used to taking orders from anyone with a rank less than that of a four star general and certainly not from someone with no rank at all. Whatever his reason, it was not worth arguing about so we had his wife keep track of his presence.

We began up the steep mountain in single file, stopping periodically to rest and confirm that our entire contingent was still intact. This diehard group certainly deserved a lot of credit. It was quite a struggle to negotiate the steep, bushy trail which on this occasion, following recent rains, was quite muddy. Neither was the trek facilitated by having to manipulate a flashlight in one hand. I was particularly concerned about an elderly couple, the Popes. Lillian had serious foot problems, not entirely resolved by a number of operations. Bob had suffered from other ailments and was in less than perfect health. Both might be suffering rather seriously at this point yet would be the last to complain.

As things turned out, the group crossed the mountain with flying colors and emerged with great anticipation to the pounding of surf on the cool sands of Playa Resaca.

I gathered the hikers around and had them turn off their flashlights to avoid frightening any turtles that might emerge from the sea. The light from the partially shadowed moon served amply so that we might maneuver adequately on the obstructionless beach. Deep into the nesting process, during egg deposition, sea turtles can be beaten, battered, and tormented at will, yet they will not abort their efforts and return to the water. Such is not the case when the animals first reach the beach.

Thus, it was important to be cautious. Light appears to play a role in orienting the return of turtles to the ocean. At some nesting beaches where artificial lighting had been installed, turtles often became disoriented and wandered inland instead of seaward.

Not uncharacteristic of my fortunes in the field, as soon as we hit the beach it began to rain. Not a relentless downpour or anything like that, but just an annoying drizzle. Since the sky had been clear several hours earlier while we were preparing to leave camp, few people had come prepared for this contingency.

Ignoring the price nature was making us pay for our exploratory urges, we excitedly, though cautiously, patrolled the upper beach for sea turtles. No luck. But it was still early, only ten thirty or so at this point. The night was young and anything could happen.

The group gathered loosely, small contingents trying to find shelter from the rain which was falling intermittently as each individual rain cloud passing over the beach dropped its due share of nature's perfect liquid and moved on. Between the dark clouds the sky was impressively clear and the open ocean well lit. During the periods we were not concentrating on obtaining better protection or patrolling the beach anew, there was the opportunity to really enjoy the wildness of the pounding surf upon the isolated beach. The remoteness of our present circumstances from the everyday world was doubtless a shocking contrast for most of us. Having made our sacrifice to submit to nature's domain, who knew how we might be rewarded.

As is the case with marine mammals such as the seals, porpoises, sea otters and the like, sea turtles represent formerly terrestrial creatures that have adapted to life in the ocean. The earliest marine turtle fossils date back to about 70 million years ago, the age of that monster turtle from North America's former inland sea. Over the course of time, turtles have become so efficient at living in the sea, that in many respects they have left even whales in their wake. Though sea turtles are bound to the land by the process of laying eggs, while whales, dolphins, and manatees give birth to live young in the sea, turtles outdo these other marine denizens in a number of other regards. For example, there is much discussion as to whether whales regularly stay under water for much over an hour, and I have yet to hear a suggestion that they can remain submerged for more than two. In the case of sea turtles a few hours is no sweat; record submergences are not discussed in the range of hours, days or weeks, but rather months! Granted, sea turtles are not active during these long underwater stints; nevertheless, their mastery of the deep breath is unquestionable. Diving? A big to-do is made, and rightly so, about a sperm whale getting caught in a submerged transoceanic cable 3,700 feet beneath the surface. The pressure at such a depth is awesome, over 100 times that at the surface. Yet a leatherback sea turtle was recorded to depths of over 4,000 feet and was still diving when the depth gauge strapped to it blew.

Though the aquatic feats of sea turtles are extraordinary for air breathing animals, other components of their life histories are equally impressive. At the time our group sat on Resaca Beach, it was believed that female sea turtles of most species bred for the first time no earlier than the age of seven. Upon emerging from the sea, the female green sea turtle, whose behavior is reasonably typical of sea turtles generally, paddles up the beach to well above the tide line where she excavates a nest chamber in the sand with her flippers. In this she deposits approximately 80 to 150 white, soft-shelled, mucous coated eggs and then seals the chamber with sand. As mentioned earlier, the female will emerge from the sea two to four times in a season to carry out this same egg laying ritual at intervals of nearly two weeks. It will then be two, three, or even four years before this cycle is again repeated. The developing embryos incubate in the closed chamber receiving warmth from the sun-heated sand above, oxygen exchange from open space left in the nest, moisture from the surrounding beach sand, and calcium directly from the eggshell itself. Incubation lasts for approximately one and one half to two and one half months, depending on the latitude. The young emerge from the nest in small cohorts at which time the hatchlings are scarcely an inch long.

The life of a hatchling sea turtle is precarious to say the least and only one to three percent are believed to ever reach maturity. The fact that they have a copious yolk supply so they do not have to feed for a few days after hatching is small compensation. Upon emerging from their nest, hatchlings immediately scurry down the beach to the sea. The chances for survival during this dash, however brief, are poor since numerous predators are attracted to the beaches during the hatching period. Dogs, cats, raccoons and rats, not to mention crabs and even the frigatebird which picks up its prey on the wing, all take advantage of the feast of defenseless morsels scampering suddenly out on the open sand.

The situation scarcely improves once the hatchlings reach the sea. Predatory fish of all sorts attack the defenseless turtles as soon as they are through the surf. Heavy losses are sustained virtually throughout the movement seaward, doubtless lessening to some degree once the hatchlings reach the home of their "lost year."

The "lost year" in the life cycle of sea turtles, particularly the green sea turtle, represents the first year in their life cycle. This is because practically nothing was known until recently about green sea turtles during this year due to a scarcity of observations. The latest evidence suggests that the frantic paddling of hatchling turtles in the Western Atlantic likely delivers them to the Sargasso Sea where they find both food and protection. The Sargasso Sea refers to beds of the floating seaweed *Sargassum* with its associated marine fauna and flora which cover vast stretches of the ocean surface. Young turtles can find protection among the dense mats of seaweed while at the same time feed upon the multitude of minute plant and animal life that makes these beds their home.

The mortality of sea turtles is so intense during the first few days after hatching that probably the majority perish. Such severe losses to species also suffering from intensive human pressures have caused great concern among scientists and conservationists. This high mortality of hatchlings has resulted in efforts to save sea turtles being focused on beaches. Here females coming to nest and young leaving the nest, both highly vulnerable to human and natural predation, can be managed to enhance their chances of survival.

Needless to say, our expedition had no specific conservation aim, though it probably served during that given evening to thwart the efforts of any turtle poacher who might have considered spending the night at Resaca.

To address the problem of heavy egg and hatchling sea turtle losses on beaches, conservationists had devised various programs. The simplest was merely to patrol a beach to keep away two footed, four footed, eight footed, no footed and sundry footed predators.

While beach patrolling helped protect the green and two species of ridley sea turtles which nest colonially, it did little for those species which nest loosely. Widely scattered nests are impractical to patrol. In response to this dilemma, a program became widely established of transplanting turtle eggs to fenced areas of the beach where they could easily be attended in artificial nests. Predation of eggs and hatchlings on the beach could be significantly reduced by this approach though once the young entered the sea they still took a shellacking.

To ameliorate this last problem, the epitome of turtle projects came into being – that of "head-starting." Head-starting consists of raising young sea turtles in captivity until they are one year of age. At this point they may be approximately a foot in length with a nice hard shell that substantially enhances their chances of survival. They are released and voila! Zilch predation occurs on the young.

The scheme sounds great. It is also relatively easy to implement, even where technical skills and financial resources are limited. Head-starting thus took off as a major sea turtle conservation strategy. Initially one-year old sea turtles were released from beaches where they had originally been deposited as eggs. Subsequently this program expanded to include releases on beaches from which sea turtles had been extirpated many decades before.

At the time of our beach watch, sea turtle programs were going great guns, but I could not help having serious misgivings. For example, relocating the eggs on the beach sounds innocuous enough. But, are the true conditions of a nest being recreated

– especially when it was not uncommon to incubate eggs in artificial styrofoam containers? Do such unnatural conditions simulate the appropriate temperature, humidity, and gas exchange required for the embryo to develop properly?

Even more serious in my mind was head-starting. Let's review some facts.

We have already learned that hatchling green sea turtles have an urge to paddle for up to three days, likely to the Sargasso Sea. We also know that many sea turtles return to nest on the beach upon which they were born. But we did not discuss just how finely developed this ability is to find the beach of origin. Green sea turtles born on Ascension Island, a minuscule outcrop five miles across, lying in the vast reaches of the Indian Ocean, return there year after year – these are turtles which spend most of their lives in the seas off the east coast of Brazil, 1,400 miles away. The migration of these sea turtles is one of the great feats and unsolved mysteries of nature. How does an adult turtle return to such a remote breeding ground? What cues does it use? What basic chemical signals did it pick up while in the egg on the beach or during its mad dash to the surf that enable it to, many years later, perform such a miracle of migration?

While we may not know the specific senses and stimuli that drive sea turtle migration and homing capacities, we can pick up some relevant information from other animals which should guide any management programs we develop.

Conspicuous to any biologist with a background in animal behavior is the fact that animals which depend upon instinct for survival cannot modify their behavior to cope with unnatural changes in their environment. It is for this reason that a bald eagle finding a foreign object in its nest will incubate it as though it were an egg. This includes bottles, plastic floats, or virtually anything that the bird can manage to sit on. Eagles are accustomed to only having eggs in their nests and nothing else. Over the millions of years that eagles have existed, there simply has been no survival value to being discriminatory about what it treats as an egg.

In another vein, in some bird species, their song is learned only during one critical period in the early life of each individual.

If the song of the species is not heard during this time, it will never be learned regardless of how often it is heard thereafter. If a kid is taken away at birth from a female goat and returned to her after one hour, she will reject it. But if she can lick and smell it for only five minutes before its removal, the return of the kid will be accepted. The point? There are sensitive periods, of limited duration, in the life cycles of animals when basic tools for survival are acquired. These critical moments cannot be tampered with.

Applying these observations to the turtles, might embryos raised in a styrofoam container have been denied some fundamental chemical cues inherent in a sand nest? I think so. Can we be so sure that releasing a one-year old turtle on a beach will have in any way enhanced its chances for survival? Certainly any urge to swim for three days, as do the hatchlings, is gone, so it certainly won't head for the Sargasso Sea. Can it survive elsewhere? We had better hope so. Is there really a reason to believe that a turtle one year of age will have any capacity to pick up cues from the beach so that it will return there to breed? I believe not. Where might it go to breed? Who knows. At best I expect one can only hope that it has an urge to go somewhere. What about the turtle's immediate future – its second year? Where will it spend that?

Maybe I am being overly critical, but my senses tell me that considering the scanty amount known about sea turtle biology, some efforts in the name of conservation, particularly head-starting, have gone too far. This is not because head-starting was tried. I think it was a reasonable experiment. Rather, I am disturbed by the extent to which the practice was implemented. Head-starting has been carried out worldwide on a massive basis. I hazard that many hundreds of thousands of sea turtles have been head-started. At what cost? I would not want to surmise. The practice is implemented as though it were a long-standing, time-tested technique. Unfortunately this was far from the case at the time of our Resaca visit.

At that time no one really knew what became of head-started turtles. It was not anticipated that they should be seen on the beaches until about six years after their release because that was believed to be the age at which they became mature and bred for the first time.

Well, six years passed since the first head-started sea turtles were released in the late 1960's and none of them showed up on a nesting beach. Seven years passed. The same result. In the late 1980's it had been about twenty years since the release of the first head-started turtles, and we were still waiting for that first female to show up on a nesting beach and demonstrate that all was not for naught! Pretty much the same was true for the 90's.

Yet, the situation, though gloomy, may not be entirely hopeless. Relatively recent investigations indicate that earlier estimates are incorrect that suggest sea turtles begin to breed at approximately seven years of age. It has now been determined, for green sea turtles at least, that age of first breeding may occur when the animals are thirty, forty, or possibly even fifty years old! Consequently, we may have a long wait indeed before we know for sure whether head-starting in fact works. In the meantime, head-starting has been all too slow to call it quits. Though hundreds of thousands of sea turtles of most species have been head-started at the cost of tens of millions of dollars there remains little to show for it. Slowly, ever so slowly some of these programs have finally shut down. It would be interesting to explore the justifications presented by those programs that continue on.

One obvious question is how estimates of turtle breeding ages could have been so far off. Well, in the case of the green sea turtle this resulted from early estimates of breeding age being based on growth rates of animals raised in captivity. Early on it was clearly not possible to track a sea turtle from birth until maturity. It still isn't. Therefore, the only way to get a fix on turtle maturation rates was by recording the rates at which captive animals grew to the size of breeding adults in the wild. What was not considered in these calculations was that captive and wild turtles do not grow at nearly the same rates.

The reason for the substantial differences in growth rates is, not surprisingly, food supply. While captive turtles may benefit from all types of protein fortified, ultra-vitaminized, and macro-nutritionalized food, wild turtles must eke out a living. In the case of the green sea turtle, "back to nature" is hardly a blessing when it comes to nutrition. Greens, at least in the Caribbean, survive primarily on *Thalassia*, somewhat appropriately referred to as turtle grass (though a major food of turtles, it is not a grass). As nature would have it, few organisms eat turtle grass because it is so tough (45% cellulose) and lacks nutritional value. To compensate, green sea turtles possess various adaptive strategies for utilizing these plants. For one thing, they have hindgut fermentation. Microbes in the rear of the gut break down 90% of the cellulose. Greens also recrop certain portions of the *Thalassia* beds leaving other areas untouched. This provides the turtles with a constant supply of young leaves. Such leaves have protein levels from six to 11 times higher than do old ones. Yet, despite these adaptations, green sea turtles can only digest 50% of the protein contained in turtle grass leaves. Comparing this to terrestrial herbivores, they typically extract 75% to 80% of the proteins from the plants upon which they feed. Poor nutrient availability and extraction, coupled with a low rate of food intake (greens consume approximately one quarter of one percent of their body weight per day; this is from eight to thirty times less food than many terrestrial mammals consume), account for the green sea turtle's extremely slow growth rate despite its wonderful adaptations.

Another practical question is why an animal would wait until it is forty or fifty years old before breeding for the first time. Would it not be advantageous to begin at, say, the age of two? Well, using humans as an example, we certainly cannot do that for the obvious reason that the full maturation of the human body takes time. The same for sea turtles. And clearly the consumption of low grade foods slows this process. Nevertheless, it is apparent that this strategy, at least for tens of millions of years before dominance of the earth by humans, was extremely successful. Being "willing to wait" in an ecological sense to breed, enables green sea turtles to take advantage of an abundant marine resource that they then have all to themselves. Evolutionarily it apparently was not worth it to compete with many other organisms for highly nutritious, easily digestible food resources. As long as turtles could protect themselves from predators, which as adults they do quite effectively, why not trade off early reproduction for a guarantee of permanent and abundant food resources?

Turtles are not the only organisms to adopt this strategy of slow development and relatively low reproductive potential. Elephants, whales, manatees, rhinoceroses and sharks, are but a few additional examples. Ecologists refer to organisms which adopt such a survival strategy as K-selected species. Suffice it to say that species with K-selection characteristics tend to occupy habitats that are very stable and not constantly changing in size or location. Such stable habitats tend to be filled to carrying capacity (represented by K in ecological jargon). Since there is little space for additional individuals in habitats which are already full, species adapted to them tend not to concentrate their efforts on having many offspring. Rather, such organisms focus their developmental strategies on producing relatively few offspring but making certain that those few individuals are extremely capable of surviving on the limited resources available.

To round out the picture, r-selection is the opposite of K. Species in this category breed prolifically and, thus, are represented by r which among ecologists stands for reproduction rate. Mice, weeds, sand flies, and most other insects are a few examples of r-selected organisms. Most of these species take advantage of less stable environments which are often not at carrying capacity. An example would be rodents out on the plains. The plains regularly have severe droughts which reduce seed production by desert grasses. This in turn may cause dramatic reductions in rodent populations. Since most rodents are r-selected species, they can bounce back quickly from such disasters. Disaster relief is built into their survival strategy. At the same time, they also have the capacity to take advantage of periods of unusual bounty. Mice in a grain elevator are a sufficient example.

Returning to the turtles, it may be some while before we know whether head-starting was an example of tremendous foresight or over-zealous conservationism. Yet, each day the answer seems to be more clear.

On a not unrelated front, sea turtle conservation efforts took a serious blow when it was discovered that the temperature at which sea turtle eggs are incubated in the sand determines the sex of the offspring! Loggerhead turtle eggs incubated at 28 degrees centigrade or less resulted in all the offspring being males, and eggs kept at 32 degrees or higher produced only females. The pivotal temperature for this species appears to be approximately 30 degrees centigrade.

If the loggerhead data are applicable to other turtles, leather-back and green sea turtle eggs in Surinam incubated in styrofoam boxes at 27.5 degrees centigrade, two degrees below that of the sand, should be expected to have hatched only males. Incubation in the natural nest would have produced 60 percent females.

To what extent incubation temperatures under artificial conditions have influenced sea turtle sex ratios will never be known. What we can draw from this is simply that when we mess with nature, whether with good intentions or bad, natural processes are often more sophisticated than we first presume, and actions taken out of ignorance can frequently result in unmitigated failure. Good intentions, no matter how well-meaning, can often do more harm than good.

After two hours of futile anticipation and intermittent show-ers, I decided to call it a night and lead my bedraggled but tolerant contingent back to camp. After everyone was gathered together we counted off in preparation for the return hike over the mountain.

Well, wouldn't you know, we were two people short! So, we counted again, but met with the same result. Where in the world could we lose two people on an open beach?

"I saw two women heading towards the end of the beach a few minutes ago," put in one of the group. That was all I needed to hear. Dashing down the beach to the west I hoped I was not too late, for that was the end closest to camp and hikers unfamiliar with the area might think they could find a shortcut back via this route. Fortuitously, I was not too late, for standing at the base of a huge boulder pile at the end of the beach were the two women, evidently surveying the treacherous slope for a path over the headland separating Resaca from Flamenco Beach. I was amply irritated that two members of the group would consider going off on their own in this manner, particularly without telling me or anyone else in the party. However, my initial irritation was miniscule compared to the hardly repressible anger I felt when I saw that one of the women was none other than – you know who – the women who had arrived late at the dock and for whom I had become greasier than an axle bearing!

Trying to remain somewhat calm, I gave the two vagrants an all too mild reprimand and escorted them back to the rest of the group so that we could begin our return to camp. The trek back went reasonably well considering the trail was muddy, and we did not reach our destination until after two in the morning.

Upon finally making it to camp I stopped to talk to the Popes, as I had constantly been concerned about their condition. I knew that this messy and futile expedition had doubtless taxed their physical tolerances, and I wanted to apologize for having put them through the ringer to no avail other than a good drenching.

"Oh, don't be silly," they both insisted. "Of all the hikes we have ever taken, we have never been on anything so exciting in our entire lives!"

Maybe it was worth taking a chance to observe the sea turtles after all.

Reflections

We have scarcely scratched the surface here in learning about Culebra's wildlife. But, at least you now have a flavor of the island's uniqueness. The question is, what keeps it that way?

The answer, in a general sense, is lack of development. But let's break that down. Perhaps most obvious is difficulty of access. There is no easy way to get there. Yet, it is not quite that simple. If Culebra had gold on it, you can bet there would probably be a bridge or causeway connecting it to the mainland.

So, another reason is limited cause to go there. Of course as beaches and coral reefs on Puerto Rico proper become increasingly degraded, those on Culebra gain in attraction. Also, as nature tourism or eco-tourism gains in popularity, localities such as Culebra have a greater allure.

But, what about when you reach Culebra? What then? Well, it is downright hard to get around. There were very poor roads and limited means of transportation. This is a major point. In our increasingly convenience-driven world, most of us desire certain levels of comfort. And this tends not to include a grueling walk in the broiling sun to get from one place to another. Road construction in, near, or around natural areas, therefore, is an automatic detriment to their continued existence in their present state. Though new roads may in no way penetrate these areas, the spin-offs from their construction can prove the downfall of these reserves.

Roads mean more people. This is automatic. More people mean the need for more amenities as they travel – gas stations, restaurants, shops, hotels. This infrastructure means more pollutants, garbage, vermin, human wastes, land clearing, alien plants, fragmentation of habitats divided by the road, overall alteration and modification of the landscape generally.

Puerto Rico is full of roads. I gradually recognized that roads were, perhaps, the single most significant factor leading to the decline of the island's splendor. And yet, planning of the island's road system was not even on our radar screen as natural resource managers. Our concerns regarding road construction only emerged when one was planned that would pass directly through a protected area. If it went just outside the reserve's border, we were satisfied. Bad call!

Perhaps this shortcoming of ours was based, in part, on acceptance of the United States model for protecting natural areas – a model highly inappropriate for Puerto Rico. That model is, basically, to set aside an area of specific conservation interest and leave things at that. There is no gradual buffering of the site from outside influences. Neither does this occur via the addition of a buffer zone within the reserve, nor by careful land use planning in the reserve's vicinity. Virtually all of the wildlife refuges, national parks, and state reserves I grew up visiting were based upon this model.

Regrettably, it is a model long obsolete and one which the United States should long ago have learned does not work. But that is another story.

The fundamental point is that I and my agency as a whole failed to recognize the myriad impacts resulting from road construction and, consequently, we failed to take even the most basic measures to cope with the problem.

Returning to Culebra, there was one other major factor limiting development. That was water. Not sea water, of course, there was plenty of that. I mean fresh water for drinking. In most places we take this commodity for granted – you don't on Culebra! On a number of occasions during my visits to Culebra there was such a scarcity of water that spigots were turned on for only one hour per day. Not fun! Water is hardly an amenity for we humans, rather it is a necessity, consequently it is not something we can do without. Years after my departure from Puerto Rico a fresh water pipeline was constructed from Puerto Rico to Culebra. One of the most critical limiting factors controlling rampant development had been breached.

Political use of the Endangered Species Act to prod the Navy to leave Culebra was a first for me. It was not so much use of the Act for this purpose that was discomforting. It was the total indifference that had been directed to the Act up to this point. Only now, when it was recognized that the Act could be used to serve a political purpose, did the desire to implement it suddenly become paramount. Not only that, but we are talking here about selective implementation. There was zero interest in applying the Act to the numerous violations taking place hither and yon across Puerto Rico. This was selective application to the Navy.

This was my first engagement in high-level political jockeying. It was not a pretty picture. But only a handful of people probably knew what was going on. It reaffirmed my feelings regarding the need for checks and balances within and without the government. Without checks and balances, abuse can easily become rampant.

Discoveries!

The prospect of discovery – that is probably the most exciting thing about being a naturalist in Puerto Rico.

Practically every other year for approximately twenty some odd, both prior to and during my residency on the island, a bird, reptile or amphibian formerly unknown to science was described for the first time or a supposedly extinct species was rediscovered. The rediscovery of the Puerto Rican whip-poor-will in the 1960's, a species not recorded with certainty since it was first described in 1888, is a fascinating case I have already described. There are others just as unusual.

More extraordinary than any other discovery had to be that of the golden coqui, the most unusual little frog from among a group, or genus, noted for its uniqueness. Coqui is the local name in Puerto Rico given to a group of tiny tree frogs which go by the scientific name of *Eleutherodactylus*. The name coqui imitates the call of the island's most common species. This group of frogs derives its peculiarity from not exhibiting the typical development we all learned to expect of frogs when studying our first lessons in biology. You may recall from those lessons, and then again you may not, that all amphibians typically go through a process called metamorphosis. This means, for frogs and toads at least, that gill-bearing tadpoles emerge from their eggs. Such forms are entirely aquatic and in no way resemble adults. Only with time do the tadpoles gradually undergo a change, losing their tails and gills while acquiring lungs and legs. It is only after this metamorphosis is complete that these animals reach the adult stage.

Not so in *Eleutherodactylus*. Rather than pass through the typical stages of a frog's life cycle – egg, tadpole, adult – coquis bypass the tadpole stage. They hatch directly from the egg into the form of an adult, though certainly miniature ones at that. The tadpole stage evidently takes place entirely within the egg.

What is the advantage of skipping the tadpole stage? The advantage is that tadpoles are entirely dependent upon water for their survival and by skipping this stage coquis are able to significantly reduce their dependence on this medium.

Freed from the confines of ponds and streams *Eleutherodactylus* has been able to spread to habitats where water is less readily available such as to the leaf bases of air plants or bromeliads and palm fronds, rock crevices, and the like. This adaptation has ultimately resulted in various species of these tiny tree frogs occupying wet and moist habitats from the coastal plains to the highest mountain summits. Such is the case not only in Puerto Rico where 16 species of *Eleutherodactylus* are known, all of which are endemic, but also throughout the other islands of the West Indies.

Returning to the golden coqui, what makes this an even more extraordinary frog than its brethren is its still more peculiar reproductive strategy. The female golden coqui retains her eggs within the body cavity and hatches its young live, a process called ovovivipary. The nearly transparent nature of the golden coqui's abdomen allows for the ready observation of this process. The benefit of this strategy is evident when we consider that amphibian eggs, unlike the familiar hard-shelled eggs of birds, are gelatinous and do not possess a shell, thus they require constant moisture. By retaining the eggs within her body, the female frog can more readily supply this essential ingredient. This extraordinary adaptation for an amphibian, one replicated elsewhere in the world by only a few closely-related species of African tree toads, enables the golden coqui to occupy a habitat too dry for other amphibians, even most other *Eleutherodactylus* tree frogs.

The golden coqui is found exclusively among the leaf bases

of bromeliads in mid-elevation forests where rainfall is relatively sparse and strong winds tend to dry out the vegetation. Though ample forests meeting these criteria occur widely, for some unknown reason the golden coqui is limited in range to one extremely small portion of the island.

Along with its novel reproductive strategy for an amphibian, the golden coqui is far and away the prettiest of Puerto Rico's tree frogs. Entirely yellow in coloration, all of Puerto Rico's other coquis are drab in comparison.

Certainly the golden coqui was not overlooked by earlier herpetologists due to being confused with species of similar appearance. Rather it was the golden coqui's extremely limited range and its inconspicuous call that hid it from the eyes and ears of scientists until 1973.

On May 22 of that year Dr. George Drewery, a resident herpetologist in the Luquillo rain forest, and a group of associates were driving slowly down a back mountain road after dark, when Drewery thought he heard a peculiar sound. Stopping the car he listened intently and, yes, there was a soft, thin, high-pitched call unfamiliar to him emanating from somewhere on the hillside above. Anxiously the group sought out the unusual sound and in short order had obtained several specimens of this beautiful new frog which was ultimately endowed with the common name of golden coqui.

Up to this point the golden coqui's story is not particularly unusual other than that the discovery of the frog from a moving vehicle was quite a feat. I can vouch for this considering how difficult it was for me to discern this frog's call from all the other boisterous forest denizens even when quietly standing reasonably near to a calling male. The call is so high pitched that it ranges far above typical sounds to which we are accustomed, even those of birds. It is also given with little intensity making it that much more difficult to detect. George's moving car discovery was clearly an extraordinary accomplishment.

Upon first telling me about the frog, George had sworn me to secrecy. It would be some time before he had the details of the animal's unique reproductive biology worked out, and he wanted to publish a single treatise on the animal in one fell swoop rather than publish a scanty description of the species right away and then a more comprehensive paper on the frog's biology at his leisure. I had no problem with this approach; the decision was his, but most biologists would have urged that a preliminary note be published immediately to forestall the possibility of someone hearing about his exciting find and stealing the discovery by being the first person to describe the animal in print. I myself had been forewarned in this manner, and rightly so, concerning a discovery of much lesser consequence which I had made. Some biologists can apparently be real *bandidos* when it comes to discoveries that can enhance one's reputation.

I had known about George's discovery for several months before new events would complicate the story of the golden coqui and put my oath of silence to the test.

Performing a bird survey in Guanica Forest one morning, the home of the Puerto Rican whip-poor-will, I was surprised to encounter someone searching carefully among the rock crevices and leaf litter. Inquiring as to the purpose of this peculiar behavior, I learned that its practitioner was in quest of some local lizards and snakes and that his work was part of a survey that would result in a published checklist of the amphibians and reptiles of the West Indies. The biologist whom I had so coincidentally come upon happened to be Richard Thomas, an active herpetologist in the Caribbean, some of whose works I had read, but whom I had never met.

Considering the ultimate purpose of Richard Thomas' efforts – a checklist of West Indian herpetofauna – I felt it would be a distinct loss if the golden coqui were not included in this work. At the same time, remembering my promise to George, I was not about to spill the beans concerning the frog's existence. During our conversation, I urged that Richard visit George Drewery before leaving the island. That would give George the opportunity to tell him as much or as little as he pleased. Little did I guess what would transpire from this point on. It was some time before I learned of how events unfolded.

In the days subsequent to our conversation, Richard Thomas

worked his way eastward across the island towards George's field station in the Luquillo Mountains. On his way, wouldn't you know, he discovered a new species of frog. Yes, it was all yellow in color and – that's right – it appeared to have an extraordinary reproductive strategy!

Richard was both elated and distraught. His discovery was clearly phenomenal, but he couldn't help but wonder whether my urging that he visit George might not relate to this exact same creature. What a disaster that would be! But, there was an easy solution. If Richard left the island directly without visiting Drewery, he could then write up his discovery with a clear conscience. Knowing that Drewery had a discovery of his own, Richard could get his published quickly just in case it was the same as George's. Besides, Richard knew that George was slow and methodical so there would be no trouble beating him into print.

Yet, this approach bothered Richard Thomas. Had Drewery discovered the frog first, he was entitled to describe it. This, regardless of Richard having made his discovery independently. Gearing up to the prospect of a severe letdown, Richard went to see Drewery. And, of course, his worst expectations were realized; Drewery had already discovered the golden coqui.

A particularly peculiar episode of discovery in which I was again involved interwove both a pretty, little bird and a weird-looking local toad. Let's first look at the toad, commonly referred to as the crested toad.

Though Puerto Rico supports 16 species of *Eleutherodactylus* tree frogs, it sustains but a single species of native toad. Not quite endemic to Puerto Rico, the crested toad, or sapo concho as it is named locally, is nearly so since the only other locality to which it is native is Virgin Gorda, one of the small British Virgin Islands. Furthermore, on Virgin Gorda the crested toad is known from a single specimen collected there in 1915 and one more recent

217

record. It is generally believed to be on the verge of extirpation from that island if not already locally extinct. The crested toad in Puerto Rico has scarcely fared much better. First discovered in 1868, this animal is so rare that subsequent gaps between sightings span 30, 40 or even 50 years. Not only that, but such rediscoveries usually involved only a few individuals, most or all of which were immediately pickled in collecting jars. Such an approach to rediscovering so rare an animal hardly serves that critter's best interests. But what can I say, herpetologists are a peculiar lot. Clearly this animal, if it still existed, was extremely rare and local in distribution.

One factor that now made the possibility of locating the crested toad somewhat more difficult was the introduction and establishment of the Surinam or marine toad. Brought to Puerto Rico intentionally around 1919 to combat major insect pests of sugar cane, the Surinam toad spread rapidly and was soon common over the entire coastal plain. A very large amphibian, the Surinam toad measures about a foot in length with legs outstretched. Introduction of this alien toad could lead to it competing with or feeding on the native species. The latter has recently been shown to be the case. To be sure, the presence of the abundant Surinam toad made it difficult to locate the rarer form simply because of the tendency searchers develop to ignore all toads, presuming them to represent the common form.

This certainly tended to be the case with me, but not to such an extent that my attention was not caught by a small aberrant looking toad I happened to stumble upon on the golf course of Dorado Beach Hotel of all places.

Now it may not seem that a golf course is an appropriate place to find an endangered toad, but my discovery happened to be made only a short distance from a very unusual habitat in Puerto Rico – a *Pterocarpus* swamp. *Pterocarpus oficinalis* commonly known as swamp bloodwood due to a blood-red substance in its bark, grows on the island in pure stands where pools of fresh water accumulate, periodically inundating the roots to depths of from a few inches to several feet. What other niche characteristics limit the distribution of this species I do not know, but they are narrow enough that only four or five small patches of swamp bloodwood were then known to exist in Puerto Rico.

Such *Pterocarpus* forests are fascinating places to visit. For one, they are just downright lovely. Swamp bloodwood distinguishes itself from practically any other tree in Puerto Rico by the form of its spectacular buttress roots. These tree supports wind out like serpents for as much as ten feet from the trunk and create all kinds of interesting patterns. The trunk and branches are also typically embellished by an impressive array of ferns and orchids, much more amply adorned than most lowland forest trees. These forests also appear to have associated with them a number of unusual animals. Most important, from my perspective, was the potential of finding the extremely rare West Indian whistling-duck, a species nearly extirpated from the island. Locally named the chiriria, a rendition of the bird's curious whinnying call, this large and apparently tasty duck had been hunted to near oblivion. Nevertheless, some of the few leads I had for still locating these birds were referable to two other *Pterocarpus* swamps further east near the towns of Loiza and Humacao respectively. Apparently whistling-ducks use these forests to roost during the day, since they primarily feed at night. Or, they might even breed here as the West Indian whistling-duck primarily nests in tree cavities.

It was in search of this duck that I found myself out on the Dorado Beach golf course for I am not a golfer, having never progressed beyond miniature. The *Pterocarpus* swamp, being next to the course, made it far and away the most accessible of any such swamp remaining, besides being well protected on the hotel grounds. I was merely traversing the golf course after having spent a fruitless dawn searching in the swamp for those elusive waterfowl.

Any frustrations I may have harbored at not locating whistling-ducks were immediately swept away when I caught sight of this peculiar toad. Not only was it much smaller than any self-respecting Surinam toad should be, but it also seemed to have unusual facial ridges that reminded me of the complicated descriptions I had read in the scientific literature describing the crested toad. By a stroke of good fortune I happened to have my camera with me and so was able to simply photograph the toad without having to incarcerate the animal until it could be properly identified.

A long week passed before my developed slides arrived in the mail. Examining them through a viewer I was pleased that I had gotten an excellent close-up of my toad, and I was anxious to obtain a definitive confirmation of its identity.

The following evening, with my precious slide in a protective box carried in my shirt pocket, I drove east from San Juan for a full hour along the coastal highway. Then turning sharply inland through the country town of Mameyes, I proceeded up the steep, winding road that penetrates the rain forest of the Sierra de Luquillo via the great mountain of El Yunque. Cattle pastures on the lower slopes soon gave way to experimental forestry plots of kadam and pine. Still higher began the natural forest, edged by clumps of introduced bamboos along the road and dissected by numerous fast-coursing streams which drained away the rains that bathed the mountain daily. Here the rain forest at night took on an aura all its own, water dripping from the vegetation, mist swirling about, and all the while a medley of innumerable tree frogs sustaining a chorus matched in few other of the world's realms. On top of all this, the ubiquitous yagrumo tree, a standout during the day by virtue of its two-foot wide leaves, is by night even more imposing. It is only after dark that one notices the silvery undersides of the leaves which on a breezy, moonlit night dance over the forest like a great festival of ghosts. El Yunque at night certainly has a wild and eerie atmosphere all its own, one of which I never tired. But on this trip my mind was on other things: it was set on verifying the rediscovery of Puerto Rico's endemic toad.

Since George Drewery was out of town at this time, I had decided to take a shot at seeing Cam Kepler, who was working in the forest to conserve the extremely endangered Puerto Rican parrot. Cam, though primarily a bird specialist, was an excellent all round biologist who, even if he could not confirm the identity of my toad, was a friend with whom I looked forward to sharing my discovery. Since he and his wife Kay had no phone in their mountain-side dwelling, I took a risk that they would be at home that evening working up their day's field notes. My hunch proved correct for as I approached their house from the steep, curved driveway, the lights were on indicating their presence.

I always enjoyed going up to see the Keplers because, aside from their pleasant company, I usually came away having learned new tidbits about birds and ecology generally. One of the most profitable ideas I had gotten from the Keplers came coincidentally from discussions concerning new birds they had found on the island. Among these were several exotic species that had become established – the Java finch from the South Pacific, the Hispaniolan parrot from Puerto Rico's western neighbor, and the canary-winged parakeet native to portions of South America. Just in the course of their other work around the island, the Keplers had stumbled upon these birds, all of which were apparently now breeding locally. Of course birds from such distant lands had not arrived in Puerto Rico naturally. All three of these species were common cage birds and had doubtless been imported. At some point enough individuals either escaped or were released by owners tired of caring for them that they were able to find mates and reproduce in the wild. What interested me was that the Keplers had discovered these newly established species only coincidentally. Could there be others? Since cage bird escapees occur where there are people and people are most common in cities, wouldn't it be likely that the best chances of finding established exotics would be in parks and greenbelts in and around urban areas?

My deductions proved correct. Initiating surveys in undeveloped portions of San Juan, I was quickly paid off one dawn when I encountered a small flock of half a dozen unusual finches with pretty brown ringlets marking their white breasts. It took me some while to track down just what these exotics were, and it turned out they were nutmeg mannikins native to portions of Southeast Asia. I was ecstatic. I continued my green-area searches.

The results were remarkable. I was discovering new birds previously unknown from Puerto Rico hand over fist. On one occasion I discovered the presence of the Indian silverbill in a seemingly abandoned naval reserve in the center of San Juan. While tracking this small flock, it took off across the Martin Pena canal into Santurce, a heavily inhabited portion of the city. I wondered where they might find appropriate habitat in this crowded environment. Pulling out my map, I noticed that a local college lay along the flight path the birds had taken. Anticipating the grounds might have ample green space, I hopped in my car and headed to the campus. Having guessed correctly, I found my silverbills there. But that was not all. While searching the campus for the silverbills, I was drawn by an unusual call up in a tree. This turned out to belong to a different exotic – an entirely yellow bird with a fiery orange crown – it was the beautiful saffron finch, a bird native to South America. I had found two bird species new to Puerto Rico in one day!

My luck did not stop with these birds. Over time I managed to discover about 15 species that were now probably breeding on the island and had never previously been recorded. In addition, I discovered many other species that were represented by only one or a few individuals. This bonanza of new birds, apparently established over the previous one or two decades, had gone undiscovered due to a lack of recent ornithological activity on the island.

Besides the Keplers who confined their work to more natural environs, the only other reputed bird authority on the island at this time was a fellow by the name of Nathan Leopold. Does that name ring a bell? It did to me. Leopold, many years earlier, had made a name for himself by trying to commit the perfect murder. He and his associate, Richard Loeb, both young boys from wealthy families, had failed in getting away with their crime and thanks only to the efforts of the great defense attorney Clarence Darrow, did they manage to get off with imprisonment rather than the death penalty. This did Loeb little good because he was murdered in jail, but Leopold was freed after nearly 13 years of confinement. When I met him, not without a certain amount of trepidation, he was an ailing old man who had long passed being active in the field. Nevertheless, we did go to the field together on a few occasions, the highlights of which were his relentless display of egotism and a totally unwarranted diatribe against police which was set off simply by seeing one walk by. Nathan Leopold passed away not long after I had gotten to know him, and I offered to buy his two collecting guns from his fine wife. Upon reporting these to the police to obtain clearance for the purchase, I was informed that the guns were in fact unregistered and that he had possessed them illegally. They were confiscated.

Leopold did have an interest in making dramatic discoveries during the period I knew him, but his numerous ailments forced him into inactivity. Though he lived in San Juan, he discovered not a single exotic species there. That left quite an opportunity for me.

During my visits to the Keplers on El Yunque, we always exchanged our latest discoveries. On this occasion, with the toad photo in my pocket, I expected to clearly have made the biggest discovery since our last get together. I could not have been more wrong.

"We discovered a new bird," Cam said to me with a big smile after initial hellos and introducing me to a famous scientist from the States who had come down for a brief visit.

"Oh, that's neat," I responded, not too surprised. I had already discovered several introduced species by this time and there were likely others to be found. "Where is it from?" I asked, wondering whether it was an escapee from South America, Africa, or elsewhere.

"You don't understand." said Cam. "I mean we discovered a totally new species of bird. A new endemic for Puerto Rico."

Unbelievable! That's all there was to it. Unbelievable.

A new species of bird had not been discovered on any island in the West Indies in over 40 years, since 1927 to be exact. And where were those discoveries made? Not in anyone's backyard, I can tell you that. Two discoveries happened to have been made in 1927, in Cuba and Hispaniola respectively, both requiring expeditions of many days to reach the habitats of the undiscovered birds. Relatively speaking, practically every inch of Puerto Rico could presently be reached by road leaving scant refuge for any bird to remain undetected. Puerto Rico also had been fairly well combed by such capable ornithologists as Wetmore, Danforth, and McCandless. No new species had been discovered during the entire twentieth century.

Clearly the bird had to be a doozy. It would make sense that the species was nocturnal and had an insect-like call, thus throwing off ornithologists. Or, another reasonable possibility was a drab, ground-dwelling form that stayed among thick vegetation, rarely flew, and had a feeble call. Neither of these proved to be the case.

What the Keplers had discovered was a diminutive bird, not drab at all, but rather boldly marked in black and white. It had gone undetected for several reasons. First, the species is practically confined to an extremely limited, inhospitable, and remote habitat. It inhabits the windswept and rain-soaked dwarf forest or elfin woodlands which cover exposed ridges and the highest peaks of Puerto Rico's mountains. Even in this habitat, however, the species is an uncommon one and is only spottily distributed. Also, despite its seemingly conspicuous coloration, the bird is easily lost to view among the dense tangles of vines of the forest canopy which is its abode. Not least important is the fact that the bird's call is extremely similar to that of the most common bird of the dwarf forest, and virtually everywhere else for that matter, the ubiquitous bananaquit. The new bird's appearance is also coincidentally disguised by another species. For three quarters of the year Puerto Rico's forests support a large number of migratory species which come south to winter. Among these is a bird quite similar to the new species in both shape and appearance and known as the black- and- white warbler. Since this migratory warbler is so common much of the year, most observers struggling with their binoculars to follow the movements of a black and white bird through the vegetation would casually identify the species as being the migrant. As a case in point, the Keplers themselves had worked in the forest an entire year before it occurred to them that they had a new bird on their hands. The coincidental similarity of the new bird's call with one common forest species and of its coloration with another were enough to thwart its detection well into the twentieth century. This was truly a major new discovery, and it was exciting to be one of the first to know about it.

For a while I completely forgot about the toad slide which had been burning a hole in my pocket while Cam and Kay told me of how it had gradually dawned on them that they had a new species, literally in their backyard. Seeing black and white birds in the dwarf forest when all the migrants should have left was one important clue. They then proceeded to show me the few priceless specimens they had managed to collect as scientific documentation of the bird's existence. Considering the bird's limited habitat preference, the Keplers chose to name the bird after that environment, selecting the catchy phrase "elfin woods warbler."

It was some time after the Keplers' spectacular discovery that they learned they had almost been beaten to the punch. Apparently some years earlier an extremely adept bird watcher had observed an unusual warbler in Puerto Rico and, realizing he had something special, drew its picture. Taking this to a museum in the States he was informed that though his drawing seemed to represent a new species, he would have to collect a specimen for confirmation. He never did.

A very puzzling attribute of the elfin woods warbler is why it is practically confined to dwarf forest – an ecological mystery that is still unsolved. During the fall, 27 species of warblers migrate to Puerto Rico. Here they spend the winter scattered throughout most of the island's numerous habitats, then returning in the spring to their breeding grounds in the United States and Canada. Subsequent to the departure of the migrants, only three native warblers remain in Puerto Rico to breed. Not only are the number of warbler species present remarkably low in the summer, but the three resident forms are all extraordinarily limited in their habitat distributions. The elfin woods warbler is confined to but a few mountaintops. The yellow warbler is just the opposite, occupying only mangrove forests fringing the coast. The remaining species, Adelaide's warbler, occurs only in the lowlands and foothills in the western half of the island. That leaves a tremendous amount of habitat unoccupied during the summer by any warbler species at all. Since most of these areas support various warblers during the winter, it is difficult to explain why they are empty in summer.

The most reasonable explanation for the shift is that insect populations may decline during summer months depriving warblers of their principal food supply. Yet, even if an insect decline occurs, it is hard to imagine it being so dramatic as to prohibit the survival of a single warbler species in many habitats. One argument against a decline in the summer abundance of invertebrates is that the black swift, a species which feeds exclusively on insects, breeds in Puerto Rico during the summer and then migrates southward in winter. This behavior is reputedly pre-cipitated by a lack of prey during winter, a case contrary to that of the warblers. Several other bird species which breed on the island apparently also leave during winter, reputedly the result of insect scarcity. Whatever the explanation for the nearly six-fold reduction in Puerto Rico's warbler population, it appears not to be a simple one.

An intriguing question deriving from Puerto Rico's peculiar warbler fluctuations is whether the island possesses a significant number of unfilled ecological niches, at least in summer. Some scientists tend to believe that mother nature does not like to leave significant amounts of unutilized niche space. Puerto Rico's summer warbler situation suggests the contrary. It will probably be some time before we understand the evolutionary factors which have resulted in the dramatic differences between Puerto Rico's sparse summer warbler populations and copious winter bounty.

Another peculiar aspect of the elfin woods warbler's limited range related to it having few similar species with which to compete during summer. In comparing bird species that inhabit islands with those from continents, several interesting differences have been found. One of these relates to distribution. Generally speaking, on continents, each species of bird appears to be relatively limited in the number of habitats which it might occupy. Some species are limited to coastal mangroves, others to lowland forests, still others to mountain slopes between 2,000 and 4,000 feet, and so on. Conversely, island birds tend to be broadly distributed among habitats. For example, many species which occur in Puerto Rico's coastal mangroves are likewise present in mountain rain forests. Moreover, such broad distributions on islands are the rule rather than the exception. What factors might explain these differences between island and continental species?

The standard explanation for island species being habitat generalists is referable to a concept termed ecological release. This idea derives from the belief that very few mainland species ever stray far enough offshore to potentially colonize oceanic islands. The lack of colonizers on islands allows those few species which are successful to expand, using all available habitats, since competitors for these habitats are few or none. In other words, the lack of competition allows successful colonists to release into unoccupied habitats from which they were excluded on the mainland.

If this concept is true, might we not expect Puerto Rico's native warblers to experience ecological release and spread much more broadly across the island once the numerous North American migrants leave, and then once again contract their ranges when the migrants return in the fall? There is presently no evidence that such shifts in fact occur to any significant degree. Puerto Rico's eastern foothills and lowlands, excluding mangroves, remain totally uninhabited throughout the summer by any warbler species. Ecological release is a very interesting concept which requires rigorous testing. Puerto Rico seems like an ideal locality for such investigations.

Another scenario that explains equally well the broad distributions of island birds might be termed the hurricane-hedging hypothesis. I have coined this phrase for I have not seen this explanation described anywhere else. In the Caribbean, and other island areas where tropical storms are common, hurricanes rather than competition might well be the principal environmental factor influencing where birds will tend to distribute themselves on islands. Unlike birds on continents, island species have finite limits set decisively by the size of the island as to where they might expand their ranges. In other words, no matter how adaptable the bird, even if it can occupy every inch of a small island, its range can only be small. Now, having a limited range is a dangerous proposition. A serious epidemic may strike the island; where can a portion of the population find refuge from the scourge? Likewise, many island archipelagos, such as the West Indies, are in tropical storm belts. More often than not hurricanes in the Western Hemisphere typically leave their mark on one or more Caribbean islands. Relating this to birds, there is no need to be reminded just how delicate these feathered creatures are, consequently, 100 mile per hour winds are hardly inconsequential to their plumage! There is also the indirect impact caused by damage to food plants, nest trees, and the like. It does not seem unreasonable to expect that nearly every individual bird might perish which has the misfortune of being directly in the path of a severe hurricane. If this is the case, there is a fundamental strategy for species of small islands which is essential to their long-term survival: spread out as much as possible! In this way, a hurricane annihilating everything on a particular mountaintop may leave a few survivors on the coast, and so on. Broad distribution enhances survival.

There are several cases of locally distributed birds in Puerto Rico nearly being extirpated by hurricanes. The troupial, a type of oriole, likely introduced to the island long ago, was common only around the town of Quebradilla late in the nineteenth century. That is, until it was virtually extirpated by the devastating hurricane San Ciriaco of 1899. The Puerto Rican flycatcher nearly succumbed following hurricane San Filipe in 1928. Other examples exist from other islands.

The elfin woods warbler would certainly be in jeopardy if it were confined only to the dwarf forest of the Luquillo Mountains. Field work would have to be done to determine its total range, and the Keplers invited me to participate in the exciting survey. This I did, and we later enjoyed a number of memorable days hiking and camping in the forest seeking out this elusive bird. Fortuitously, subsequent to our work, other observers found the elfin woods warbler at the other end of Puerto Rico in the Maricao forest. Two widely separated populations of the bird existed, a very important condition as a hurricane hedge. Today four disjunct populations of this warbler are known for the island.

Having lapped up every detail of the new discovery, I wanted to hear many facets of the story once again if for no other reason than for the sheer magnitude of the event alone. It was, therefore, some time before we moved away from the most historical ornithological discovery to be made in Puerto Rico in decades to the matter which had brought me to the rain forest that night in the first place – my enticing toad slide.

"I don't feel entirely comfortable making this identification, being that we're dealing with an amphibian," put in Cam as I delicately removed the slide from its protective wrapping.

"That's alright," offered the Kepler's distinguished scientific visitor who suddenly appeared to have received a shot of adrenaline. "Project the slide up on that bare wall and dig up Karl Schmidt's 'Scientific Survey of Porto Rico and the Virgin Islands.' Let's have a go at it," he commanded, now taking charge.

The idea of using Schmidt's work, the classic on Puerto Rico's herpetofauna published in 1928, had not gone unconsidered by me as a tool for verifying my toad's identity. The problem was the descriptive text was virtually unintelligible. Perhaps this big name scientist would have better success.

"The superciliary crests are extraordinarily elevated, having an arched outline and descending steeply to the loreal region." I almost caught what that meant. The expert, with brow furrowed, glanced at the projected photograph with the toad now 100 times larger than life. "That fits. Next."

"It is angulate posteriorly, joining the almost equally developed supratympanic ridge." I was starting to get lost. "Okay," boomed the authority.

"Loreal region very concave, canthus concave and very close together." I was lost. "Fine," he went on.

"Parotoids broad oval, directed obliquely downwards, covered like the remainder of the upper surfaces of the body and limbs, with numerous closely placed subround tubercles, with rugose surfaces." Oh, for those rugose surfaces, they are really something, aren't they? We awaited the verdict of the authority who was obviously in his element. Considering he was a bird specialist, his mastery of toad lingo was awesome. "No doubt about the rugose surfaces," he proclaimed. "So far, so good."

From there we went on to the corneus ridge which everyone knows is on the inner margin of the tarsus and then to the half webbed toes with strong dermal margins. Lastly, but certainly not least, were the two strong carpal tubercles, features which might drive a frog specialist mad but for which at this point I had no compunction to search.

"That's it!" shrieked the renown scientist who had become ever more animated with each rugose tubercle and corneus ridge that we encountered. "Your photo is of *Bufo lemur!* You have rediscovered the Puerto Rican crested toad!"

That pronouncement was enough to change my mood and then some. From a state of awe at this expert's confidence and skill in an area that was not his specialty coupled with a feeling of inadequacy at being spectator to a matter well over my head, I transformed into a state of euphoria at having my discovery corroborated.

Puerto Rican crested toad

A new species of bird and a supposedly extinct toad had both made news in the annals of the island's natural history virtually at the same moment. It was indeed late before I left the Keplers and their guest, driving down the mountain with a feeling of pride and fulfillment. So absorbed was I in reliving the night's events that even the ghostlike yagrumo leaves dancing in the wind failed to distract me from the bliss of this moment.

Though corroboration of the toad's identification no longer seemed necessary, I had left the slide with Cam so that he could show it to George Drewery upon his return to the island. Surely George would be interested in seeing evidence of the discovery.

It was some weeks before I chanced to see Cam again, and it

and social system. Gifford Pinchot, Aldo Leopold, Rachel Carson, are a few of these luminaries. Science, however, is a method of looking at things. It is not a set of ethics or morals. Science is about testing hypotheses – Is the hypothesis correct or incorrect.

There is nothing in science about right or wrong. There is nothing in science about taking pride in one's natural heritage. There is nothing in science about conserving the earth for future generations. There is nothing in science about educating people and elevating communities. There is nothing in science about – well, you get the picture.

Since scientists in the U.S. were among the first to detect the deteriorating condition of our environment, they turned to what they knew best to convey their concerns to the American public. They used numbers and graphs and figures and tables. There was limited attention to the development of an environmental ethic as a moral imperative.

What has been the result? The U.S. methodically wiped out the gray wolf via a relentless campaign of hunting, trapping and poisoning. The mountain lion, hardly a serious threat to humans, has been virtually eliminated from the eastern U.S. and has been driven to the most remote forest tracts in the west. The grizzly bear, a legitimate threat to humans and their livestock, number but a few hundred individuals in the lower 48 states where they survive only in parks and remote backcountry. The American bison, not even a true pest, was reduced from many millions of individuals to only a few thousand at present. And this does not even count the decimation we have caused to totally harmless species such as the ivory-billed woodpecker, passenger pigeon, Carolina parakeet, Eskimo curlew, Bachman's warbler, and many others.

Let's compare this to the situation in India. India has over one billion people. The U.S. has less than one-third of that. That one billion people is squashed into a land mass only about one-third the size of the U.S. – that is to say, it is rather crowded. So, India has approximately 250 people per square kilometer compared to approximately 27 per square kilometer in the U.S. And what of these people? For one thing, over one-third of them, a number greater than the entire population of the U.S., live in

235

abject poverty – a circumstance not conducive to caring about the environment. On top of this, India's scientific capabilities in the area of natural sciences, though admirable, are not in the same league as those of the U.S.

Why do I offer these figures? To suggest that India should be a basket case with regard to wildlife conservation if we use measures so admired if not revered by Americans – reduced population size, high standard of living, and science as the driving force for conservation.

Yet, what else might we say about India? India has approximately 3,000 tigers roaming at will in the wild. It also has countless leopards known to have preyed on humans from time in memorial. India sustains approximately 25,000 Asian elephants which make terrible neighbors for rural farmers. There are estimated to be at least 2,000 wolves ranging freely over the countryside. These, not to mention innumerable "muggers" the huge, deadly crocodiles which used to take thousands of lives per year throughout that nation. And let us not forget the various cobras, including the king cobra, a notorious threat to humans, even to the present day.

Why? Why can animals of all sort, even the most dangerous imaginable, survive in India in close proximity to humans while, in the U.S. all efforts are made to exterminate them? I believe the answer lies with India's conservation ethic. Most Indians have it built into the moral fabric of their being, and that of their society, through religion. Children learn from their earliest years to have the highest regard for animals, not based upon scientific studies, but upon moral teachings.

Contrarily, in the U.S. the case for wildlife conservation is not a moral one. It is more one of scientific debate. "Prove to me the species is declining and then I will think about saving it." or "Quantify that the species provides some benefit to me to counteract my belief that it is a nuisance."

U.S. scientists who were among the first to recognize the need for conservation and to this day are world leaders in this field still have not learned how to achieve this goal. There remains the propensity to ask for far too much scientific study and not nearly enough education, education specifically regarding our ethical and moral perceptions about wildlife and the entire natural world. While scientists focus on researching, monitoring, assessing, counting and inventorying of every last critter in need of conservation, many of these plants and animals will likely pass into oblivion long before their data collecting is done and they are prepared to initiate active conservation measures.

This is not to say that scientists do not have an important role in conservation, they do. What I am saying is that science is not the backbone of conservation as is often claimed. Or, if it is, environmental education and development of a true environmental ethic are the heart and soul of conservation – the essence of the matter.

The Waterless Swamp

It is not fair to give the impression that everything that went on in Puerto Rico was a comedy of errors. I had some outstanding coworkers who, despite great limitations with regard to equipment, gasoline and vehicles, as well as administrative and supervisory support, performed outstanding field work in every corner of the island not to mention its most remote offshore cays. George Drewery, who discovered the golden coqui, was just one example.

The island showed signs, as well, that individuals with great vision and commitment had been at work decades before us. Probably the most outstanding reflection of this was the complex of Commonwealth forests located around the island. These dozen or so forests had not been located just randomly. Rather, their placement had clearly been thought out so as to cover a wide array of Puerto Rico's unique natural features. These included, among others, the huge mangrove forest on the north coast, the fascinating haystack hills, various mountainous areas spanning the central spine of the island, dry southwestern coastal forest, and even Puerto Rico's most distinctive offshore island – Mona.

Furthermore, not only had these special areas been set aside as far back as early in the 20th century, but most were dramatically augmented by trail systems and simple infrastructure during the 1930's by impressive efforts of the Civilian Conservation Corps.

One of these areas, the Boqueron Commonwealth Forest, turned out to be a site which I came to know fairly well and which taught me a lot of lessons regarding wildlife conservation.

Let me begin by clarifying that the Boqueron Commonwealth Forest was no longer a forest. It was a swamp. And it was usually a dry swamp at that. Of its more than 400 acres, 399 were usually dry as a bone. Well, not really. I don't want to exaggerate. Let's say about 350 of its acres were as dry as a bone. The remainder had shallow puddles and meandering channels fringed with mangrove.

There was evidence that Boqueron had once been a forest. Dead snags of formerly huge trees occurred widely throughout the reserve, and many more had toppled over forming a maze of dead timber across much of the landscape.

The most dramatic human-made feature of the site was a dike, perhaps 10 feet high and more than wide enough for one vehicle to drive, but barely wide enough for two, so that passing a second vehicle required some caution. This dike virtually enveloped the reserve. The dike formed a square, the outer border of which was edged by water channels, except for the western side which was bordered by the sea.

Through the dike, at various locations, were water control structures. These structures were simply culverts under the dike which allowed one to control the inflow or outflow of water by manipulating by hand sets of wooden planks which served as adjustable dams at one end of each culvert.

Apparently what had happened here was that an impressive mangrove forest had been intentionally enclosed by construction of the dike. By cutting off the natural penetration of sea water from tides and storms, the vast majority of the mangrove trees had died.

What was not so apparent was why this had been done. Or rather, not so much why, but why here?

The "why" was evidently to create an open wetland for waterfowl. This wetland was to replace two other wetlands formerly not far distant, Anegada and Guanica lagoons, which had been entirely drained in the 1950's for conversion to agricultural and pasture lands.

The "why here" was more challenging. Boqueron reserve is located near Puerto Rico's extreme southwestern corner. This is the absolute driest part of the island. Only a few miles south of the reserve is an area where it might not rain even once during an entire year. Channels outside the dike were constructed to provide fresh water to the impoundment. Typically, however, these channels contained so little of that substance that water levels did not rise high enough to pass through culverts into the reserve.

Absence of water in the channels, coupled with the near absence of rain, compounded by the cutting off of tidal waters, exacerbated by clogging of the channels by invasive aquatic vegetation, all of these conspired to create one heck of a dry waterfowl impoundment. Were the fallen trees to be taken away the impoundment would have served better as baseball diamonds than as waterfowl ponds.

So "why here"? Evidently the brain-trusts who devised this plan wanted to replace the drained lagoons with equivalent habitat in a nearby area. Converting the Boqueron forest to a waterfowl impoundment likely was the only alternative in this water-stressed region.

It was my responsibility for the better part of two years to conduct waterfowl studies for the Department of Natural Resources. A particular focus of the studies was to determine the status of Puerto Rico's native breeding waterfowl, particularly the ruddy duck, West Indian whistling-duck, and white-cheeked pintail. As circumstances would have it, the latter two species had become so reduced in numbers by the time of my study that they had virtually disappeared from the island. That left only the ruddy duck in adequate numbers for me to collect meaningful data. And, you guessed it, Boqueron refuge was a site I visited to seek out this bird.

My study focused on these three waterfowl species because they were important to hunters, were declining, and because they nested in Puerto Rico. That they nested in Puerto Rico was especially important. Such species tend to occur on the island year round giving us much greater potential to manage them.

This circumstance was counter to that for the vast majority of other waterfowl such as blue-winged teal, green-winged teal, northern pintails and American wigeon, to name but a few, which were seasonal migrants and do not nest on the island. These birds breed far north in the pothole region of Canada and the central United States, only visiting Puerto Rico during their lengthy migration south and, perhaps, for a few months of winter.

Migratory waterfowl were still moderately common, only in a relative sense, in Puerto Rico. These birds too had declined, primarily due to habitat destruction, but they were not nearly as decimated as the native forms. They were better off simply because they were replaced annually by other individuals ranging from their expansive breeding populations in North America. Only a handful of the huge populations of these migratory waterfowl depend upon Puerto Rico as a stop-over or wintering site. Thus, these birds are relatively unimpacted by whatever hunting practices Puerto Rico might choose to implement. If Puerto Rico severely over-hunted the birds one year, others would come to take their place the next.

This was opposite the case for the three resident waterfowl. Resident waterfowl, almost by definition, do not move around a lot. Generally, they only move under duress – loss of habitat, inadequate food, intensive hunting, things like that. Thus, if local waterfowl are killed off, birds from neighboring areas would only be likely to stray sporadically to Puerto Rico. Exacerbating the problem is the fact that the West Indian whistling-duck, in particular, has a total world population confined to but a few islands of the Caribbean, not the expansive plains of a huge continent. The Caribbean subspecies of the ruddy duck is nearly in the same boat. Additionally, the resident species were under severe pressure on most other Caribbean islands similar to that which they were facing in Puerto Rico.

The ruddy duck is the only one of the three species of waterfowl I was studying that occurs in North America, and it does so widely. Most of Puerto Rico's ruddy ducks, however, do not migrate to the continent. Rather, they remain in Puerto Rico or on adjacent islands the year round and have become so isolated from their North American cousins that they have become a distinctive Caribbean subspecies. Among other characteristics, local Caribbean ruddy ducks tend to have scattered black spots on their distinctive white cheeks. The males that is. Male ruddy ducks are also characterized by an overall reddish-brown coloration, a bright blue bill during breeding season, and a short, stiff tail, often held erect. Females share the stiff tail, but are dark brown overall and have a distinctive horizontal dark stripe below the eye.

A compilation of hunter bag data demonstrated a continuous and precipitous decline of this bird over the previous few decades that showed no signs of leveling off. My field observations corroborated this – ruddy ducks had become exceedingly scarce on the island. It was my job to find out why, and fast, or the bird would become so scarce we would be unable to collect enough data to understand the cause of the decline and thus take actions to reverse it.

As dry as Boqueron refuge was, it did support a few ruddy ducks. Also, the dike gave hunters access to otherwise remote portions of the swamp, consequently the refuge was favored by these camouflaged intrepids. It did not take a genius to recognize that a quick and invaluable source of useful data would be to set up a station at the entrance to the refuge and check the breeding condition of all ruddy ducks shot. So that's what I did.

Ruddy duck

And did I learn something – and quick! Checking of each female's reproductive tract indicated that nearly all of them were in the midst of their reproductive cycles! Some had enlarged ducts, a sign that eggs had recently been laid. Others had eggs in differing stages of development still in their oviducts. Of about a dozen females shot, more than three out of four were in the midst of breeding.

The ramifications of this were obvious. No animal can sustain its numbers when, in the midst of its breeding season, a stream of people invade their environment with guns and shoot at them at every opportunity.

You will also recall that I mentioned only about a dozen

females were shot. This is the total shot by more than a hundred hunters over several weekends. Not much of a harvest! That is because Boqueron had so little water the ducks had nary a place to swim nonetheless breed. And you can bet that the concentration of hunters in the limited pockets of water in the refuge was such that few if any nestling ruddy ducks survived long enough to leave the nest. Tramping through the refuge and seeing broken ruddy duck eggs floating in one of the channels only served to corroborate the tragic conditions that likely had been playing out for these beautiful ducks year after year in Puerto Rico's wetlands.

And the hunting of ruddy ducks was not off limits!

Hunters were scarcely happy about this situation. They were frustrated for sure. Who wouldn't be. You get up at four o'clock in the morning to get to the refuge well before dawn. You slog through mud, climb over logs, and put up with mosquitoes and no-see-ums while you find your favorite spot. And then you sit there and wait for just a few ducks to come to this one pond which you are sharing with far too many compatriots with the same goal as you. I do not recall the numbers, but it was the rule, not the exception, that following hours in that inhospitable swamp far more hunters than not had failed to bag a single duck.

It certainly was not ruddy ducks that kept hunting alive in Puerto Rico. Waterfowl hunting is sustained by the migratory ducks which breed in much safer wetlands in North America as discussed earlier. These birds come to Puerto Rico as full-grown individuals and, consequently, have at least some chance to survive the gauntlet presented by Puerto Rico's hunter-choked wetlands in the fall and winter. Nearly a dozen species of waterfowl fall within this category. Blue-winged and green-winged teal are among the most common of these migrants. These are followed by the American wigeon or baldpate, the latter name derived from the white stripe down the center of the male's crown giving the appearance of baldness. Northern pintails and northern shovelers are next trailed by a host of rarer species such as the ring-necked duck and fulvous whistling-duck.

Further threatening to the survival of the ruddy duck was the fact that the hunting season was divided into two components. Waterfowl hunting ran from October to November. Then there was a hiatus of nearly a month, and it started up again in December running into January. The purpose of the hiatus was to give waterfowl a chance to revisit areas from which they had been frightened. Thus, restarting the season in December would offer better hunting. Unfortunately, the downside of this approach, heretofore unknown, was that this extended the misfortune of nesting ruddy ducks for a full five month period. No wonder the bird was experiencing a relentless decline.

Drainage of wetlands in Puerto Rico, as exemplified by Anegada and Guanica lagoons in the southwest, had resulted in freshwater marshes being one of the scarcest habitats on the island. Coupling of this habitat loss with poorly thought out hunting regulations was more than enough to threaten the survival of even the most prolific species.

Based upon the information I had collected, and holding of a number of public hearings, I drafted new hunting regulations for Puerto Rico. I believed three steps were necessary to try and reduce the negative impacts of hunting on the ruddy duck. First, was to take the ruddy duck off the list of game species. This would make hunting them illegal. Second, it was essential to eliminate the split hunting season. This action would reduce by approximately one month the period of time hunters would be wading through the swamps hunting and, unintentionally, impacting the birds while they were breeding. Third, I thought it important to close off one or two areas entirely from hunting so that at least some ruddy ducks would have a fair chance to raise their young in peace.

It is a significant understatement to say that these recommendations were highly controversial. The numbers of ducks of all types shot by hunters had been declining for years. What with the steady draining of wetlands, their overgrowth by cattails and water hyacinths due to the influx of fertilizers, plus the decline of native breeding waterfowl, this was no wonder. The last thing Puerto Rico's hunters wanted was a further curtailment of their already suffering pastime.

I shall not describe further the gyrations I went through

to adopt and implement these modifications to the hunting regulations. That is another story. What is significant here is that I had taken a number of steps which had upset the hunting community and it was important to try and show that these new restrictions had been made with their best interests, and that of the waterfowl resource, at heart. Easier said than done.

Improvement of Puerto Rico's wetlands as waterfowl habitat seemed an important way to show some positive initiative by the DNR that the hunter community would appreciate. But what improvements might we undertake?

Boqueron was an obvious basket case, but perhaps something could be done to improve its productivity for waterfowl. So, I began asking around as to why the U. S. government had invested so much money to build dikes in a swamp which had no water. No one in Puerto Rico had any idea. Several of my associates who worked for the U. S. Fish and Wildlife Service did not know. Then I got lucky and found someone who had been around at the time the decision was made to impound Boqueron. The answer I received was quite revealing. "Why, aren't you fellows pumping water into the refuge to maintain water levels?" was the response.

How about that. A pump! Why hadn't I thought of that! That's what the DNR got for hiring a science teacher to do the work of a wildlife biologist! But okay, I got the picture. Here was a way, in one simple step, that we could improve Boqueron overnight. Fantastic! I'd see to it right away. Waterfowl would benefit and the hunters would be ecstatic. This would be the first major step taken in decades that would improve their lot, significantly improve conditions for waterfowl and, in the bargain, likely have spin-offs that would favor native waterfowl breeding. What an opportunity!

I rushed to the management division responsible for day to day operations of Boqueron and Puerto Rico's other protected areas to inform them of my discovery and urge them to obtain a pump. They were less than impressed.

"We don't have the money," their chief responded.

"I'll get you the money."

"We don't know where to order it."

"I'll prepare a requisition."

"It won't matter, we don't know how to install a pump or use it."

"I'll arrange for training."

"There's no regular staff at the refuge, so that won't work."

And so it went. This was typical of my dealings with the management division. When the Department of Natural Resources was first formed, it had received personnel from an array of agencies. The Department's first secretary figured it would be a long time before our agency was prepared to manage its protected areas so he deliberately placed his least skilled and least motivated personnel in the management division figuring he would fix things later on. Well, it was now "later on," he was gone, and nothing had been fixed. I had a dilemma. This would have to be elevated.

I went to see my boss to arrange an immediate meeting with the Secretary. Once the Secretary understood the benefits of a pump for Boqueron, he would shape up the management division fast enough. My boss did not share my enthusiasm.

"I don't think so," he said in a rather forlorn tone.

"Why not? What's the problem?" I queried somewhat surprised.

"Well," he retorted, "I'm not on the best terms at this moment with the Secretary." He paused. "And we would be taking on the management division, which is his pet program."

"His pet program?" I responded. "How can that be? That program does absolutely nothing!"

"It doesn't matter," he said glumly. "He's down on us right now, so we don't stand a chance."

"Not in this case," I offered with gusto. "We have an iron-clad argument. Boqueron is dry as a bone and serving no positive purpose. By getting the management division to purchase a pump, we can take a major step forward at minimal expense."

"You might think so," my boss offered, "but you are wrong. The Secretary will find something wrong with your position and we will end up with the short end of the stick."

"No way!" I was determined. "This is a fool-proof case –

black and white – a no-brainer. I can't even imagine an argument that might counter our position."

"Okay." My boss had surrendered. "I'll arrange the meeting. But I am telling you. You are going to lose."

It was but a few days before my boss and I were seated before the Secretary with our counterparts from the management division on hand for a discussion of Boqueron refuge. I laid out the issue quickly and waited for the Secretary's response. It came quickly.

"Does Boqueron refuge have a management plan?"

"No sir."

"You haven't written one?"

"No sir. Only a few of our protected areas have such plans. Most have nothing. There are teams busy preparing plans for two other protected areas, but Boqueron may not be gotten to for some time."

"Well then, there's nothing to discuss."

"But sir, what we are talking about here is an interim measure. Boqueron refuge was set aside to enhance waterfowl conservation. Presently it in no way serves that purpose nor achieves that goal. By purchasing a pump we can take a major stride in the right direction and, at a later date, fine-tune matters with a detailed management plan. If we wait for the drafting of a management plan, we could lose years of the refuge not fulfilling a positive function."

"Perhaps you did not hear me clearly. I said that until there was a plan, we had nothing to discuss. Now, if you will excuse me, I have other business to attend to."

I walked out of the Secretary's office in a fair state of shock. How could he be so callous? My boss, on the other hand, without saying a word, clearly communicated, "I told you so." He had long before premonitioned the outcome and had resigned himself to it.

⌒

The plan was long in coming. And the pump, even longer.

There was simply no way, even with a pump, that the refuge could be filled with water when desired. As mentioned, Boqueron was in the driest part of Puerto Rico and the drainage canal running by it rarely supported a significant water flow. That meant the impoundment would have to be subdivided.

This had several important benefits in addition to allowing for our limited access to fresh water. The refuge was at the end of the Lajas Valley drainage system. Consequently, the canal water was primarily runoff from the irrigation system, water full of fertilizers, among other things. These fertilizers, from our experience, would lead to a major infestation of cattails, a pretty plant, but not one conducive to waterfowl or waterbird production. By subdividing the impoundment we could treat one area to eliminate cattails while keeping others in good condition for waterfowl. Subdividing would also enable us to set aside some portions of the wetland for hunting while protecting others for nesting ruddy ducks. Finally, the additional dikes would facilitate patrolling the reserve to ensure hunters were complying with regulations.

I was proud of the plan when I had finally completed it. The modifications were ambitious, but the arguments for subdividing the refuge was overwhelming. At least, I thought so.

Regrettably, a well placed individual outside the Department thought the plan was terrible. His argument was that increasing the number of dikes would reduce the actual amount of wetland. That was his whole case.

While this was true, I agreed, the relative amount of wetland to be lost would be minimal. Besides, without additional dikes, it was somewhat far-fetched to call Boqueron a wetland. It held that status pretty much on paper only.

My arguments went unheeded. Only a small part of the plan was accepted – and that was to buy a pump!

Needless to say, the pump was long in coming – very long indeed.

Then, it wasn't quite the right pump for the job.

Needless to say, the pump soon broke down.

But, replacement parts were expected soon.

The parts never came.

I don't recall that I ever saw the pump in action.

I left Puerto Rico several years after this whole incident of the pump had started. They were still waiting for replacement parts. The ruddy ducks could not wait.

Reflections

Much to derive from this.

Why didn't the U.S. Fish and Wildlife Service see to it that their investment in Boqueron was followed up on effectively? The probable reason is that this was not considered an investment. Boqueron was probably impounded to compensate hunters for the loss of two other important wetlands. Once the pressure from hunters abated, there no longer was an issue. Had local hunters continued to complain, more likely than not, something would have been done much sooner to improve the refuge.

Why were the hunter's voices not heard? Two reasons. For one, they were not well organized. I heard virtually nothing from hunter groups during the several years I was in charge of wildlife planning. This is quite the contrary when it came to individual hunters. They had a lot to say. It happens, however, that individual voices get lost in the system unless they are very well connected. Second, the hunter community generally was uninformed. They did not have a clue how the system worked, what resources were available, how they were being spent, and so on. Ignorance is not bliss under such circumstances. Understanding the system takes time, money, and is anything but fun, yet, that is how to make a difference.

Was what happened at Boqueron unique? Not at all. And I do not just refer to Puerto Rico. An idea may be a good one (not that the Boqueron impoundment was), but it takes follow-through. And, regrettably, the later stages of projects such as the Boqueron impoundment are not nearly as glamorous as, nor do they receive the recognition of, the initial phase. Costs of maintenance and operations simply are not glitzy and, consequently, are often ignored or under-funded. This is reality not from a managerial perspective, but from a political one. And it is the politicians who usually provide the money.

Who presented such weak arguments against subdividing the impoundment? A biologist. In fact, one of the better trained biologists on the island. Regrettably, the biology most of us learn at universities and other academic institutions hardly provides us with the common sense, broad perspective, ability to communicate, to listen and to observe, that is essential to conduct effective wildlife conservation.

Would impounding Boqueron refuge have been a good idea had it been executed properly? That depends upon your perspective. In its natural state, pre-impoundment, the Boqueron mangrove doubtless was an important nursery for fish, perhaps shrimp, and many other marine organisms. It also served the many other functions described for mangroves in an earlier chapter. Construction of the impoundment virtually eliminated these benefits. With proper on-going management, however, the impoundment could have improved available habitat for various waterfowl and other freshwater organisms. Freshwater habitat was extremely scarce in Puerto Rico, consequently there was an argument for creating more of it. At the same time, choosing to do so in the most arid corner of the island where fresh water habitat could be sustained only at major expense hardly seemed like a particularly wise undertaking.

Why isn't it a good idea for other countries simply to adopt wildlife management practices developed in the U.S.? It is not a good idea because their natural environment is different. Let's look at waterfowl. In the U.S. the breeding seasons of all waterfowl are very much prescribed by the length of summer. Hunting seasons then are built around this circumstance. In the tropics and sub-tropics, however, areas which are much less seasonal, waterfowl breeding is less bounded by season and could occur in almost any month. Consequently, the tropical wildlife manager has to take into consideration varying parameters with which his or her temperate zone counterpart is not familiar. The direct application of U.S. hunting regulations to Puerto Rico appeared to be a direct cause of decline for most of the islands native breeding waterfowl.

Postscript

First of all, I have never been back to Rat Island. One can only hope that the sand flies have met a timely demise.

Monkey removal has been attempted several times since Desecheo was acquired by the U.S. Fish and Wildlife Service and designated a national wildlife refuge. These efforts have extended well over a decade. All have failed. On the positive side, the number of monkeys on the island has been reduced to the point that at least a few seabirds may now be breeding successfully. Yet, seabird populations remain a shadow of their former levels. Also, should efforts to remove the monkeys be curtailed, the monkey population will increase resulting once more in the total devastation of seabird nesting.

The monkey situation on Puerto Rico proper has degenerated. Monkeys of two species have spread widely over the southwest portion of the island. They are raiding crops and causing significant damage. Farmers are now filing law suits against the government concerning these depredations.

Rhesus macaques now range to Guanica forest, the Puerto Rican whip-poor-will's stronghold. Local residents and the reserve manager himself periodically observe small numbers in or around the forest. I fear this situation will worsen before it gets better. Hopefully, the aridity of the forest is inhospitable enough to keep monkey numbers at a very low level. Otherwise, regrettable consequences could be in the offing for the whip.

The parasitic shiny cowbird has now spread through the West

Indies and as far north as Florida in the United States. Contrarily, the brown-headed cowbird expanded its range eastward across the United States and southward into the Bahamas and Cuba. Consequently, those islands now have two avian nest parasites in sharp contrast to a few years ago when they had none.

It remains to be seen whether the brown-headed cowbird will continue its expansion through the Greater Antilles to Puerto Rico and the remainder of the Caribbean, an expansion exactly the reverse of the shiny cowbirds. While this is quite possible, it is difficult to speculate at this time concerning what additional impacts this bird may have beyond the devastation already caused by it shiny cousin.

The situation caused by the shiny cowbird in Puerto Rico remains grim. The yellow-shouldered blackbird is barely holding on, chiefly thanks to intensive cowbird control efforts. The only good news is that the small Mona population is thriving and has suffered no ill effects from the few cowbirds thus far recorded there.

The manatee? The manatee still survives in Puerto Rico. Subsequent aerial surveys to our first effort periodically recorded numbers in the twenties. Extrapolating for individuals not observed, it is estimated that between 50 and 150 animals survive. Though this can hardly be considered a healthy number of individuals, there is reason for hope. An effective public awareness and law enforcement campaign can still save this animal on the island.

The golden coqui has disappeared! It is not clear why. George Drewery, the frogs discoverer, speculates that the cause may be acid rain. Acidities as low as a pH of five reputedly have been recorded in mountain rains in parts of Puerto Rico. Additional support for this hypothesis regrettably comes from the disappearance of another coqui, *Eleuterodactylus karlschmidti*, a more widespread species common only two decades ago. The habitats of both these tree frogs have not been degraded in any obvious way.

It is noteworthy that in recent years there has been a mysterious decline in numerous frog species worldwide. The problem has become so serious that international conferences have been held to examine the issue and in 2004 a Global

Amphibian Assessment was published with input from 500 scientists representing 60 countries. The assessment found that an alarming 1,856 species of amphibians are threatened with extinction, 32.5 percent of all amphibians known. Of these, 435 are in rapid decline. No fewer than 113 species have gone unrecorded in recent years and may already be extinct joining nine others considered extinct since 1980. A fungal disease, chytridiomycosis, has recently become a serious threat to many high elevation and streamside frogs and very possibly played a role in the disappearance of Puerto Rico's two missing ranids. Clearly the amphibians of the world could be facing the greatest decline of any group of animals and as a consequence may well be one of our best natural indicators of environmental health, much like the use of canaries in coal mines in days gone by to detect toxic gases. While the mystery facing the world's amphibians continues to be sorted out, it appears that any solution will have come too late to save the golden coqui.

Little by little head-starting of sea turtles is being abandoned. It has taken all too long, but at least it is happening at last!

What ever happened with the ruddy duck? For some time the species continued to decline. In fact, about seven years after my departure from Puerto Rico the hunting season was again split in two, doubtless to the further detriment of these poor birds. By that time ruddy duck numbers were so low they could no longer be studied in the wild. More recently sager regulations have been promulgated. And, even more significantly, formerly drained wetlands have been restored, most notably at Humacao and Tiburones. Overall, this has resulted in a net improvement of habitat conditions for Puerto Rico's waterfowl. Hopefully, this will have positive repercussions for the ruddy duck.

New threats are now impinging on Puerto Rico. The green iguana, a common pet trade animal from Central America, is showing up in every corner of Puerto Rico and proving a pest in many ways. Growing to over four feet in length, tolerant of a broad range of habitats, and highly diverse in the plants and animals it will eat, the green iguana has the potential to raise ecological bedlam on the island.

And then there are the released caimans, rather nasty crocodiles, introduced from South America which have become established in a few water bodies. But, enough is enough. Those are stories for some other occasion. Doubtless they make fascinating natural history tales. Let us hope that their endings are more comic than tragic.

Printed in the United States
74375LV00001B/1-99